ROMMEL'S

AFRIKA KORPS

EL AGHEILA to EL ALAMEIN

GEORGE R. BRADFORD

STACKPOLE
BOOKS

Published by
STACKPOLE BOOKS
5067 Ritter Road
Mechanicsburg, PA 17055
www.stackpolebooks.com

Cover illustration by George R. Bradford

Printed in China
10 9 8 7 6 5 4 3 2 1
FIRST EDITION

Library of Congress Cataloging-in-Publication Data

Bradford, George R.
   Rommel's Afrika Korps : El Agheila to El Alamein / George R. Bradford. —
1st ed.
      p. cm.
   Includes bibliographical references.
   ISBN 978-0-8117-0419-9
   1. Germany. Heer. Panzerarmeekorps Afrika—History. 2. Rommel, Erwin,
1891–1944—Military leadership. 3. World War, 1939–1945—Campaigns—
Africa, North. 4. World War, 1939–1945—Tank warfare. 5. World War,
1939–1945—Regimental histories—Germany. I. Title.
D757.55.A4B73 2008
940.54'1343—dc22

                                        2008025752

CONTENTS

Acknowledgments

A book of this nature is never prepared without the able assistance of fellow enthusiasts, and I would like to thank the following individuals for their support and participation in this enterprise. Dr. Leo Niehorster of Germany for much of the D.A.K. organizational data; Miles Krogfus of the USA for support in a number of areas; Dick Harley of Scotland for answering my call for 1st K.D.G. organization; Dr. Nicola Pignato of Italy for supplying the T/O&E for the 132nd "Ariete" Armored Division; Richard Garczynski of the USA for coaching me on the lesser known incidents of the Desert War; John Reynolds and Vance Holliday of the USA for data on the 8th Army; Peter Brown of England for his help with nomenclature and photo captions; Nic Sabatini of Canada for translating and helping with Italian formations; Theo Lammers of Canada, for German translation; Edmond Baker of the USA for supplying some of the rare 8th Panzer Regiment photographs; and my dear wife, Susan, who gallantly put up with my highs and lows while burning the late-night candle.

Introduction

The North African Campaign of World War II leaves its imprint on the minds of anyone who has taken the time to study it. No other theater of operation ever matched the ebb and flow of battle which took place on the endless sands of the Western Desert, nor the achievements and defeats that seesawed back and forth between the armies involved. This was also about the only large campaign of World War II where the combatants fought with equal respect for the other and did their best to treat captives fairly.

This book is meant as a tribute to the men who fought on both sides, but in particular to Field Marshal Erwin Rommel and his Afrika Korps, whose determination and daring earned him the respect of combatants on both sides of the conflict, even if the OKW in Berlin was not overly impressed with his antics at times. Even the British commanders got upset when Rommel took matters into his own hands and disobeyed orders coming from Berlin, since they did their own planning based on German radio traffic intercepts. The photo content of this book is an attempt to show as much previously unpublished material as possible, accompanied by some of the more exotic shots to be found in archives around the world.

From his first daring envelopment of the British Cyrenaican outposts in early April 1941, until the gradual disintegration of his cherished Afrika Korps on the road to Cairo, we will attempt to relive the tank battles that swirled across the Western Desert, on and off, for almost two years. Many books have already been written on this subject, but we will confine ourselves to the more dramatic high points of the ground war, with some emphasis on the Tables of Organization and Equipment (T/O&E) charts to illustrate how the various units were composed and just how many vehicles were used. In the desert much depended on the steady flow of materiel, fuel, water, troops, and replacement vehicles for both sides in determining which side could take the initiative. Often during and after a battle these vehicles fell under control of the enemy, if it was he who controlled the territory after the battle ended. Captured trucks, fuel, and foodstuffs were always a welcome bonus for the weary troops.

The Deutsches Afrika Korps, or D.A.K., was originally forged from the 5th Panzer Regiment of the 3rd Panzer Division and a number of other units, to become known as the 5th Light Division (later named 21st Panzer Division), and soon after joined by the 15th Panzer Division in Africa. Alongside the D.A.K. fought a considerable Italian force, the most prominent of which was the 132nd "Ariete" Armored Division. All of these and other units were eventually incorporated into Panzerarmee Afrika, more or less directly under Rommel's command. These forces were pitted against the British 8th Army, which in many instances had a numerical superiority but inferior firepower, and the victor of the day was usually the one with the most deceptive moves or the deadliest anti-tank shield.

Although the Italian forces in Libya had made overtures suggesting a serious threat against the British in Egypt, at no time did they have the initiative, except in numbers. Although they had lost most of Libya and thousands of men to the British by the time Rommel's forces arrived in 1941, this chronicle will concentrate mainly on the achievements of the Afrika Korps from the first encounters at El Agheila in February 1941 through to their withdrawal from El Alamein in November 1942. The make-up of certain 8th Army units will be covered to a lesser degree, where possible, to reflect the vehicles deployed by the British and for comparison purposes.

The British would continually suffer from the inadequate armor and main guns on their cruiser tanks, with the standard issue 2-pdr on both their cruiser and infantry tanks. To add to their misery, all their cruisers tended to suffer from both mechanical and track-shedding problems. The British tank industry simply seemed unable to "get it right," while at the same time they were under pressure to produce even more of what they had on the lines.

The Germans on the other hand, were ahead with the quality of their vehicle armor and main guns, but would always be fighting in the shadow of the great battles on the Eastern Front. Africa simply did not seem to be in Hitler's plans, and the Afrika Korps more or less was sent whatever leftovers could be found. However, in many cases those supplies were often sunk just trying to reach Africa.

THE ROAD TO AFRICA

8th Panzer Regiment in Europe, 1940–41

Most of the units which would eventually make up the early Deutsches Afrikakorps were drawn from formations which had already served in Europe. Many of the photos in the first part of this book came from the belongings of a German prisoner of war captured at Bitche, Germany, in 1945. He was obviously a member of 8th Panzer Regiment and his photos start with their participation in the invasion of France 1940 and end around July 1941 in Africa. Speculation might suggest that he was seriously wounded about this time and shipped back to Germany

Advance elements of 8th Panzer Regt. moving through Luxembourg on their way to the Ardennes, at which time they met with no resistance. May 10, 1940.

to sit out the rest of the war in an office staff position. These photos give us an insight into the early activities of the tank regiment which would soon become the spearhead of the 15th Panzer Division in Africa

ORIGIN OF 8th PANZER REGIMENT

The 8th Panzer Regiment was raised at Böblingen, Wehrkries V (near Stuttgart), in November 1936. It consisted of 2 battalions, each with a headquarters and 3 light tank companies. Along with 7th Panzer Regiment, it was assigned to the 4th Panzer Brigade in November 1938. By September 1939 it had been mobilized and

The crew of this PzKpfw.II was obviously involved in the heavy fighting around Sedan or Amiens, as witnessed by the numerous penetrations on their vehicle (near the Balkankreus), and which has now been loaded onto a tank transporter.

This photo was obviously taken at a point in the campaign when 8th Panzer Regiment was being directed south toward Château Thierry. Their regimental "Wolfsangel" symbol can be seen on this N.80 road sign directing them toward Saulieu.

attached to Schaal's 10th Panzer Division and participated in the Polish Campaign as part of OKH Reserves. In December they moved west to Eifel, as part of 16th Army, Armeegruppe A, during the French Campaign in May–July 1940. During this period it was part of Guderian's XIX Panzer Korps under Panzer-Gruppe Kliest, and on May 10 they struck through the Ardennes Forest region to emerge just south of Sedan and then crossed the Meuse River.

By May 16 they had breached the French defenses and on the seventeenth and nineteenth were challenged by the French 4th Armored Division of Col. Charles de Gualle. Once on the move again they struck out for the coast, but were heavily engaged around Amiens and Pèronne on June 9–11. At this point von Kliest's forces were directed south past Paris toward Château Thierry on the Marne River.

By June 18 they had passed through the Lyons area of southern France, and when the fighting ceased, 8th Panzer Regiment remained in France as part of XII Armeekorps, 2nd Army, Heeresgruppe C. From November 1940 to January 1941, they acted as 1st Army Reserves for Heeresgruppe D. On January 18 they were re-assigned to 15th Panzer Division and likely returned to Germany.

WITH 15th PANZER DIVISION

During this period 8th Panzer Regiment was assigned to the newly formed 15th Panzer Division which had come into being November 1st, 1940 at Darmstadt, Germany, near Frankfurt. This new armored division had been built from the main elements of the 33rd Infantry Division plus the 8th Panzer Regiment. It remained at Darmstadt, converting and training until March 1941, and during that time was assigned to the XXIV Armeekorps (mot.), 2nd Army, Heeresgruppe C. Their tactical insignia was the "Wolf's Hook" and can be seen on the vehicles and the sign board directing them to Paris.

Although these photos do not concern themselves directly with the desert war, it was felt that they would give the reader an insight into where the 8th Panzer Regiment had fought before it was scheduled to go to Africa and what the crews had experienced. It also gives us a look at their tanks, which often had arrived in Africa with their old unit markings still intact, although by this time most of the tanks were oversprayed with a desert sand color before or upon arrival in Tripoli.

ARRIVAL IN AFRICA

The first elements of 15th Panzer Division under Gen. Heinrich von Prittwitz reached the front by April 9, 1941, but without the 8th Panzer Regiment, and it would be mid-June before the complete division had arrived in Africa. Both the 1st Battalion of the 115th Motorized Infantry Regiment and 33rd Engineer Battalion took part in the abortive attack on Tobruk on April 30, and both suffered heavy casualties.

When 8th Panzer Regiment eventually started off-loading in Tripoli harbor on April 14 it was made up of five tank companies, 1, 3, 4, 5, and 6. However, by mid-September 1941 it would be expanded to eight tank companies. The 3rd and 7th (medium) companies were redesignated as 4th and 8th (medium) companies, and completely new 3rd and 7th (light) companies were raised.

It should also be mentioned here that on April 16 the ship transporting a portion of the 15th Panzer Division staff and vehicles was sunk with heavy losses.

A group shot of an 8th Panzer Regiment crew assembled on their PzKpfw. III medium tank, accompanied by two of their staff officers. This photo was taken in the yard adjacent to their billet in Merroles, France, 1940.

A motorcycle with side car of 8th Panzer Regiment in France, carrying their "Wolfsangel" insignia on the front fender of the bike.

This distinctive regimental symbol travelled to North Africa with the 8th Panzer Regiment. In Europe, while it was part of the 10th Panzer Division, it usually appeared in white on the bow plate of its tanks, which were painted the regulation "Dunkelgrau" (panzer grey). However, during its days with the D.A.K. in Africa it began to appear in red on the rear of the turret stowage bin. This rune was historically known as a "Wolfsangel" and in English translates roughly as Wolf's Hook or Wolf's Trap.

THE BIRTH OF THE
AFRIKA KORPS

THE BIRTH OF THE AFRIKA KORPS

In September 1940 the British watched as the Italian Tenth Army, consisting of nearly 250,000 men, began crossing the Egyptian frontier. In North Africa Mussolini had begun to get grandiose ideas of conquest and ordered Marshal Graziani to confront the Western Desert Force with the intention of driving the British out of Egypt. Britain had taken the defensive on all fronts by now, and Mussolini calculated that it would be an ideal time to topple its Middle East empire.

Germany was cautiously happy to see the Italians finally take the offensive after almost two years of hesitation, but at the same time was quite leery about how well they would do in an all-out Mediterranean war against the British. The Suez Canal and the oil fields beyond were essential to British naval domination in the region and as a link to the rest of the Commonwealth. If Germany could bolster the Italians in this venture it would certainly be to their mutual benefit.

The advancing Italian Tenth Army masses were skilfully screened by elements of Lt. Gen. Richard O'Connor's desert-wise but sadly worn Western Desert Force. On December 9, with a force never to exceed 36,000 men, O'Connor attacked the Italian advance camps in Egypt as they were preparing for the next phase of their offensive.

THE BRITISH XIII CORPS STRIKES

On January 1, 1941, his command became the XIII Corps, and on the third he unleashed the green 6th Australian Division and 23 Matilda II tanks of 7th RTR against the 45,000-strong Italian garrison at Bardia, which was the bulwark of Libya's defenses, and captured thousands of Italian troops. The British infantry tanks were so well armored that Italian anti-tank gunners could not penetrate them, and the Italian lines simply collapsed. By the twenty-first, with only 18 Matildas he had captured another 32,000 prisoners in Tobruk. By February 8, all of Cyrenaica down to El Agheila and over 130,000 POWs were in British hands. O'Connor's force was now extended to its limit, and Wavell's attention was turning to Greece, where Churchill felt they must send assistance. At this point Germany decided to support the Italians in Libya by sending an expeditionary blocking force to Africa.

The British Navy and Air Force did everything in their power to thwart any massive movement of Axis troops and equipment between Sicily and Tunisia, but to no avail. In the period February 1 to June 30, 1941, a total of 81,785 Axis troops were disembarked at Tripoli, along with 450,000 tons of weapons, fuel, and ammunition. The Axis air attacks on Malta had neutralized the British influence in the Mediterranean during February and March,

Men of the 15th Panzer Division chat with two Italian soldiers (center) during their voyage across the Mediterranean to Tripoli. These men appear to be members of a supply unit, so vital to the long-range operations in the desert. Note that the two Germans on the left have already been issued their tropical-style high-laced boots.

Above: Scenes from the docks at Tripoli in April 1941 as the equipment for the fledgling Afrika Korps begins to arrive from Italy. The initial purpose of this force was merely to act as a static blocking force to defend the Libyan capital from the advancing British, but Rommel, after assessing the situation, had other ambitions.

Below: Early elements of 15th Panzer Division leave Tripoli on their way to the front, stacked high with water and fuel containers in neat rows of "jerry cans" strapped to the top of their turrets. This column has halted for the moment and is made up mainly of PzKpfw III Ausf G medium tanks, with wheeled vehicles following.

Some of the 8th Panzer Regiment troops sailed for Africa on the Italian battleship Giulio Cesare. Here we see them being photographed with Italian seamen.

allowing the Italian "Ariete," still equipped with L3/33 tanks, and "Trento" Divisions, along with the German 5th Light Division, to arrive safely in Tripoli.

On February 6, 1941, Generalleutnant Erwin Rommel was appointed to command the German forces in Africa, and by mid-February the first units of the 5th Light Division were disembarking in Tripoli. Rommel landed in Tripoli on February 13, 1941, to greet his arriving troops and report to General Gariboldi, who had recently relieved Graziani. The vanguard of the 5th Light Division was Motor Vehicle Workshop 13, Water Columns 800 and 804, plus Field Hospital 4.572. The following evening the 3rd Reconnaissance Battalion and 39th Anti-Tank Battalion started to come ashore.

Rommel was there to greet them and gave them 5 hours to disembark and be ready to march. On the morning of February 15 they were inspected and then headed east on the 26-hour drive to the front lines at Sirte. Once the panzers were unloaded, Rommel was quick to see how small his forces were at this point and proceeded to parade

Here again, a shot of the men trying to sort out all their equipment and vehicles as they are unloaded on the docks.

Axis troops prepare their vehicles after arrival in Africa.

them twice around the Governor's Palace in Tripoli to give the impression of a much larger force.

A NEW FORCE TO BE RECKONED WITH

The D.A.K. came into being on February 19, 1941, when Hitler decreed that the German forces in Africa under Generalleutnant Rommel would henceforth be known as the "Deutsches Afrika Korps." Previous to this announcement the headquarters staff for the German Army in Africa had carried the title "Aufklärungsstab Rommel" since February 6, when it became known that Rommel was to be their commanding officer. With the influx of men and materiel to the African theater, Rommel's command eventually achieved the status of a Panzergruppe on August 15, 1941. This encompassed the 15th Panzer Division, 5th Light Division, 90th Light Division, and six Italian divisions (Ariete, Trieste, Pavia, Bologna, Bescia, and Savona). The three aforementioned German divisions now made up the "Afrika Korps." On January 30, 1942, "Panzerarmee Afrika" came into being and this title would remain in effect until February 23, 1943.

From mid-April to the end of May, the rest of the Deutsches Afrika Korps, or D.A.K., would arrive, along with most of the 15th Panzer Division.

At this stage of the war, Rommel was to take his orders from General Gariboldi, and he was quite pessimistic about the ability of his Italian allies to withstand a sustained attack. On the British side, O'Connor had made it clear to Wavell that with reinforcement for his 7th Armoured Division, he was ready to move forward into Tripolitania and had even planned coastal amphibious landings against Buerat and Misurata in support of his planned offensive. However, this was not to be, since the British War Cabinet had chosen instead to send all available armored forces

A German Pz.Kpfw. III of 5th Panzer Regiment moving through the streets of Tripoli in mid-February 1941.

to try to halt the German invasion of Greece. This was the break that Rommel needed, and he was soon to take advantage of the situation.

Because of Britain's decision to support Greece with as strong a force as it could muster, O'Connor's forces in western Cyrenaica were stripped bare to the point that his 2nd Armoured Division was equipped with captured Italian tanks as the final insult. The newly arrived forces sent to Greece included the 6th Australian and 2nd New Zealand Divisions and over half the British 2nd Armoured Division. Had these units and the ones withdrawn from O'Connor's grasp been directed to the west, the final scenario in North Africa might well have taken a completely different course. However, this is all hindsight, and at the time Britain was trying to convince the world that support of Greece came before its own self-interest.

O'Connor did have the 3rd Indian Motorized Brigade at his disposal, but the 7th Armoured Division had been ordered back to the Nile delta by Wavell for refitting. Had those repair shops been moved forward to Tobruk instead, Rommel would have had a much harder time of it in the month ahead. Obviously, Wavell had gambled that Rommel was not capable of any major counteroffensive, and even Brauchitsch and Halder of O.K.H. back in Germany had no thoughts of launching Rommel into the attack much before the end of May, by which time the remaining elements of 15th Panzer would have arrived in Africa.

CYRENAICA UP FOR GRABS

The 2nd Armoured Division positions at El Agheila included an armoured car regiment and a support group deployed in defensive positions extending inland from Marsa el Brega, with the 3rd Armoured Brigade patrolling the front each day, but returning to laager in the hills near Agedabia each night. The daily reconnaissance was done by the King's Dragoon Guards in their light Marmon-Herrington armored cars, and they would be the first to glimpse the forward elements of Rommel's forces. The division work shops and supply troops were based at Msus. When 2nd Armoured Division relieved the 7th Armoured, the division inherited three regiments: 6th RTR, 3rd Hussars, and the 1st Royal Horse Artillery. The British had captured 112 Italian M13/40 medium tanks at Beda Fomm, and the best of these were upgraded with British radios and passed on to 6th RTR to replace their earlier losses. The Mark VI Light tanks of 3rd Hussars were also bolstered by equipping B Squadron with M13/40 tanks. Such was the makeshift army opposing the German and Italian forces at this time, and Rommel realized that opportunity was knocking.

Members of Stab. I, 8th Panzer Regiment, 15th Panzer Division, have their picture taken outside their barracks shortly after their arrival in Africa. Note the facine bundles in the rear decks of the tanks, likely intended for use in unditching in soft sand or simply as firewood, which was at a premium in the desert.

Above: The crew of a PzKpfw II of 15th Panzer Division meet their first baby camel. This crew was issued Dutch pith helmets (confiscated from stores in Holland) because of short supply of the standard German "Tropinhelm." These are recognizable by their significantly smaller and somewhat more rounded brim.

Below: A PzKpfw III of 8th Pauzer Regiment, Company 1, the crew already having switched to the visored field caps. Their Axis allies in the foreground are colonial Libyan soldiers serving under Italian command, and belong to the 9th Battalion "Agadabia", as indicated by their black and green waistbands.

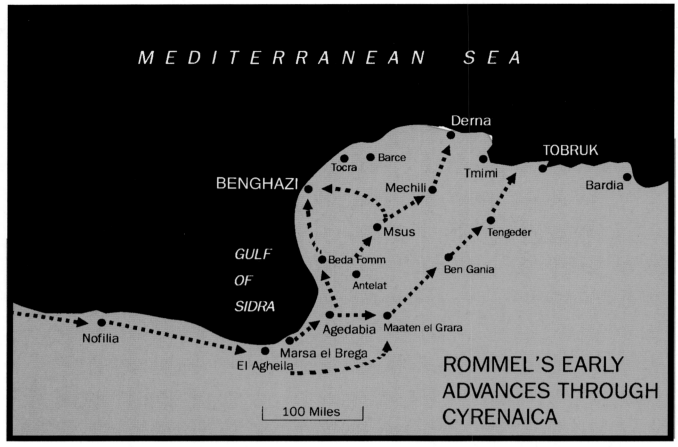

MEDITERRANEAN SEA

Derna

Barce
Tocra

BENGHAZI

Mechili

TOBRUK

Tmimi

Bardia

GULF

OF

SIDRA

Msus

Beda Fomm

Antelat

Ben Gania

Tengeder

Nofilia

Agedabia   Maaten el Grara

Marsa el Brega
El Agheila

100 Miles

ROMMEL'S EARLY
ADVANCES THROUGH
CYRENAICA

The great distances covered by the 5th Light Division to reach the front and then cross the Cyrenaican bulge were staggering, as shown by the mileage scale on this map.

Rommel has always been acknowledged as a superb tactician on the field of battle, but as a strategist who could grasp the overall situation in the Mediterranean theater of operations, he was surely lacking. He never seemed quite capable of understanding that sound strategy must link land, sea, and air forces into a combined effort to ensure safe passage of supplies from Italy to North Africa. His direst request to Hitler that Luftwaffe squadrons be diverted from their task of neutralizing Malta to support his forces in their mad rush across the desert just may have been his downfall. Had the submarine, bomber, and torpedo-bomber forces based at Malta been held in check, much of the fuel and supplies he later begged for would likely have reached him.

The German forces sent to North Africa were far from prepared for the rigors of desert life which would confront them. Their staple rations on the continent had been white bread, butter, and potatoes, but because of possible spoilage, these were now changed to black bread, olive oil, sardines, and legumes. The greatest deficiency was in fresh fruit and vegetables, and the only meat available for the first four months was Italian tinned meat, which was detested by the troops. By April 1941 Bakery Company 531 was in operation and fresh bread was finally made available, although the wood for the ovens still had to be shipped over from Italy.

Water supply was a completely different situation. Here the German General Staff had overshot the mark, with special water procuring and filtration companies and a special water transporting company. These units were under the command of engineering officers and were even capable of drilling deep water wells and erecting pumping

Although the standard "jerrycan" with white cross was the popular water carrier, there were also aluminum "Trinkwasser" containers issued to the troops.

stations. Their only weak point was that the water was delivered in jerry cans or barrels, since they had no tankers at their disposal.

In the early going the German tanks lacked both adequate oil filters and air filters for desert conditions. During the day the temperature often reached 120 degrees Fahrenheit, and the cooling systems for the engines simply could not stand up to these conditions. Since the evenings were much cooler, the Germans normally moved their tanks forward at night to keep the engine breakdowns at a minimum. Sudden sandstorms often penetrated the turret bearing mechanisms so severely that the turrets had to be removed and cleaned before they would become functional again. Even the Italian maps of the area left much to be desired, and many a troop found themselves wandering around in the desert far off the mark. One by one these problems were overcome, and the Afrika Korps would emerge as an experienced desert army, capable of long marches under the harshest conditions imaginable.

ROMMEL GOES ON THE OFFENSIVE

In the early dawn of February 24, elements of the 3rd Recon Battalion, "Advance Unit Wechmar," had probed towards El Agheila and exchanged fire with a British patrol, destroying three British scout cars in what was the initial contact between German and British troops in Libya.

On March 19 Hitler awarded Rommel the Oak Leaves to the Knight's Cross, but gave him no instructions to hold back. Agedabia was to be his first target and Benghazi the final objective of his spring campaign, but Rommel saw that Benghazi was indefensible and that the whole of Cyrenaica was ripe for picking.

On March 24 the 3rd Recon Battalion made a reconnaissance in force on El Agheila, only to find that the British forces there had pulled back to Marsa el Brega. These new positions placed them in a defensive line between the Gulf of Sirte and impassable salt marshes to the west, about 50 miles from Agedabia.

Knowing that if he waited for the final elements of 15th Panzer to arrive he would loose the initiative, Rommel decided that he would strike before the British could react to his probe and reinforce Marsa el Brega. The attack by 5th Panzer Regiment went in early on March 30, but massed artillery fire halted them in their tracks. However, a more concerted attack the following day, supported with a flanking action by the 2nd Machine Gun Battalion on motorcycles, succeeded. Assisted by air support from their Stukas, the attack continued throughout the day, and by late afternoon they had breached the 2nd Armoured's line of defense.

By April 2 the Afrika Korps, followed by the Ariete Armored Division and Brecia Infantry Division, had reached Agedabia and taken about 800 prisoners. This was two months ahead of the schedule laid down by O.K.H. In this first raid Rommel showed some of his cunning as a commander by utilizing prefab dummy tanks on Volkswagen chassis to give the appearance of a much larger attack force than he actually had at his disposal.

All of this was done on his own initiative, and although his German and Italian superiors tried to make contact with him, he always managed to evade their communiqués. At this point Gariboldi set out after Rommel himself, but upon arrival at Rommel's forward camp, he found himself rebuked by his subordinate, who in the meantime had just made several more gains over his British opponents. However, Berlin finally signalled its approval and the Desert Fox was now on the move. The reconnaissance group of the 5th Light Division reached Benghazi on the night of April 3 and proceeded west toward El Mechili.

The tank strength of the British 3rd Armoured Brigade had been reduced to twelve A13 Cruisers, twenty M.13-40 Mediums, and eighteen Mark VI Lights, caused mainly by mechanical breakdown and fuel shortages. Later that day an RAF recon plane reported a sizeable tank force together with motor transport moving against the fuel dumps at Msus, so the garrison torched their fuel dumps.

The following morning, when the 3rd Armoured arrived to refuel, they were met by huge columns of black smoke. In actuality, the force spotted had been a Long Range Desert Group patrol and a Recovery Section of 3rd Armoured Brigade out looking for damaged tanks that they could recover. Such was the confusion on this day.

At British headquarters in Cairo the swiftness of Rommel's successes caused almost as much confusion as he had with his Italian superiors. Realizing that the situation was serious and that an organized retreat was fast turning into a rout, Wavell called on O'Connor to take stock of the situation. In a bizarre turn of events, on a night trip to Tmimi made by Generals Neame and Carton de Wiart for a staff meeting, they were stopped by a German advance patrol near Derna and taken captive. It appears that their driver had taken a wrong turn and gone north instead of veering eastward to Tmimi. In this same period General Gambier-Parry, commander of the 2nd Armoured Division, was also captured near Mechili, along with a good portion of his 3rd Armoured Brigade and most of the 3rd Indian Motorized Brigade. Among

Panzers moving forward along the coastal road had to pass through Mussolini's "Arco dei Fileni" (Marble Arch), built as a symbol of his conquest of Libya. It was located just west of El Agheila and was a favorite watching spot for the Long Range Desert Group, who kept track of all traffic passing through.

A rare shot of a captured British Mk.VIA Light Tank accompanied by a proud Italian soldier.

the booty captured here was a British general's command Dorchester heavy truck, and as it was being unloaded, an ever-vigilant Rommel reached forward and claimed an oversized pair of sand and sun goggles. These he promptly clamped over his peaked cap, where they would remain as the hallmark of the Desert Fox in numerous photographs taken of him in the months to follow.

Rommel's thrust across central Cyrenaica was no cake walk, and the severe terrain took its toll on his meager motorized forces. As a means of keeping abreast of his advancing forces, he went aloft in his Fiesler Storch light observation plane and on several occasions found himself taking fire from the bewildered Italians below.

A German Junkers 52 transport unloading supplies of every description.

The German armored elements became dispersed after first being ordered to make for Tobruk and then being reined in by Rommel when he changed his mind and decided to concentrate all his forces on Mechili instead. Numerous breakdowns were caused by pushing the tanks and other motorized vehicles to the limit over treacherous terrain with limited fuel, and at times his troops reached the breaking point. The advance units, ordered to make for Derna to cut the coast road, were in such dire straits that they were forced to siphon the remaining fuel from most of the vehicles so that a small force could reach the objective. The rest of the troops were now stranded and forced to camouflage their vehicles and wait it out in a small wadi.

Meanwhile, the supply column had started the 1,000-kilometer trip back to Tripoli for more fuel and supplies. In desperation the Germans attempted to fly fuel forward to the beleaguered 5th Panzer by landing on a nearby dry salt lake. However, on several occasions the British Hurricane fighters caught these Ju52 transports on the ground, with disastrous results.

After a three-day battle Mechili was finally taken on April 8 in the midst of a blinding sandstorm. Mechili gave up 1,700 prisoners, with 70 British officers among them, and a goodly amount of badly needed supplies. It was here that Rommel captured his prized "Mammut" AEC armored command vehicle, which would travel everywhere with his Panzergruppe from that day forward.

Rommel, as a commander was very demanding, and his immediate staff was expected to endure any hardships required to get the job done. He was quite abrupt and outspoken with his officers, but once he was convinced of their efficiency and loyalty, he would treat them with respect.

His most disruptive tendency was to interfere with minor details which should have been the responsibility of his chief of staff, and to make things worse, he insisted that the chief of staff accompany him on his numerous visits to the front. This left junior staff officers with some pretty heavy decisions to make during critical battles.

During these visits to the front to check on his troops, he was very popular with the common soldiers and cracked many a joke with them. However, if he felt that one of his commanders was shirking his responsibilities, he would dress them down right there in front of his men. Many a time he was wrong in his actions and proved quite willing to listen to the officer's side of the story and finally square things away with him.

His endurance on these extended inspections was amazing, and he would spend the whole day in the scorching heat until he had completed his tour of the front to his satisfaction. His lifestyle was quite Spartan, and he insisted that he and his staff officers be fed the same rations that the troops were given. In some ways this might sound magnanimous, but actually he left himself and his staff officers open to the many health problems which afflicted all troops fighting in North Africa. The choice of tinned foodstuff and brackish water over fresh vegetables and pure water often left his vital officer staff and himself open to dysentery and other ailments common to the desert.

After taking Mechili on the eighth, Rommel had struck out straight for the coast in an attempt to cut off the British forces retreating from Benghazi, but as luck would have it the rearguard of the Australian brigade had already fallen back on Tobruk. Rommel knew that the port of Tobruk was essential for the fuel and materiel he would need to continue an all-out move on Cairo and the Suez. However, the British had been improving the old Italian fortifications around Tobruk since mid-March and

Rommel discussing the battle situation with his staff.

they were now close to impregnable. Rommel had no idea how well defended Tobruk was, and he still hoped that he could strike before the British built it up. He was soon to learn that it would be a tough nut to crack and that the "Desert Rats" were equal to the task of defending it.

Wavell realized that although Rommel could easily bypass Tobruk, he would be forced to use up precious fuel hauling tons of supplies overland from Benghazi and Tripoli for any further advances he contemplated. Tobruk would also remain as a thorn in Rommel's side, since from there the British could counterattack at any time and cut his supply route along the Via Balbia.

The Tobruk garrison consisted mainly of the 9th Australian Division, commanded by General Morshead, reinforced by a brigade of the 7th Armoured Regiment, with 45 armored cars. In all, they numbered about 36,000 men within the Tobruk perimeter, supported by an A.A. brigade with 16 heavy and 59 light guns for air defense.

German tanks began to probe the outer defenses of Tobruk on April 11, but were driven back by heavy artillery fire. Even so, Rommel still felt that a full-scale armored assault planned for the fourteenth would bring a quick victory. At the first light of dawn tanks of the 5th Light Division broke their way through the outer wires and found little resistance as they moved forward. However, the Australians had planned to withhold their fire until the infantry supporting the tanks had passed through the outer defenses. At this point the German infantry was decimated by murderous fire from their rear. In the smoke and dust of battle the tanks moved on, only to find themselves trapped two miles inside the perimeter with the Australians firing on them with heavy field artillery and anti-tank fire at close range. By the time they realized that they were caught in a planned crossfire, they had already lost 17 tanks and barely managed to withdraw before they lost more. As for the infantry, the German 8th Machine Gun Battalion had suffered 75 percent casualties.

Rommel was furious at this failure and ostracized General Streich, commander of the 5th Light, for not rolling up his flanks as he moved through the perimeter. A second attack went in two days later on April 16, and this time Rommel himself took personal command. Unfortunately he chose to use the Ariete Division, supported by Italian infantry, and watched as the Italian tanks took refuge in available wadis the minute they were fired upon. The infantry was then faced with an Australian counterattack and dutifully surrendered on the spot. The end result was 800 Italian prisoners taken and 90 percent of Ariete's tanks out of commission, due mainly to breakdowns.

It was at this point that Rommel realized that he had better build up his forces before trying another attack on Tobruk. At the same time, Morshead had informed his troops that Tobruk was going to hold, no matter what, and even began to harass Rommel's troops by sending out twenty-man night patrols intended to launch surprise attacks. One successful patrol of Indian warrior-caste Hindus was accused by the Australians of exaggerating their nightly kills, and in response to this challenge they returned the following night with a bag full of thirty-two human ears. In another case, Rommel saw the results of these night raids for himself when he casually approached

A FIRSTHAND REPORT FROM A PANZER OFFICER OF THE 5th LIGHT DIVISION, APRIL 1941

Tobruk. 10 April 1941. Toward evening we reached our advanced positions 17$\frac{1}{2}$ miles in front of Tobruk. We had covered 100 miles and wearily we pitch camp. Vehicles are checked over. I have to force the louvres open with a hammer, the sand has jammed them so badly.

Tobruk. 11 April 1941. At 0900 hours we move off into the desert again to the southeast in order to cut off Tobruk from the south. With us are anti-tank, machine gun, and anti-aircraft guns.

Ten miles south of Tobruk and already the enemy's artillery is giving us an H.E. welcome. As soon as they get the range we withdraw 100–200 yards. Their fire follows us—their observation must be good. At 1630 hours we attack with two half-squadrons. The artillery puts down a barrage, but can make little impression on us.

We are through! We charge onward for 1,000 yards and then turn carefully through a minefield. As the smoke lifts, I see barbed wire and anti-tank trenches. "Halt!" Gun Flashes. "Gun, 9 o'clock. A.P. shell, light-coloured mound, fire!" A hit. Again—10 yards to the right . . . with six shots we have finished off the anti-tank position. We move along the wire looking for a gap and the leading tank finds one, and in doing so runs onto a mine of course. Another goes to its rescue, while I give covering fire.

Tobruk. 14 April 1941. At 0010 I am contacted, and ordered to report with the company commander at 0100 hours. Situation: Machine gunners and engineers have worked a gap through the anti-tank defenses; 5th Tank Regiment, 8th Machine Gun Battalion, anti-tank, and anti-aircraft artillery will cross the gap under the cover of darkness and overwhelm the position. Stuka attack at 0645 hours. 0715 hours. Storming of Tobruk. With least possible noise 2nd Battalion, Regimental HQ Company and 1st Battalion move off completely blacked out. Bitterly cold. Of course, the enemy recognizes us by the noise and as ill luck will have it, a defective spot-light on one of the cars in front goes on and off.

Soon artillery fire starts coming in, getting the range. The shells explode like fireworks. We travel six miles, every nerve on edge. From time to time isolated groups of soldiers appear - men of the 6th Machine Gun Battalion—and suddenly we are in the gap. Already the tank is nose down in the first ditch. The motor whines; I catch a glimpse of the stars through the shutter, then for the second time the tank goes down, extricating itself backwards with a telltale thud, the engines grinding. We are through and immediately take up file in battle order.

In front of us 8th Company, then 2nd Battalion HQ Company, then 5th Company. With my troop I travel just left of the (6) company commander. With 2nd Battalion HQ about 60 men of 8th Machine Gun Battalion with Oberst Ponath are marching in scattered groups. Tanks and infantry?—against all rules. Behind us follow the Regimental HQ Company and 1st Battalion plus the other arms. Slowly, much too slowly, the column moves forward. We must, of course, regulate our speed by the marching troops, and so the enemy has time to prepare resistance. The more the darkness lifts, the harder the enemy strikes. Destructive fire starts up in front of us now —1-2-3-10-12-16 bursts and more. Five batteries of 25-pounders rain hail on us. 8th Company presses forward to get at them. Our heavy tanks, it is true,

fire for all they are worth, so do we all, but the enemy with his superior force and all the tactical advantages of his own territory makes heavy gaps in our tanks.

Wireless: "9 o'clock anti-tank gun, 5 o'clock tank!" We are right in the middle of it now, with no prospects of getting out. From both flanks A.P. shells whiz by. Wireless: "Right turn, left turn, retire." Now we come slap into the middle of 1st Battalion, which is following us. Some of our tanks are already on fire. The crews call for doctors, who alight to help in this witch's cauldron. English anti-tank units fall upon us, with their machine guns firing into our midst; but we have no tome. My driver, in the thick of it, says, "The engines are no longer running properly, brakes not acting, transmission working only with great difficulty."

We bear off to the right. Anti-tank guns 900 meters distant in the hollow behind, and a tank. Behind that in the next dip 1,000 yards away another tank. How many? I see only the effect of the fire on the terrace-like dispositions of the enemy.

Above us Italian fighter planes come into the fray. Two of them crash in our midst. The optical instruments are covered with dust. Nevertheless, I register several unmistakable hits. A few anti-tank guns are silenced, some enemy tanks are burning. Just then we are hit, and the wireless is smashed to bits. Now our communications are cut off. What is more, our ammunition is giving out. I follow the battalion commander. Our attack is fading out. From every side the superior forces of the enemy shoot at us.

"Retire!" There is a crash just behind us. The engine and petrol tank are in the rear. The tank must be on fire. I turn around and look through the slit. It is not burning. Our luck is holding. Poor 8th Machine Gunners! We take a wounded man and two others aboard, and the other tanks do the same. Most of the men have bullet wounds. At its last gasp my tank follows the others, whom we lose from time to time in the clouds of dust. But we have to press on to the south, as that is the only way through. Good God, supposing we don't find it, and the engines won't go anymore!

Close to the right and left flanks the English shoot into our midst. We are hit in the tracks of our tank, and they creak and groan. The minefield lane is in sight. Everyone hurries toward it. English anti-tank guns shoot into the mass. Our own anti-tank guns and 8.8cm guns are almost deserted, the crews lying silent beside them. The Italian artillery, which was to have protected our left flank is equally deserted.

We go on. Now comes the gap and the ditch! The driver can't see a thing for dust, nor I either. We drive on instinct. The tank almost gets stuck in the two ditches blocking the road, but manages to extricate itself, with great difficulty. Examine damage to my tank. My men extract an AP shell from the right hand auxiliary petrol tank. That petrol tank was shot away and the petrol ran out without igniting!

Tobruk. 14 April 1941. At 1200 hours we retire into the wadi south of us. We cover up. Heavy cumulus clouds cover the sky. Every 10–30 minutes 2 or 3 English bombers swoop out of them to bomb the tanks. Every bomber drops 4–8 bombs. Explosions all around. It goes on like this until 1900 hours without a pause. Casualties in 2nd Battalion of 5th Tank Regiment, 10 tanks, apart from five 7.5 cm guns of 8th Co.! A few dead, several wounded, more missing. The anti-tank units and the light and heavy AA were badly shot up and the 8th Machine Gunners were cut to pieces. The regiment has lost all of its doctors—presumably captured. The regiment is practically wiped out!

Tobruk. 15 April 1941. Artillery fire from 700 hours. The bombers repeat yesterday's game. My troop has two heavy tanks again. Tank No. 625 isn't running any longer, however. It only serves as a pillbox. According to orders, I report at the brigade commander's office at 1200 hours. Once more the principal subject discussed is the action in front of Tobruk on 14th April. We simply cannot understand how we ever managed to get out again. It is the general opinion that it was the most severely fought battle of the whole war. But what can the English think of us! A weak battalion, only two squadrons strong, bursts through the complex defense systems until it is just a mile from the town, shoots everything to bits, engages the enemy on all sides, and then gets away again.

The war in Africa is quite different from the war in Europe. That is to say, it is absolutely individual. Here there are not the masses of men and material. Nobody and nothing can be concealed. It doesn't matter whether it is a battle between opposing land forces, or between airforces, or both; it is the same sort of fighting, face to face, each side thrusting and counter-thrusting. If the struggle were not so brutal, so entirely without rules, you might compare it with the jousting of knights. And now before Tobruk.

Tobruk. 20 April 1941. In the afternoon tank No. 623 rolls up with a new engine. Now I have the strongest squadron in the regiment: Four PzKpfw II tanks, four PzKpfw III. Gradually, however, the job of squadron commander is becoming difficult. I have absolutely nothing to go by, everything is in the desert. Where are the tanks, where are the HQ cars and squadron office? And I have no command tank and no motorcycle - and then the reports and the paper-war which begins as soon as the last shot has been fired!

Tobruk. 23 April 1941. The journey I planned has been postponed owing to the arrival of Lt. Grim with 6 tanks. The engines of the tanks are partly new. Partly overhauled in the factory. They have new gears, transmission, brakes, etc. The British do not miss the chance of sharing the welcome with some well-aimed fire. The faithful 625, which is the only heavy tank of the squadron remaining with us, will now be sent back to have its six shell wounds cured. Whilst in the workshop it will have its engines changed.

Tobruk. 29 April 1941. 50 dive-bombers circling over Tobruk. Tank 622 turns up. They tell us about the desert—of hunger and thirst, of Benghazi, and of Derna. Since tank 625 is still in the workshops, I am getting No. 634 as my fifth tank, with Sergeant Schafer, my driving instructor from Wunsdorf.

Tobruk. 30 April 1941. Put finishing touches to our preparations for battle. 1745 hours. March to assembly place. Strong Stuka attacks. 2000 hours: our own strong artillery bombards the enemy heavily, 8th Machine Gunners in front. 1st Engineer Battalion and 1st Battalion of Assault Engineers break through and demolish the barriers on either side. The light signals show that the attack has begun. At 2200 hour sleep under the tank.

Tobruk. 1 May 1941. We intend to take Tobruk. My fourth attack on the town. Up at 0330 hours, leave at 0430 hours. We lose touch in the darkness and dust, and then join up again. We file through the gap where many of our comrades have already fallen. Then we deploy at once, 6th Sqn. on the left, 5th Sqn. on the right, behind HQ, 8th and 7th Sqns. The regiment is now Hohmann's Mobile Battalion and consists altogether of about 80 tanks. The English artillery fires on us at once.

We attack! No German patrol goes in front to reconnoitre. Tier upon tier of guns boom out from the triangular fortification before us. The two light troops of the company and my left section are detailed off to make a flanking movement. I attack. Wireless message: "Commander of 6th Co. hit on track." Then things happen suddenly. A frightful crash in front and to the right. Direct hit by artillery shell. No! It must be a mine. Immediately send wireless message: "Commander Schorm on a mine, will try to get old direction."

Move five meters back—another detonation! Mine underneath to the left. Now it's all up with driving. Wireless message: "Getting back went on mine again." Now mount tank 623. Back through the artillery fire for 100 meters and got in. Wireless: "Tanks active behind ridge. Men of the mined tank all right."

Back carefully. Then with the last tank in Company HQ and Lt. Roskoll I give cover to the north. 9 heavy and 3 light tanks of the squadron have had to give up owing to the mines. Of my troop, the commander's tank and both of the section leaders' tanks are damaged. Of course the enemy went on shooting at us for some time. A slight change of position: forward—right—backwards—left! With the commander's approval I am to move up in front to salvage tanks. Whilst we are on the way we are fired at by MGs and anti-tank guns from about 500 yards. I silence them with HE and drive in the tracks of 624.

I bring up the rear and then the laborious work of salvaging begins. The anti-tank gunfire starts up again and has to be kept in check by constant fire. At last I move off slowly with 624 in tow, through the gap and on another 800 yards. 250,000 Marks saved. The crew is really delighted to have its tank back. It is now late afternoon. Dive-bombers and twin-engine fighters have been attacking the enemy constantly.

In spite of this, the British repeatedly make counter-thrusts with tanks. As soon as the planes have gone the artillery starts up furiously. It is beginning to grow dark. Which is friend, and which is foe? Shots are being fired all over the place, often on your own troops and tanks in front on their way back. Suddenly a wireless message: "British attacking gap with infantry." It is actually true.

Two companies get off their motor lorries and extend in battle order. All sorts of light signals go up - green, white, red. The flares hiss down near our own MGs. It is already too late to take aim. Well, the attack is a failure. The little Fiat-Ansaldos go up in front with flame-throwers in order to clean up the triangle. Long streaks of flame, thick smoke, filthy stink. We provide cover until 2345 hours, then retire through the gap. It is a mad drive through the dust. At 0300 hours have snack beside tank. 24 hours shut up in the tank, with frightful cramp as a result—and thirsty!

Tobruk. 2 May 1941. Heading out to recover tanks . . .

Here the diary ends, as this panzer officer was captured by the British.

A group of captured Italian M11/39 and M13/40 medium tanks used by the Australians in the defense of Tobruk.

The German 88 was capable of engaging and destroying a target at a range of nearly two miles. Dug in on the open desert, they could literally destroy any tanks of an advancing British column before they ever got within responding fire range.

A PzKpfw III Ausf F of 15th Panzer Division, 8th Pz. Regt. preparing their vehicle for desert action. The crew has affixed a sturdy wooden chest to the rear deck for carrying their belongings. Tropical dress has already succumbed to more casual attire to better suit the hot desert conditions.

the Italian sector of his lines one morning, only to find the ground covered with discarded plumed helmets of the supposedly crack Italian Bersaglieri rifle regiment.

Through all this the Luftwaffe had continued to pound any supply vessels entering the port, and the harbor was littered with rusting hulks of supply ships. However, during the night some managed to get through, and with the troops dug in deep underground, they suffered only minor discomfort during these air attacks.

By April 10 light German forces had moved eastward along the coast road and taken Bardia, then crossed the Egyptian frontier to capture Fort Capuzzo on April 14, and Sollum also fell to an enveloping attack shortly thereafter. The advance German units then managed to nudge the British off the heights at Halfaya Pass on April 25, but the German force was so small it could do little more than consolidate its position. Halfaya Pass was the gateway to the Egyptian coastal plains, and as such was a key defensive position, guarding over the slope that led up to the high plateau.

OPERATION BREVITY
Wavell realized its importance also, and in mid-May ordered Operation Brevity in an attempt to recapture the pass, along with Sollum and Capuzzo. This led to some very confusing encounters around Halfaya Pass and the border post of Fort Capuzzo. He had managed to scrape together about 30 heavy Matilda II Infantry tanks and 29 Mk.II (A10) Cruiser tanks. These cruisers would intercept

any attack from the desert flank, while the heavy infantry tanks would reclaim Halfaya Pass. Thrown in with this mix were about 15 Mk.VIB light tanks of 3rd Hussars and another 28 Mk.VIB light tanks with the 6th Australian Cavalry Regiment.

By April 28 the 4th RTR had 33 Matilda Infantry tanks and 6 light tanks, and these were moved forward by rail to Maaten Bagush. From there they moved forward to Bir Scheferzen, and late on May 8 the 4th RTR began a 100-mile march to Sofafi. They arrived there with 26 remaining Matildas and 3 light tanks.

At that time Halfaya Pass was being held by a company of the 15th Motorcycle Battalion supported by an Italian artillery battery. At dawn on May 15 the British 22nd Guards Brigade overwhelmed the Axis defenders at Halfaya Pass, and only twelve survivors escaped. Sollum and Capuzzo both fell soon after, and Rommel was forced to dispatch the 8th Panzer Regiment to try to snuff out this advance. However, the British had by then already withdrawn to consolidate their occupation of Halfaya Pass.

This area was quite barren, with few defensive positions, and the British were forced to fortify the pass as best they could and mine all approaches to deter the enemy.

OPERATION SKORPION
Rommel knew that the British would soon be reinforcing the Halfaya Pass positions and ordered Kampfgruppe Herff to retake it. Kramer's 8th Panzer Regiment left its

staging area at Sollum and arced across the open desert to strike from the rear, while a company of 104th Rifle Regiment, led by Hauptmann Bach, made a concerted frontal attack. After a short battle the pass was again in German hands, and this time it was heavily fortified in anticipation of the inevitable counterattacks to come.

Also on May 12 the British Tiger shipment convoy had arrived at Alexandria, after making a hazardous voyage through the Mediterranean. It arrived with a total of 238 tanks and unloaded 135 Matildas IIA Infantry tanks, 67 Crusader, Mk.VI Cruiser tanks, 21 Mk.VI/C light tanks, plus 43 brand new Hurricane fighter planes. However, during the voyage one ship, the *Empire Song*, which was carrying 57 tanks and 10 Hurricanes, had gone down after striking a mine. With these reinforcements Wavell was once again urged by Churchill to go on the offensive.

Although the Tiger shipment had arrived, it still had to be unloaded and all the vehicles checked over in the Cairo workshops, some requiring complete overhauls. So it wasn't much before the end of the month that unloading of the heavy Matilda IIs had been completed.

However, although Churchill was still pressing for another attack, Wavell had his own reservations, stating, "Our armoured cars are too lightly armoured to resist the fire of enemy fighter aircraft, and, having no gun, are powerless against German eight-wheeled armoured cars which have guns and are faster. This makes reconnaissance difficult. Our Infantry tanks are really too slow for a battle in the desert. Our cruisers have little advantage in power or speed over German medium tanks. Technical breakdowns are still too numerous. We shall not be able to accept battle with perfect confidence in spite of numerical inferiority as we could against the Italians."

To add to all of this, his Matilda tanks, which were meant to sweep a path through the enemy defenses and challenge enemy tanks, could fire only 2-pounder anti-tank armor-piercing solid shot, which was of little use against enemy troops that were well dug in. The German PzKpfw. III medium tanks on the other hand could fire both armor-piercing and high explosive from their 50mm cannons, which gave them an added advantage.

Naturally, while planning his moves, Rommel would take full advantage of the slow speed of the heavy Matilda II Infantry tanks and constantly used his faster vehicles to outmaneuver them and his 88s to stop them.

OPERATION BATTLEAXE

In the early hours of June 15 the British offensive opened on a wide front, attacking along the desert plain as well as the high plateau. The strategically emplaced 88s and anti-

8th Panzer Regiment crewmen pose with their PzKpfw III Ausf G that was knocked out during the June 16–17 British Battleaxe offensive. Note the captured Matilda II tanks in the left background. These men had fought in temperatures over 130 degrees and now don their Dutch pith helmets. 15th Panzer Division managed to gain possession of the battlefield and were thus able to salvage all but 25 of their most seriously damaged tanks.

Two different views of a PzKpfw III Ausf G of 8th Panzer Regiment knocked out during the fighting around Capuzzo on June 16, 1941. It is in the process of being salvaged, the tracks and drive sprockets already having been removed. Note the additional face-hardened driver's bow plate, the new-style cupola, and the partially open escape hatch on the lower hull side.

tank guns on the Halfaya perimeter destroyed the British heavy armor of 4th Indian Division while it wallowed in a well-prepared series of obstacles and minefields along the coastal plain.

On the plateau the 7th Armoured Division was successful in capturing Fort Capuzzo again on June 15. The now fully operational 15th Panzer Division counterattacked and eventually managed to dislodge the 4th Armoured Brigade but suffered considerable losses. This was the first battle for the newly arrived Crusader tanks, and their mechanical unreliability proved their undoing. With the tanks of 5th Light Division sweeping round Hafid Ridge on the evening of June 15, the British advance was thwarted, although the fighting continued for several more days. Meanwhile the 7th Armoured Division had blunted itself while challenging the German anti-tank screen on Hafid Ridge and was finally forced to

withdraw. With this, possession of the battlefield went over to the D.A.K., and when 15th Panzer looped south to try to ensnare the British armor, Wavel decided to withdraw his remaining forces. An escape corridor was held open and two Matilda squadrons managed to hold off the German tanks for the better part of a day while their armor withdrew south.

In most cases final control of the battlefield was crucial to both sides, since the victor had the opportunity to reclaim lost vehicles in order to salvage and repair them. Many times a disabled tank could merely have its tracks or suspension damaged and otherwise be in good working order. Every tank salvaged was a bonus, and above and beyond this they could also lay claim to any guns, transport vehicles, and serviceable tanks left behind by the enemy to bolster their own ranks. During this battle a good number of both Matildas and Crusaders were claimed by the D.A.K.

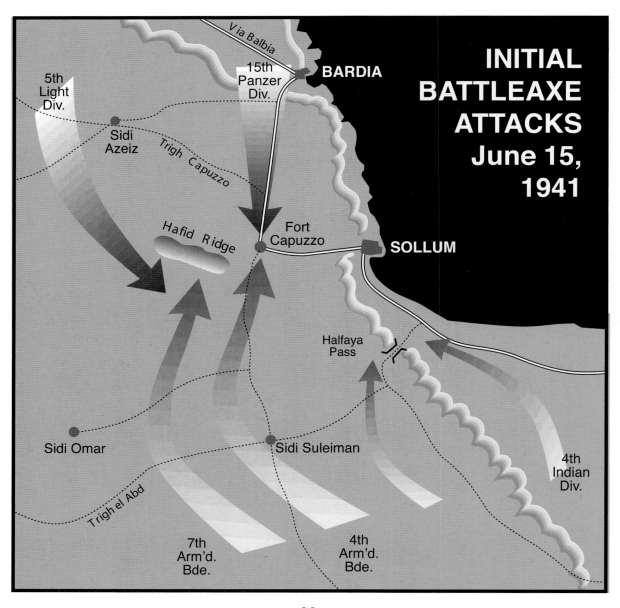

Rommel greeting one of his commanders in the field. In the background is his captured British AEC Dorchester command vehicle still displaying its British caunter pattern camouflage. Rommel affectionately named it Max and has it well marked with red German flags to ward off any friendly German or Italian aircraft who might recognize the shape as of British origin.

Wavell had lost 101 of his 190 tanks, and the RAF had suffered the loss of 36 planes. The Axis had lost only 12 tanks destroyed, 50 damaged and recovered, plus 10 aircraft shot down. Rommel's well-organized defenses and his quick judgement of when units could be shifted from one part of the front to another appear to have made the difference. In contrast, the unimaginative and almost incompetent conduct of the three-day battle by the British commanders led to a costly defeat.

The German 88 had come into its own as a weapon to be reckoned with, and Rommel had impressed his nominal Italian masters to no end. They immediately agreed to proceed with the construction of a bypass road skirting Tobruk. This road would not only loop to the Via Balbia on either side of the Tobruk defenses but would also serve the troops holding the perimeter and investing the fortress. The Italians completed this bypass road in a record three months, and it was given the name *Achsenstrasse* (Axis Street).

His latest victories had elevated Rommel to a new plateau where even his adversaries were beginning to admire the cunning of the Desert Fox. On the other hand, Wavell had come into disfavor with Churchill and on June 21 he was relieved and replaced by Gen. Sir Claude Auchinleck. Auchinleck would prove far more popular with his troops and come to be seen as a cool and skillful commander, using his armor with far greater understanding than his predecessor.

The period following these ill-fated offensives by the British was used by both sides to build up their depleted forces. However, Hitler's Operation Barbarossa had channelled most of Germany's armor into the massive offensive in Russia, and Rommel would find it even harder to gain support for his D.A.K. The Axis supply convoys were still being battered by British naval superiority, and the garrison in Tobruk continued to be supplied by sea.

In August of 1941 the "Afrika Division zbV" was formed and within a week was renamed as the 90th Light Afrika Division. Although it lacked tanks and was only four battalions strong, the 90th Light sported three field gun batteries, an anti-tank battalion, and an 88mm flak battalion. By October the 5th Light had been redesignated the 21st Panzer Division, while at the same time being strengthened by receiving the 104th Motorized Infantry Regiment from 15th Panzer.

A British Cruiser Mark I (A9) of 7th Armoured Division captured by 8th Panzer Regiment during the fighting in the Fort Capuzzo area, June 15–16, 1941. These older models were gradually replaced by the newly arriving Cruiser Mark VI and Crusader I and II.

5th LIGHT MECHANIZED DIVISION: March 15, 1941
5. LEICHTE DIVISION (motorisiert)

DIVISIONAL HEADQUARTERS
Headquarters
200th Mapping Detachment
    200th Printing Detachment
    200th Motorcycle Messenger Platoon
    3rd Signal Company/39th Signal Bn.

5th PANZER REGIMENT
Headquarters
    Armored Signal Platoon
    2 Light Tank Platoons
    Band
    Armored Maintenance Company
    Tank Reserve Detachment

1st Armored Battalion
Headquarters
– Headquarters Company
    Headquarters
    Light Tank Platoon
    Armored Signal Platoon
    Motorcycle Reconnaissance Platoon
    Engineer Platoon
    Anti-Aircraft Platoon
2 Light Tank Companies
1 Medium Tank Company

2nd Armored Battalion (same as above)

200th INFANTRY REGT. HQ (motorized)
    for special purposes
– Headquarters
– Signal Platoon

2nd Motorized Machine Gun Battalion
Headquarters
– Headquarters Company
    Headquarters
    Signals Platoon
    2 Motorcycle Platoons
– 3 Motorized MG Companies
– 1 Heavy Company
    Headquarters
    2 Anti-Tank Platoons
    1 Mortar Platoon
– 2nd Company/33rd Engineer Battalion
– 2nd Company/39th Engineer Battalion

8th Motorized Machine Gun Battalion
Headquarters
– Headquarters Company
    3 MG Companies
    Heavy Company as 2nd MG Battalion
– 1 Engineer Company
– 1 Anti-Tank Company

39th MOTORIZED ANTI-TANK BN.
– Headquarters (with Signal Platoon)
– 3 Anti-Tank Companies

3rd ARMORED RECONNAISSANCE BN.
– Headquarters (with Signal Platoon)
– 1 Armored Car Company
– 1 Motorcycle Reconnaissance Company
– 1 Motorized Heavy Company
    Headquarters
    Light Infantry-Gun Platoon
    Anti-Tank Gun Platoon
    Engineer Platoon

1st BN./75th MOTORIZED ARTILLERY REGT.
– Headquarters (with Signal Platoon)
– 3 Light Field Howitzer Batteries

605th HEAVY ANTI-TANK BATTALION
– Headquarters (with Signal Platoon)
– 3 Self-Propelled Anti-Tank Companies

606th LIGHT ANTI-AIRCRAFT BATTALION
– Headquarters (with Signal Platoon)
– 3 Light Anti-Aircraft Companies

Attached from Luftwaffe
1st Motorized Bn./33rd Flak Regt. (Lw)
– Headquarters
– 3 Motorized Heavy Flak Batteries
– 2 Motorized Light Flak Batteries

Upon arrival in North Africa the 5th Light Division vehicles still carried this tactical insignia of its parent 3rd Armored Division. Raised hastily for service in North Africa, the 5th Light Mechanized Division was an abnormal unit. It was put together from bits and pieces taken from the 3rd Panzer Division, small sections of several infantry divisions, and rounded out with various GHQ Troop units. It was then strengthened and reorganized as the 21st Panzer Division by October 1, 1941, although its organization would remain non-standard.

German Vehicle Identification Numbers, 1941

The impact that German armored formations made on modern warfare in the early battles of World War II was in part due to their fetish for organization and training. In many instances it was simply the superior chain of command which won the day against a more numerous or better equipped opponent. To accomplish this, the company or platoon commander had to know exactly where every vehicle was during the action so that the initiative could be taken when it presented itself.

To this end German tanks carried turret identification numbers which indicated their position within the formation. In the early stages of the war German tanks usually carried a small, removable, rhomboid-shaped plate on the lower side of the hull which displayed the vehicle's identification number. Later these small plates were often dispensed with altogether, and only the large turret numbers were used.

However, in Africa there were instances where these plates were kept, or the small number was still painted directly onto the forward hull sides, accompanied by a single large company number only on the turret sides, plus a small divisional insignia and the common Afrika Korps palm tree symbol. The 15th Panzer Division marked many of its tanks in this manner, with the large number in red rimmed with a bold white outline for greater visibility at long distance. However, in the early fighting for Halfaya Pass, the 8th Panzer Regiment displayed only a large red number with no discernible outline. This large company number would appear on both sides of the turret and on the rear of the turret stowage bin.

The 5th Light and 21st Panzer Division, on the other hand, tended to stick more to the large three-digit numbering system in black with white outline, and here again the large numbers would appear on both sides and rear of the turret.

LIGHT TANK COMPANY 1 (5th Light Division, 1941)

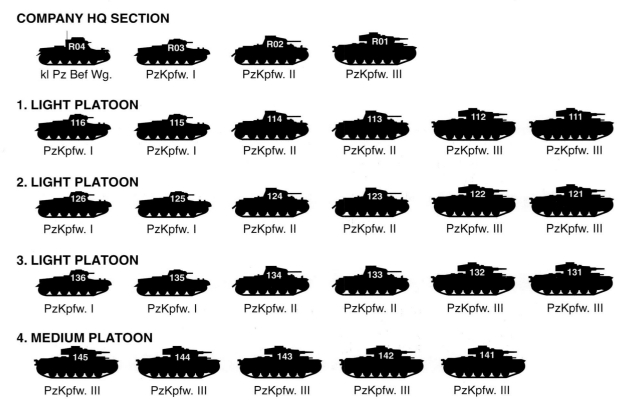

COMPANY HQ SECTION

R04	R03	R02	R01
kl Pz Bef Wg.	PzKpfw. I	PzKpfw. II	PzKpfw. III

1. LIGHT PLATOON

116	115	114	113	112	111
PzKpfw. I	PzKpfw. I	PzKpfw. II	PzKpfw. II	PzKpfw. III	PzKpfw. III

2. LIGHT PLATOON

126	125	124	123	122	121
PzKpfw. I	PzKpfw. I	PzKpfw. II	PzKpfw. II	PzKpfw. III	PzKpfw. III

3. LIGHT PLATOON

136	135	134	133	132	131
PzKpfw. I	PzKpfw. I	PzKpfw. II	PzKpfw. II	PzKpfw. III	PzKpfw. III

4. MEDIUM PLATOON

145	144	143	142	141
PzKpfw. III	PzKpfw. III	PzKpfw. III	PzKpfw. III	PzKpfw. III

These numbers designated the company, platoon, and vehicle within the platoon, in that order. Therefore 314 would designate 3rd Company, 1st Platoon, fourth vehicle. The Company Headquarters Section used the zero for its position within the company. Thus 302 would designate 3rd Company, HQ Section, third vehicle.

Regimental command vehicles used a similar system with an "R" for the first digit. This R01 was carried on the regimental commander's vehicle, and R02 for the regimental adjutant, R03 for the signals officer, and R04 and upwards for other regimental staff vehicles.

Battalion command vehicles used a toman numeral for the first digit. Thus I01 was the tank of the 1st Battalion commander, I02 was the battalion adjutant, I03 was the battalion signals officer, I04 was usually the battalion ordnance officer, etc. Finally, II01 would be from 2nd Battalion, and III01 would be from 3rd Battalion. In many instances the final two digits were much smaller than the Roman numeral portion.

With regard to these command tanks, I02 was considered the spare tank for the battalion commander in the event his vehicle broke down or was damaged. This was because only the low-digit vehicles had command radios installed in them.

Naturally, as with any system, there are variances from the norm, and North Africa was no exception. At times, when new tanks were rushed to the front to rebuild Rommel's forces, there appears to have been no time to properly mark them. This seems especially prevalent with the newly arriving PzKpfw. III Ausf L and PzKpfw. IV Ausf F2 models.

MEDIUM TANK COMPANY 3 (5th Light Division, 1941)

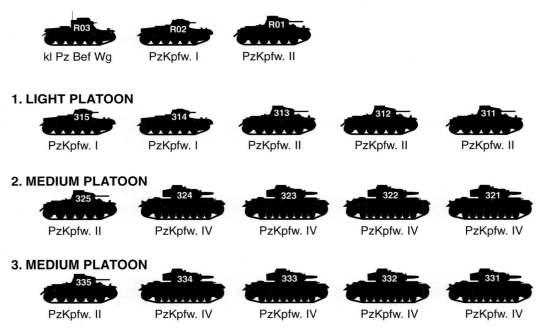

COMPANY HQ SECTION

kl Pz Bef Wg   PzKpfw. I   PzKpfw. II

1. LIGHT PLATOON

315   314   313   312   311

PzKpfw. I   PzKpfw. I   PzKpfw. II   PzKpfw. II   PzKpfw. II

2. MEDIUM PLATOON

325   324   323   322   321

PzKpfw. II   PzKpfw. IV   PzKpfw. IV   PzKpfw. IV   PzKpfw. IV

3. MEDIUM PLATOON

335   334   333   332   331

PzKpfw. II   PzKpfw. IV   PzKpfw. IV   PzKpfw. IV   PzKpfw. IV

Above: A survivor from 605th Anti-Tank Battalion poses with his burned-out Panzerjäger I Ausf B during the aftermath of the Battleaxe offensive.

Below: A PzKpfw IV Ausf E being directed into position in a new bivouac area. Note the spare track on the rear deck and the old-style number plate affixed to the rear just above the smoke candle rack.

Above: A squadron of Marmon-Herrington Mk.II armored cars being briefed during the early fighting around Msus. The vehicles at each end mount captured Italian Breda 20mm guns. 4th S.African Armoured Car Regiment.

Below: A disabled A10 Cruiser of A Squadron, 5th Royal Tank Regiment. The empty 2-pounder casings strewn on the ground suggest that it continued to fight from a stationary position, possibly after track damage.

British 2nd Armoured Division: N. Africa, March 31, 1941

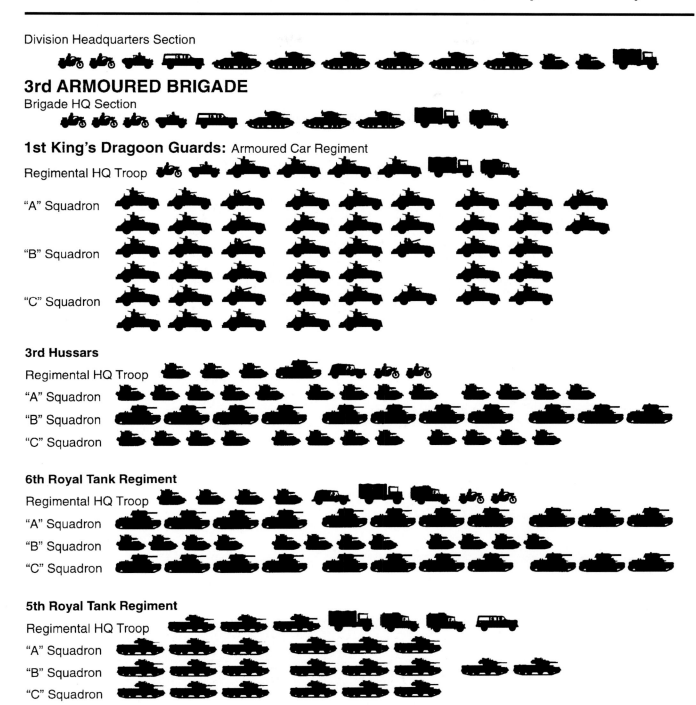

Division Headquarters Section

3rd ARMOURED BRIGADE
Brigade HQ Section

1st King's Dragoon Guards: Armoured Car Regiment
Regimental HQ Troop

"A" Squadron

"B" Squadron

"C" Squadron

3rd Hussars
Regimental HQ Troop

"A" Squadron

"B" Squadron

"C" Squadron

6th Royal Tank Regiment
Regimental HQ Troop

"A" Squadron

"B" Squadron

"C" Squadron

5th Royal Tank Regiment
Regimental HQ Troop

"A" Squadron

"B" Squadron

"C" Squadron

This is a brief outline of the vehicles available to the British 2nd Armoured Division around March 31, 1941. As such it represents only the armored elements, including the Italian M.13-40s pressed into service with 3rd Hussars of 6.RTR The light vehicles in the HQ units are merely representative, and the rest of the regiment's 100 "B" echelon supply vehicles are not shown.

There was also an accompanying Infantry Motor Bn., the Tower Hamlets Rifles, which had 4 rifle companies in carriers and 15cwt trucks. The support group consisted of the 102nd Anti-Tank Regt., RA with 2-pdrs, the 15th L.A.A. Regt., RA, with Bofors, and the 104th Regt., Royal Horse Artillery with 25-pdrs. The 3rd Armoured Brigade HQ Section would normally have had 10 cruiser tanks, but it is doubtful that this was the case. Wartime figures state the Brigade could muster only 86 tanks by March 31 (not including the M.13-40s), but this figure overlooks the few A9s known to be with the HQ Section.

Two shots of the Morris C9A Light Armoured Cars of 11th Hussars in early 1941. Note the Boys anti-tank rifle mounted in the turret as ultimate armament.

FORTRESS TOBRUK
& OPERATION CRUSADER

FORTRESS TOBRUK and OPERATION CRUSADER

During the war in the Western Desert both sides had managed to intercept and decipher messages to their mutual advantage. However, this could work both for and against the military planners, since many times false information was planted in the transmissions. The other feature that was most disconcerting to the British was that Rommel rarely ever did what he was told by Berlin or Rome, and ignoring his directives, he would decide to attack much earlier than predicted or at some other distant target.

The desert war was also the first true experiment in modern armored warfare fought on endless open terrain. Here the opponents had ample room to maneuver or to move overland at night for a surprise dawn attack. Rommel had studied Guderian's concepts on how armored formations should be deployed and made full use of these methods. Using the cover of a dust storm, a mobile division could disappear and turn up in an attack position on the opponent's flank before he realized what had happened. The desert, for all intents and purposes, was used like a huge ocean with each opponent trying to outmaneuver the other, while the elements and terrain took their toll on the men and equipment.

Rommel's one obsession at this time was the capture of Tobruk, and to boost morale and sharpen their fighting spirit, he instigated a limited operation which was code-named "Unternehmen Sommernachtstraum" (Midsummer Night's Dream). Their main objective would be the British supply dump at Bir Khireigat, about fifteen miles on the other side of the wire. Having lived on British rations in the past, it was not hard to entice his men into another round-up of British supplies. "Midsummer Night's Dream" was meant to solidify the front before his intended

Rommel, on one of his frequent forays to the front lines, is briefed by a local commander.

With the main battlefield far ahead of them, this PzKpfw III moves forward to better assess the situation. Note the extra track pins protruding from the spare roadwheel on the rear fender.

attack on Tobruk and, if possible, to capture information on the enemy's order of battle.

On September 14 the 21st Panzer Division slipped out of its assembly area and moved southeast. The division split into two battle groups, Kampfgruppe Stephan and Kampfgruppe Schutte. Kampfgruppe Schutte would steal the booty while Stephan fought off any challengers. As a cover for this operation, 3rd Reconnaissance Battalion was ordered to move along the frontier at speed, raising large clouds of dust and transmitting confusing wireless messages. Von Ravenstein's tanks, with Rommel at the head, swung deep into the British positions but netted nothing. The British 7th Support Group under Brig. "Jock" Campbell simply pulled back from the frontier and left Rommel empty handed.

At this time the British Ultra intercepts were playing havoc with Rommel's plans. The British had broken the German code and were quietly spying on every directive that Rommel put on the air. It is highly possible that Campbell was given ample warning

of this impending attack and thwarted it by making a calculated withdrawal from the area. The one good bit of luck from the raid was the capture of a broken-down staff vehicle of 4th South African Armoured Cars, with important documents and cipher material aboard. However, there is speculation that even these documents were planted, in an effort to mislead Rommel into believing that no major offensive was planned for the near future.

To make things even worse, the 21st Panzer Division ran out of fuel and was bombed mercilessly by two squadrons of the South African Air Force. Rommel's AEC Mammoth was hit, he had the heel of his boot blown away, and his driver was badly injured. This enterprise netted nothing, and Rommel indignantly retraced his steps back into Libya.

Now it was time for a serious move against Tobruk. The Panzergruppe was steadily growing in strength, and Rommel's timetable demanded the fall of Tobruk by early November. His long-range plans went as far as neutralizing any British attack that

Examples of the canvas "sunshield" disguise applied to British tanks in the lead-up to Operation Crusader in an attempt to hide the armored units from the Germans.

winter and reaching the Suez Canal by spring. From there he would drive on into Iraq, seize Basra, and sever the Allied supply route to Russia. These were grandiose ideas, and since Africa was increasingly playing second fiddle to the war in Russia, there was no way that he would glean the required supplies for such an ambitious enterprise.

The British situation was quite the opposite, with General Auchinleck, the new British theater commander in the Middle East, getting full support from Churchill. He received an unending stream of tanks and supplies to bolster the units of the new Eighth Army. According to the British Official History, by the end of October 1941, a total of 300 Crusaders, 300 Stuarts, 170 Valentines, 34,000 trucks, 600 field guns, 200 anti-tank guns, and 900 mortars had reached Africa.

With this massive build-up the Eighth Army, under General Cunningham, would again challenge Rommel's armor and destroy it by attrition. Once the Afrika Korps had been rebuffed, they would link up with the Tobruk garrison and together they would then challenge the remains of Armeegruppe Afrika. The name of this operation would be Crusader, and

German troops moving along the outer fringe of the main battlefield.

Rommel was about the only one who could not convince himself that it was coming.

As a ploy to try to hide this mass of new equipment, the British used the talents of peacetime illusionist Jasper Maskelyne to help disguise the armor they were moving forward. This came in the form of what would come to be known as "sunshields," which were actually huge canvas-frame contraptions that were fitted to the tank on side rails to make it look like a British lorry. When moving forward they would look like a truck convoy.

On October 26 Rommel ordered his troops to prepare for an attack on Tobruk between November 15 and 20. Then, in early November, Rommel and von Ravenstein flew to Rome to plead for supplies and to lodge objections to Jodl's order to forget Tobruk and prepare for Auchinleck's attack. On November 15 Rommel's wife met her husband in Rome, and with the von Ravensteins they celebrated his fiftieth birthday.

On this same night, two British submarines (*Torbay* and *Talisman*) surfaced in a quiet inlet on the coast of Cyrenaica. A unit of British commandos, led by Maj. Geoffrey Keyes came ashore and made their way toward Beda Littoria. Their target was the

two-story Prefettura building, which supposedly housed the headquarters of Panzergruppe Afrika and Rommel himself.

They were later to learn that Rommel had long since vacated these lush surroundings for more austere quarters closer to the front at Ain Gazala. During a storm, shortly after midnight on November 17 this group of about twenty commandos stormed the building, hoping to eliminate Rommel and the nerve center of the German command. Keyes and several of his men were killed in the ensuing skirmish, along with some of Rommel's staff. Three of the commandoes did eventually make it back to the British lines, but the others were all captured when the Arabs they were hiding with decided to cash them in to the Germans for 100 pounds of corn and flour.

4th Armoured Brigade crewmen mount their Honey in preparation for action. The turret of another Honey can be seen in the distance.

When Rommel learned of this attempted assassination, he ordered that Colonel Keyes be buried with full military honors at Beda Littoria along with the other four Germans that had died that night as well. The true folly of this raid was the fact that Rommel had moved his headquarters several times since he used Beda Littoria, and the British Secret Service had not even twigged to these moves, let alone the fact that Rommel was out of the country.

Upon his return from Rome on November 18 Rommel was confronted by an even greater threat; Operation Crusader had begun in earnest. On the night of November 17 the tanks of the British XXX Corps moved forward to their jump-off points. To emphasize the expected unreliablility of the British armor, the 7th Armoured Division managed to loose 22 of its 141 tanks on the way forward, and 22nd lost 19 of its 155 tanks to breakdowns as well. The fact that even the newer British-built Crusader Mk.VI cruiser

Rommel in his tropical tunic and the distinctive sand goggles that he acquired from the booty of the early fighting, which resulted in the capture of British generals Neame and O'Connor near Tmimi.

tanks were still proving unreliable would continue to haunt the British commanders and crews. Only the speedy little Honeys of the 4th Armoured Brigade reported no mechanical problems, as the American-built M3 Stuarts rolled forward into their first major battle of the desert war.

OPERATION CRUSADER

General Auchinleck had reorganized the troops taking part in Crusader into the Eighth Army, which was commanded by Gen. Sir Allan Cunningham fresh from his victories over the Italians in Abyssinia. At the opening of the Crusader battles, the eighth Army was deployed as follows:

TOBRUK: 70th Division under Maj. Gen. Scobie, who also commanded the whole garrison; Polish 1st Carpathian Infantry Brigade Group under Maj. Gen. Kopanski; and 32nd Army Tank Brigade under Brig. Willison.

RIGHT FLANK: XII Corps under Lt. Gen. Godwin-Austin, which was made up of: New Zealand Division (Maj. Gen. Freyberg; 4th Indian Division (Maj. Gen. Messervy); and 1st Army Tank Brigade (Brig. Watkins).

LEFT FLANK: XXX Corps under Lt. Gen. Norrie, made up of: 7th Armoured Division (Maj. Gen. Gott); 4th Armoured Brigade Group (Brig. Gatehouse); 1st South African Division (Maj. Gen. Brink); and 22nd Guards Brigade (Brig. Marriott).

This formation was fully motorized, with an armored force spearheaded by the 7th Armoured Division fielding 469 tanks, with 210 Crusaders and

A Pz.Kpfw. III Ausf F that appears to have lost a track. These panzers were lost in the fighting in the Belhamed sector south of Sidi Rezegh in November 1941.

An excellent shot of the early Crusader Mk. I with external mantlet, early dust guards, roadwheel covers, and possibly early air filter replacements.

165 American M3 Stuarts. Since the British still used tanks for infantry support, the Tobruk garrison and XIII Corps both had their share of Cruiser and Matilda II tanks. On this day the eighth Army could count on a total of 713 gun-armed tanks, with another 200 in reserve.

Panzergruppe Afrika at this time, theoretically under General Bastico's command, was deployed as follows: Italian XX Mobile Corps under Gen. Gambara, made up of the following:

"Ariete" Armored Division (Gen. Balotta), and "Trieste" Motorized Division (Gen. Piazzoni).

Panzergruppe Afrika commanded by Lt. Gen. Rommel, made up of:

The Afrika Korps, under Lt. Gen. Crüwell, composed of 15th Panzer Division (Maj. Gen. Neumann-

PzKpfw III's of 15th Panzer Division left on the battlefield after the fierce fighting at Sid Rezegh.

Silkow); 21st Panzer Division (Maj. Gen. von Ravenstein); Afrika Division (Maj. Gen. Sümmermann); and "Savona" Division (Gen. de Giorgis); plus the Italian XXI Corps under Gen. Navarrini, composed of: "Brescia" Division (Gen. Zambon); "Trento" Division (Gen. de Stefanis); "Bologna" Division (Gen. Gloria); and "Pavia" Division (Gen. Franceschini).

Panzergruppe Afrika had been formed on August 15 and this now allowed Rommel to designate General Crüwell as commander of the Afrika Korps. The original 5th Light Division was then renamed the 21st Panzer Division, but basically remained the same. The newly formed "Afrika" Division was made up of two infantry battalions recruited from former German volunteers in the French Foreign Legion. By early December it also had been renamed as the 90th Light Division.

Rommel's plan was to use the Italian XXI Corps to overrun Tobruk, while the Afrika Korps and some German units along with the whole "Savona" Division would confront the British on the line Sidi Omar–Capuzzo–Halfaya–Sollum. The 15th and 21st Panzer Divisions were ordered to position themselves

One of Rommel's favorite modes of travel in the field was this SdKfz. 250/3 radio/command vehicle name "GREIF."

near Gambut and be ready to move in any direction when called upon. Gambar's "Ariete" Armored Division was placed around Bir el Gubi and his "Trieste" Motorized Division at Bir Hacheim.

Against Cunningham's 713 tanks the Germans could field only 174 panzers, along with 146 Italian

A group of exuberant "Tommies" overrun this captured PzKpfw. IV in an attempt see the inside of an enemy tank and maybe assess the damage done by their anti-tank fire.

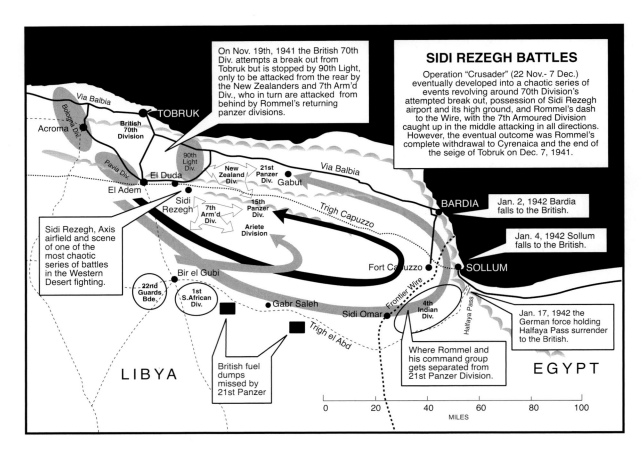

On Nov. 19th, 1941 the British 70th Div. attempts a break out from Tobruk but is stopped by 90th Light, only to be attacked from the rear by the New Zealanders and 7th Arm'd Div., who in turn are attacked from behind by Rommel's returning panzer divisions.

SIDI REZEGH BATTLES

Operation "Crusader" (22 Nov.- 7 Dec.) eventually developed into a chaotic series of events revolving around 70th Division's attempted break out, possession of Sidi Rezegh airport and its high ground, and Rommel's dash to the Wire, with the 7th Armoured Division caught up in the middle attacking in all directions. However, the eventual outcome was Rommel's complete withdrawal to Cyrenaica and the end of the seige of Tobruk on Dec. 7, 1941.

Jan. 2, 1942 Bardia falls to the British.

Jan. 4, 1942 Sollum falls to the British.

Jan. 17, 1942 the German force holding Halfaya Pass surrender to the British.

Where Rommel and his command group gets separated from 21st Panzer Division.

Sidi Rezegh, Axis airfield and scene of one of the most chaotic series of battles in the Western Desert fighting.

British fuel dumps missed by 21st Panzer

LIBYA

EGYPT

TOBRUK
Acroma
Via Balbia
Bologna Div.
Pavia Div.
British 70th Division
90th Light Div.
El Duda
El Adem
New Zealand Div.
21st Panzer Div.
Gabut
Via Balbia
Sidi Rezegh
7th Arm'd Div.
15th Panzer Div.
Ariete Division
Trigh Capuzzo
BARDIA
Bir el Gubi
22nd Guards Bde.
1st S.African Div.
Gabr Saleh
Fort Capuzzo
SOLLUM
Trigh el Abd
Sidi Omar
Frontier Wire
4th Indian Div.
Halfaya Pass

0   20   40   60   80   100
MILES

tanks of dubious value. The weight of numbers on the British side however is somewhat misleading. The German PzKpfw III had now been fitted with the long 50mm gun, and 139 of these tanks were available to Rommel. With this gun they could outrange the 2-pounders and 37mm guns on British vehicles and destroy them before they could move within effective striking range.

The SdKfz. 223 command and radio version of the SdKfz. 222 light armored car was used extensively in North Africa. Here we see one on the move, loaded to the hilt with tents and personal gear.

The new British Cruiser Mk.VI, Crusader Mk.I and Mk.II tanks were renowned for breaking down on the long sweeps, now so familiar in desert warfare. The sturdy Matilda, although heavily armored still only mounted a 2-pounder armor-piercing main gun that could not fire high explosive to support their infantry attacks. The M3 Light Stuart/Honey, although extremely fast and mechanically reliable, still suffered from the fact that its aero engine required special high-octane fuel and was prone to bursting into flames when hit.

The other ace that Rommel held was the anti-tank gun support that he always tried to provide for his armored formations. The legendary 8.8cm anti-aircraft gun, on a mobile carriage, was originally pressed into service by Rommel to defeat the heavy armor of the Matilda. This gun, later to be referred to simply as the 88, could control the battlefield from a great distance and had a devastating effect on armored vehicles out to a range of 2,000 yards and beyond. These, accompanied by the even more mobile 50mm anti-tank guns, were dug into prepared positions and usually blunted any British armored attack. The accompanying panzers would then counterattack the decimated British unit and hunt down the survivors.

The SdKfz. 263 was a very large eight-wheeled armored car decked out with a large frame aerial, along with a telescoping pole aerial for extra long range transmission.

The British Crusader offensive began on November 18 during a horrendous rainstorm, with one British corps taking up positions covering Halfaya Pass. The other corps moved across the desert in three columns, with the central one heading for Tobruk to link up with a planned breakout of the garrison troops. This part of the attack went well and reached within ten miles of the port and took the Sidi Rezegh airfield. However, the 22nd Armoured Brigade on the left flank ran into heavy resistance from a persistent Ariete Armored Division and lost at least fifty of its newly arrived Crusaders. 4th Armored Brigade on the right ran smack into the 21st Panzer Division and was stopped dead in its tracks.

At Bir el Gubi the Ariete, behind an extensive minefield and well-positioned anti-tank guns, had stood up well to the 22nd Armoured Brigade's attack. In this battle the sides were fairly evenly matched, with the Italians able to muster 146 M.13-40 medium tanks and supporting artillery, against 158 of the new British Crusader tanks supported by a battery of 25-pdr artillery. However, within their artillery and anti-tank screen the Italians had seven truck-mounted 102mm coastal artillery pieces firing armor-piercing shells originally designed to penetrate naval armor plate. These guns came into play and severely battered the 3 and 4 County of London Yeomanry, who were trying to outflank the Italian position.

Although caught a bit by surprise, Rommel soon realized that the British plan was to reach the Tobruk garrison. On November 22 he sent his two Afrika Korps armored divisions to recapture Sidi Rezegh, supported by the Italian XXI Corps. The battle over this airfield saw tanks on both sides go up in smoke, but it finally ended up in German hands

again. Norrie's 7th Armoured Brigade was reduced to ten remaining tanks. The 22nd Armored Brigade withdrew with only thirty-four tanks left, and on the next day the 5th South African Brigade lost 3,400 of its 5,700 men.

At the outset of the Crusader attack a 20-mile gap had appeared between XIII Corps and Norrie's XXX Corps. To fill this opening the 4th Armored Brigade with its 165 M3 Stuarts was split away from 7th Armoured Division, reducing its strength by one third. This later allowed Rommel's armor to take them on one at a time, to his delight.

THE GERMAN RESPONSE TO CRUSADER

The first sign of the British onslaught was a report of some 200 tanks moving up from the southwest. Gen. Ludwig Crüwell repeatedly warned Panzergruppe of this intrusion and insisted that it was a serious threat. However, Rommel simply was not convinced that this was anything more than a harassing operation. He had his mind set on attacking Tobruk and was in no mood to see this delayed again.

Baffled by Rommel's lack of response to their probe, Norrie had sent his 7th Armoured Division to take Sidi Rezegh and his 22nd Brigade to challenge the Ariete Armored Division. The 4th Armored Brigade was held back at Gabr Seleh to protect his left flank. His plan was to force Rommel to commit his armor, but in the process he had broken up his spearhead and diluted Cunningham's plan to draw Rommel into an all-out tank battle against a concentrated XXX Corps. The numerical advantage had been lost.

The Italians lost at least 34 tanks, but the British eventually broke off the engagement, leaving behind

A typical example of an Ariete carro armatti M. 13-40 loaded down with jerry cans for the long trip forward.

A wartime publicity shot of a squadron of Matilda II heavy infantry tanks manned by the British 4th RTR. Although extremely well armored, the Matilda tank mounted the relatively small 2-pounder cannon which could only fire armor-piercing shot, lacking a high-explosive round to support the infantry.

50 knocked-out tanks. By this time Crüwell had finally convinced Rommel that the British attack was serious. He now sent a strike force of 120 tanks of 5th Panzer Regiment, under Colonel Stephan toward Gabr Saleh to engage the enemy threatening the 3rd Reconnaissance Battalion.

By mid-afternoon Stephan's force had made contact with 4th Armoured Brigade northeast of Gabr Saleh and opened fire at 1,500 yards. The British were equipped with the new Honey M3 Stuart light tank, and these vehicles, moving at up to 40 miles an hour, charged into the ranks of 5th Panzer Regiment, creating utter chaos. The Honey mounted only a 37mm cannon and had to close rapidly with the enemy to get within effective firing range of about 1,000 yards. Interestingly enough, the Honey got its name from the first British tank commander to try one out. They shot across the desert in a cloud of dust, and when they returned, he remarked, "It's a real honey," and the name stuck.

Much of the fighting was done at very close range with disastrous results for those that happened to expose their flanks to the murderous fire from all quarters. By dusk, Stephan's force had severely damaged two regiments of 4th Armoured Brigade and withdrew to refuel and resupply.

However, the overall picture was far from clear, and that evening Rommel learned that a British force of tanks and armored cars had roared onto Sidi Rezegh airfield and seized it from the weak Italian contingent there. Air reconnaissance reported three endless British columns moving northward between Girabub and Bir el Gubi, so Major General von Ravenstein proposed that 15th and 21st Panzer Divisions be combined to destroy each column in turn. Unfortunately he read the British spearhead wrong and spent most of the day "swanning" around Sidi Omar looking for an imaginary enemy. Once he realized his mistake, he swung 15th Panzer in a wide sweep southwest, and in the late afternoon of November 20 the 8th Panzer Regiment encountered a strong enemy tank force supported by artillery and anti-tank guns.

A Valentine infantry tank debarking from a portee truck near Bardia. These large white-red-white recognition markings were used mainly during Operation Crusader.

This turned out to be the 4th Armoured Brigade, positioned around Gabr Seleh, and a furious tank battle ensued. As night came on, the British retired, and that night 15th Panzer laagered at Bagr Lachem and took on much-needed fuel and supplies. At the same time the 4th Armoured Brigade was licking its wounds and found that it was now down to 77 Honeys, with the total tank strength of XXX Corps being a meager 119 of various types.

While all this was going on, the 7th Armoured Brigade and the New Zealander Division had reinforced their positions around Sidi Rezegh airfield

A typical 25-pdr field gun position sprawled across the open desert. This advance position is manned by gunners of the 4th New Zealand Field Regiment.

The mosque and tomb of an ancient Arab saint and his son at Sidi Rezegh, which gives the site its name.

and thwarted attempts by the Afrika Division to re-take it. Rommel now realized the threat to his perimeter around Tobruk and decided that he had to attack northward from Gabr Saleh to intercept and destroy the enemy force advancing on Tobruk.

Several great opportunities had been squandered the previous day, but on November 21, the full wrath of the Afrika Korps, screened by 88s and 50mm anti-tank guns bore down on Sidi Rezegh. By noon the 7th Armoured Brigade was a pile of rubble, with a mere ten surviving Cruisers escaping. The Germans had opened fire at 2,000 yards from behind a screen of anti-tank guns, and in due time the 15th Panzer was abreast of the high ground overlooking the airfield. However, attempts to seize the airfield itself were unsuccessful.

A newly arrived British Crusader Mk. II cruiser tank being loaded onto a tank transporter for movement to the front area. Note the metal rack on the rear for carrying "flimsies," the soft metal petrol cans used by the British before they were introduced to the jerry can by the Germans.

During all this General Scobie's Tobruk garrison had attempted its planned breakout, and Rommel was busy trying to contain them. In an attempt to link up with Scobie's forces, Brig. "Jock" Campbell's 7th Support Group had plunged northward, planning to capture the Sidi Rezegh escarpment and from there to break through to the garrison forces. Scobie's 70th British Division, along with 32nd Army Tank Brigade, tolled over the Afrika and Bologna Divisions, and Rommel was forced to throw everything he had at them to close the hole in his Tobruk lines.

In the meantime XIII Corps, with the New Zealand Division at the helm, had advanced to a point where they were behind the Afrika Korps and crossing the Trigh Capuzzo near Sidi Azeiz. This development was such that Rommel was forced to order his Panzertruppe headquarters at Gambut to retire to El Adem during the night of November 21. Rommel had little or no reserves left to stave off this new threat and was resigned to sending two reconnaissance battalions eastward to keep tab on XIII Corps.

By this time the Crusader offensive had broken down into a melee of isolated actions, with German and British units scattered everywhere over a twenty-five-mile stretch of desert. The movement of possibly 35,000 vehicles of all types had pulverized the battlefield surfaces to a fine sand that was wafted into the air by the wind, along with smoke from the guns and burning vehicles until visibility was totally obliterated. Units stumbled around, drove in circles, and clashed unexpectedly for hours, leaving their commanders at a loss as to the outcome of battle or even where their units were.

Crüwell, in an attempt to escape this chaos, and knowing that his 15th Panzer was low on fuel, chose to regroup south of Gambut, while 21st Panzer moved down over the escarpment and assembled near Belhamed.

On November 22, with the Afrika Korps refuelled, Rommel chose to make an aggressive move by sending von Ravenstein's armor in a wide sweep across the Axis bypass road at El Duda for another attack on Sidi Rezegh airfield from the west. Afrika Korps infantry and Sümmermann's Afrika Division would attack the Sidi Rezegh escarpment from the north in support of this move. At the same time, German heavy artillery would pound the British positions there.

Just after noon on the twenty-second the 5th Panzer Regiment roared onto the airfield, with the

A new Crusader II displaying the latest bulbous external gun mantlet fitted to all later Mk.IIs. Also seen here are the side rails used to support the large sunshades that, from the air, gave the tanks the appearance of being trucks. The Crusader was a rakish and fast moving tank on the battlefield, but found it hard to survive with its small 2-pdr gun and light armor plate, let alone the problems of poor tactical deployment and constant mechanical problems.

British 25-pounder field artillery doing their best to quell the attack, but to no avail. The 22nd Armoured Brigade counterattacked and lost 45 of their 79 tanks, but by nightfall the airfield was back in German hands.

Later that evening Crüwell made an unexpected probe into the flank of 7th Armoured Division and stumbled upon elements of 4th Armoured Brigade laagered down for the night. The German armor was within ten yards of the British tanks before they recognized them as such, and after a short skirmish lit up by flares and burning tanks, 150 men, 17 officers, and 35 tanks were captured.

The battles of November 22 had reduced 7th Armoured Division to one-third strength. Its 4th Armoured Brigade was totally destroyed, and the 7th and 22nd Brigades were truly battered. Rommel had taken the initiative and it had paid off.

On November 23, *Totensonntag,* the date when Germans honoured their World War I dead, Crüwell ordered 15th Panzer, accompanied by 5th Panzer Regiment, across the rear of 7th Armoured Division in an effort to link up with the Ariete. From there he would sandwich the British against the infantry

and guns of 21st Panzer dug in on the escarpment south of Sidi Rezegh airfield. Roaring through endless streams of British supply columns, he linked up with Ariete and at full speed swept down on the 7th Armoured. Losses were heavy on both sides, but when the battle was over, the 5th South African Brigade ceased to exist, and the tank strength of 7th Armoured was down to next to nothing.

Rommel was in his glory, and at midnight he radioed Rome and Berlin to say that he could envisage the complete destruction of the British Eighth Army if his supplies continued to arrive as promised.

At 1030 hours on the twenty-fourth Rommel suddenly decided that he wanted to bag the whole eighth Army, and leaving Westphal in charge of Panzergruppe HQ, he rounded up 15th and 21st Panzer Divisions, about 100 tanks, and headed east for Sidi Omar in the hope of striking the British in the rear.

By late afternoon he had reached the Wire, with the whole Afrika Korps strung out behind him for over forty miles. Ahead of him the 7th Armoured Division and 1st South African Division had stampeded in all directions, and once the rear supply elements saw him coming, there was complete chaos. Rommel had ordered von Ravenstein to lead the attack with 21st Panzer Division and push straight through the frontier wire and swing north to the sea near Sollum. At the same time a kampfgruppe of a single motorized battalion with one company of tanks was to attack General Cunningham's headquarters at Maddalena. A second kampfgruppe from 15th Panzer Division was ordered to head over the escarpment to capture the railhead and adjoining fuel dump at Bir Habata. If these two moves had succeeded it literally would have beheaded the Eighth Army in the field.

When Cunningham heard that Rommel was well in his rear and bearing down on Bardia, with very little between him and Alexandria, his immediate reaction was to call off the attack and withdraw his forces back into Egypt. This was exactly what Rommel had been hoping for, but General Auchinleck intervened and flew up to Eighth Army headquarters to overrule this move. He ordered that the offensive continue, and this changed the whole complexion of the battle. Cunningham was eventually relieved and replaced by Neil Ritchie.

During this rapid advance Rommel's forces had passed within a mile or two of the British supply dump F.S.D. 63, fifteen miles southeast of Bir el Gubi, and F.S.D. 65, fifteen miles southeast of Gabr Saleh. Had these dumps been captured at the time, it would

have strangled XXX Corps, along with the New Zealand Division.

Their only protection at that time was the Guards Brigade. General Bayerlein, when questioned on this after the war, recalled that as they passed through they saw and identified the Guards Brigade, but never gave any thought to what they were doing there. Had they turned slightly and captured or destroyed these two dumps, the battle would have been won. However, the R.A.F. had done a fine job of keeping German reconnaissance aircraft well away from that area, and Rommel's staff had no idea that they were there.

This daring raid into the rear of the Eighth Army might have worked had Auchinleck not intervened and ordered his forces to hang tough and go on the offensive. With the rest of his army screaming for the return of the Afrika Korps, Rommel had no other recourse than to call off this escapade. To his horror, the 21st Panzer Division had already returned to Libya under countermanding orders from Westphal, who was well aware of how serious the situation was.

While he was away, the situation had changed considerably. During this respite the British had brought up replacement tanks and salvaged and repaired others. The New Zealanders had made a firm

A good view of an early model of the Pz.Kpfw.III Ausf J that has been recovered by a British tank transporter rig. The turret number reads 111 in white outline while the squares were a British addition.

Rommel and a group of his officers and staff.

hook-up with the Tobruk garrison, and the R.A.F. was having a field day with his supply columns. In a desperate effort to regain the initiative he drove General Freyberg's New Zealanders from Sidi Rezegh again and severed the link with the Tobruk garrison.

As of November 29 von Ravenstein was now down to twenty tanks, and Neumann-Silkow had forty-three, and with these meager forces they still managed to reclaim Duda, only to have it retaken by the British, where General von Ravenstein was taken prisoner.

On the thirtieth Rommel put everything he had into a heavy bombardment of the New Zealander's positions at Sidi Rezegh. He then sent 15th Panzer in for the kill and once again Sidi Rezegh was in German hands.

On December 1 the remaining tanks of 8th Panzer Regiment overran the 4th New Zealand Brigade at Belhamed and captured huge quantities of war supplies and hordes of prisoners. The encirclement of Tobruk was again secure and Rommel appeared to have the desert war well under control. He still had several garrisons trapped on the Sollum front, and

the two kampfgruppen he sent to liberate them were badly mauled. An attempt to recapture the El Duda prominence on December 4 also broke down under heavy artillery. Crüwell objected vigorously to these moves by Rommel but was overruled. The Afrika Korps was now only a skeleton of its former self, and Crüwell wanted to rebuild their formations before frittering away any more of his men and machines on minor objectives.

On December 5 Rommel received word from Rome that no further reinforcements would be forthcoming before January 1942. This startling news obviously struck home and he finally acknowledged that he would have to withdraw from Cyrenaica until he could rebuild his waning forces. The Afrika Korps was now down to forty tanks, and the Ariete to thirty, but Ritchie's eighth Army was steadily replacing its losses from their reserves. On this same day Neumann-Silkow, commander of 15th Panzer, was killed by incoming artillery fire. At this point the Axis forces had lost over 8,000 men and some units could no longer resist enemy pressure.

By December 12, after a masterful withdrawal protected by well-disciplined rearguards, Rommel had reached the Gazala Line. His thoughts of holding this position were dashed when the British broke through the Italian XX Motorized Corps and now enveloped him on both flanks.

The Axis forces streamed westward until they reached Agedabia, and here they made a short stand. On December 19 the *Ankara* had docked in Benghazi and unloaded twenty-two tanks, much to Crüwell's delight. With these first reinforcements since early November, an attempt to outflank the German forces by the British 22nd Armoured Brigade was smashed. Crüwell lost seven tanks in this battle, but the British force had lost thirty-seven, and once again the Afrika Korps was gaining strength.

Although Crüwell was all for setting up defenses at Agedabia, Rommel was afraid that a wide sweep through the desert could outflank this position and chose to move back to Marsa el Brega. This was now January 2, the same day that the Bardia garrison surrendered.

More than 500 miles behind these new positions, three remaining Axis garrisons had been under siege in Bardia, Sollum, and Halfaya Pass. On December 30 the British had made a concerted attack on the Bardia defenders, making use of land, sea, and air bombardment. However, it was not until January 2,

A German 4.7cm Panzerjäger I of 39th Motorized Anti-Tank Battalion waiting in a defensive mode for further orders. It appears to have been swabbed with local mud or a mop and paint to better fade into its desert surroundings.

1942, that their assault, supported by armored units, finally managed to penetrate the defenses. With the situation becoming increasingly hopeless, the city was eventually surrendered later that day.

Sollum had been occupied by the Germans since November 21, 1941, and was now defended by the 10th Oasis Company, the HQ of 300th Special Purpose Oasis Battalion, and the remnants of 12th Oasis Company. They were now down to about seventy German soldiers and managed to hold off several vigorous attacks on January 11 and 12, but finally used up the last of their food and ammunition and surrendered on the twelfth.

The defenders at Halfaya Pass, consisting mainly of the 1st Battalion, 104th Infantry Regiment, were

A German 88mm gun being towed into position. Much of the desert terrain was very rough, and this caused much wear and tear on vehicles.

A PzKpfw. III Ausf G moving forward in 1941 is loaded to the hilt with spare track and roadwheels as extra bow protection. In the desert fighting in North Africa the gunner often concocted a protective canvas muzzle cover to keep the barrel of his 5cm KwK L/42 gun clear of sand.

well dug in, and their main concern was a lack of water for the men. Their 2nd Company was chosen to lead an assault squad which recaptured a local well long enough for their water truck to fill up, thus replenishing their drinking water supply. Several attempts were made to resupply the beleaguered forces at Halfaya by air, with night flights of Ju 52 transport aircraft flying out of airbases on the island of Crete. However, these flights were discovered by the British and on the second night were intercepted and shot down by British night fighters.

In mid-January the remnants of the Italian "Savona" Division, which had been holding out farther to the west, was driven back to the pass, as the situation became more and more hopeless.

Eventually, preliminary surrender negotiations were begun with the South Africans, and on the morning of January 17, 1942, the last defenders of

Halfaya Pass marched into captivity, ending another phase in the battle for North Africa.

The fighting in North Africa would claim a heavy toll on numerous Panzer-Armee Afrika commanders, because of the unique demands placed on them. The terrain and actions demanded that they be well forward to make the vital decisions required, and Rommel expected this of them. Out of 37 generals or colonels that took over major commands during the course of the campaign, von Randow, von Prittwitz, Neumann-Silkow, and Sümmermann all were killed in action, along with Stumme, who died of heart failure while under attack. Six more—Nehring, von Esebeck, Fehn, von Bismarck, von Liebenstein, and Kleemann—were wounded, and three more were taken prisoner: Crüwell, von Ravenstein, and von Thoma. This made a total of fourteen DAK generals that were put out of action.

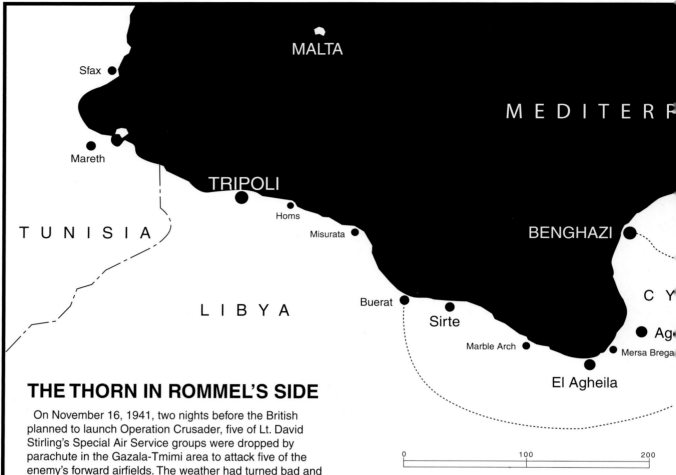

MALTA

Sfax •

M E D I T E R R

Mareth •

TRIPOLI •

Homs •

T U N I S I A

Misurata •

BENGHAZI •

L I B Y A

Buerat •

C Y

Sirte •

Ag•

Marble Arch •

Mersa Brega

El Agheila •

0   100   200

THE THORN IN ROMMEL'S SIDE

On November 16, 1941, two nights before the British planned to launch Operation Crusader, five of Lt. David Stirling's Special Air Service groups were dropped by parachute in the Gazala-Tmimi area to attack five of the enemy's forward airfields. The weather had turned bad and they were forced to jump from 500 feet into gale force winds which scattered the men and supply chutes. This air attack was a total disaster and many of the men were lost, but Stirling and some of his men were picked up by the Long Range Desert Group (LRDG) and transported 250 miles south to their Siwa Oasis base.

This experience convinced Stirling that his Special Air Service (SAS) raiders should stick to surface attacks, using the LRDG to drive them into enemy rear areas. From that point on Rommel's airstrips and supply transport were under constant threat of attack from this combined group. The men of the LRDG had originally been deployed to operate from the southern vastness of the desert and radio back reports on enemy movements and build-ups. While carrying out these reconnaissance missions, they would now also drop off and rendezvous with the SAS groups after their sabotage missions were completed. With this arrangement the SAS had immediate success, and between December 14 and 28, 1941, they struck enemy airstrips from Sirte to Agedabia, destroying 61 planes on the ground, along with 30 enemy vehicles.

On the night of January 23, 1942, in one of their greatest successes, the SAS was in position to strike at an oil supply depot in Buerat, west of Sirte. They managed to blow up eighteen enormous fuel transporters, each loaded with 4,000 gallons of fuel, along with the dock facilities and accompanying warehouses filled with everything from foodstuffs to heavy machinery. Rommel had just launched his latest offensive and was desperately short of these massive fuel transporters at this time.

They would not be easily replaced. That same night a second group also knocked out a German wireless intercept station ju east of the town.

From this point on they continually harassed airfields and supply lines of the Afrika Korps and began to earn Rommel's concern, as he mentioned their attacks in several of his report Since Rommel had once again pushed the British back to Tobi Lt. Col. Stirling chose the airfields near Benghazo as his next targets. Moving by night and navigating by the stars, several S attack groups were delivered to the Cyrenaican escarpment overlooking the city sixteen miles away. The Senussi inhabitan of these foothills were bitter enemies of the Italians and eager gave them refuge and assistance hiding the trucks. They had come equipped with a makeshift German staff car so that they could move freely along the main roads, but this outing was les than successful. They managed to blow up 15 planes at Berka airstrip, but found most of them too heavily guarded now. They had also hoped to sink shipping in Benghazi harbor, but this never reached fruition either.

On the nights of June 13 and 14, in support of the Malta convoys, it was planned that eight separate raids would take place simultaneously against German airfields. The targets we located in the Benghazi sector, Derna area, Barce, and Herakl aerodrome in Crete. Each raiding party consisted of five men, and the three airstrips near Derna would be the hardest to cra For Derna they enlisted the help of the SIG, which was made of German-speaking Palestinian Jews who had trained to work behind German lines dressed as DAK soldiers.

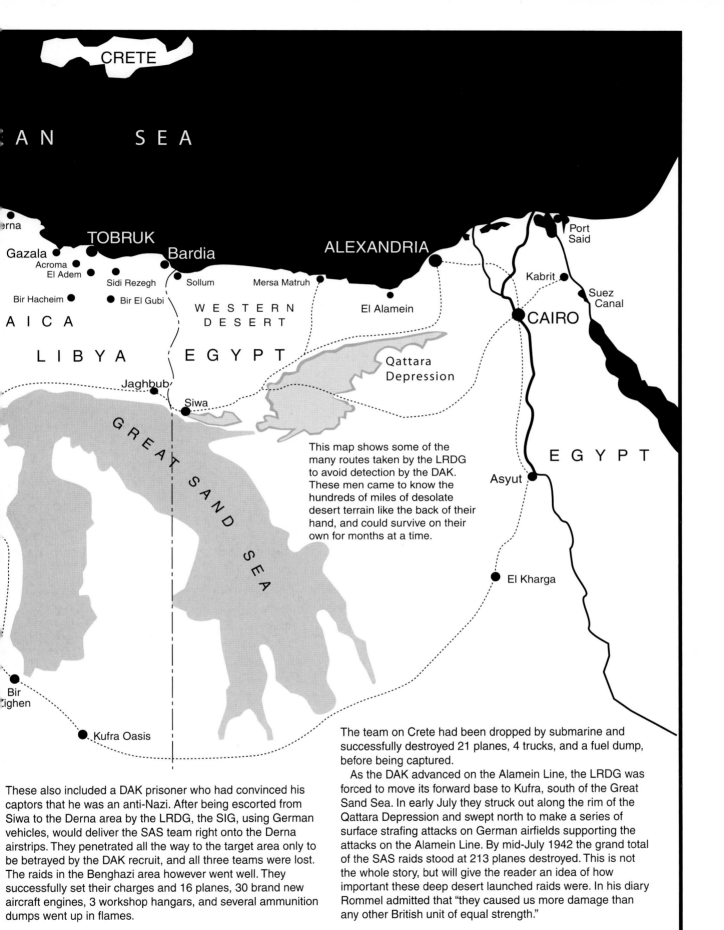

CRETE

AN SEA

erna

TOBRUK

Gazala

Acroma

El Adem

Bir Hacheim

Bir El Gubi

AICA

LIBYA

Sidi Rezegh

Bardia

Sollum

WESTERN
DESERT

ALEXANDRIA

Mersa Matruh

El Alamein

Port
Said

Kabrit

Suez
Canal

CAIRO

EGYPT

Qattara
Depression

Jaghbub

Siwa

GREAT SAND SEA

This map shows some of the
many routes taken by the LRDG
to avoid detection by the DAK.
These men came to know the
hundreds of miles of desolate
desert terrain like the back of their
hand, and could survive on their
own for months at a time.

EGYPT

Asyut

El Kharga

Bir
ighen

Kufra Oasis

These also included a DAK prisoner who had convinced his
captors that he was an anti-Nazi. After being escorted from
Siwa to the Derna area by the LRDG, the SIG, using German
vehicles, would deliver the SAS team right onto the Derna
airstrips. They penetrated all the way to the target area only to
be betrayed by the DAK recruit, and all three teams were lost.
The raids in the Benghazi area however went well. They
successfully set their charges and 16 planes, 30 brand new
aircraft engines, 3 workshop hangars, and several ammunition
dumps went up in flames.

The team on Crete had been dropped by submarine and
successfully destroyed 21 planes, 4 trucks, and a fuel dump,
before being captured.

As the DAK advanced on the Alamein Line, the LRDG was
forced to move its forward base to Kufra, south of the Great
Sand Sea. In early July they struck out along the rim of the
Qattara Depression and swept north to make a series of
surface strafing attacks on German airfields supporting the
attacks on the Alamein Line. By mid-July 1942 the grand total
of the SAS raids stood at 213 planes destroyed. This is not
the whole story, but will give the reader an idea of how
important these deep desert launched raids were. In his diary
Rommel admitted that "they caused us more damage than
any other British unit of equal strength."

57

British Infantry Tank Squadron: June 16, 1941

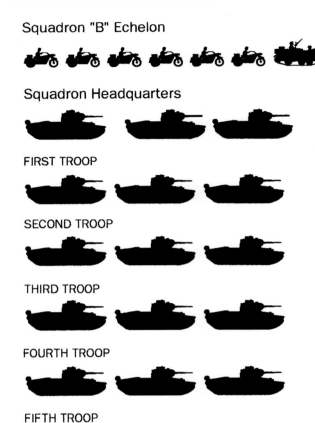

Squadron "B" Echelon

Squadron Headquarters

FIRST TROOP

SECOND TROOP

THIRD TROOP

FOURTH TROOP

FIFTH TROOP

In the early Western Desert battles against the Italians the British Matilda infantry tank ruled the battlefield. It was virtually immune to any anti-tank gun or tank gun on the field and reigned supreme until the appearance of the German 8.8 cm FlaK 36 which was being used in an anti-tank role by mid-1941. This was the first gun that was able to penetrate the Matilda's maximum 78mm armor at long range. However, the number of 88s was always at a premium, and when the infantry tanks managed to evade them, they were almost unstoppable.

During the see-saw battles for possession of the Halfaya Pass feature, nine Matildas of C Squadron, 4RTR, were sent out to cover the withdrawal of their infantry units retiring down to the coastal road. A strong German force of over 100 tanks, led by PzKpfw. IIIs, was bearing down on them, but the 37mm and 50mm shot from their guns simply bounced off the Matilda's thick armor. At 500 to 800 yards the British 2-pounder gun could penetrate any German or Italian tank of that period, and the Matildas took a heavy toll that day, with tanks of the 5th Light Division being forced to pull back out of range.

Track damage had immobilized six of the Matildas, but their crews were picked up by the three undamaged infantry tanks and they then retired down the pass to rejoin their infantry.

It would continue to be their slow speed, track damage, and the lack of a high-explosive round that would plague the Matilda to the end. There appeared to exist among the German and Italian tank crews a very real fear of the Matilda, and a serious request was made for a self-propelled Panzerjäger to be shipped to Africa that could restore the balance.

The Matilda tank squadron was comprised of both fighting and administrative (or B Echelon) vehicles. The former included all eighteen Matildas, and the latter was made up of the softskin contingent and generally accompanied the battalion headquarters. In the event that the squadron was acting independently, the B Echelon would usually be augmented with additional trucks drawn from the Battalion HQ.

In the field the Matilda squadron was attached to an infantry brigade or battalion for a particular operation. The Matildas would form up with the infantry troops and then preceded them in the upcoming advance on foot. Until the appearance of the German 88mm FlaK guns used in the anti-tank role, there was nothing that could stop such an attack except for heavy artillery fire directed at the accompanying infantry unit.

90th LIGHT DIVISION: November 26, 1941
90. LEICHTE DIVISION

AFRIKA DIVISION HEADQUARTERS
    259th Motorized Mapping Detachment
    190th Motorized Signal Company

155th MOTORIZED INFANTRY DIVISION
    Mot. Regiment HQ & Mot. HQ Company
– 1st Infantry Battalion (truck borne)
    Battalion HQ
    3 Motorized Companies (truck borne)
    1 Heavy Company (truck borne)
– 2nd Infantry Battalion (truck borne)
    Battalion HQ
    3 Motorized Companies (truck borne)
    1 Heavy Company (truck borne)
– 3rd Infantry Battalion (truck borne)
    Battalion HQ
    3 Motorized Companies (truck borne)
    1 Heavy Company (truck borne)

361st AFRIKA REGIMENT (truck borne)
    Regiment HQ & HQ Company (truck borne)
– 1st Infantry Battalion (truck borne)
    Battalion HQ
    3 Infantry Companies (truck borne)
    1 Heavy Company (truck borne)
– 2nd Infantry Battalion (truck borne)
    Battalion HQ
    3 Infantry Companies (truck borne)
    1 Heavy Company (truck borne)
– 361st Afrika Artillery Battalion (truck borne)
    Battalion HQ & Signal Platoon
    Motorized Calibration Detachment
    3 Artillery Batteries (truck borne)
    1st Company/613th AA Bn. (truck borne)

3rd BATTALION/347th INF. RGT. (non-mot.)
    Battalion Headquarters
    3 Infantry Companies
    1 Heavy Company

3rd BATTALION/255th INF. RGT. (non-mot.)
    Battalion Headquarters
    3 Infantry Companies
    1 Heavy Company

The 90th Light Division was in the process of being reorganized at this time and therefore is hard to depict with total accuracy. The term "truck borne" has been used because although both the 155th Motorized and 361st Afrika Regiments were not organically motorized, the moment that trucks from any source became available (Italian, German, or captured), they were assigned to these units. The following list indicated the number of vehicles authorized for services as of January 30, 1942.

I/155	10 Light Personnel Carriers, 15 Trucks
II/155	10 Light Personnel Carriers, 15 Trucks
III/155	10 Light Personnel Carriers, 15 Trucks
361 Regt. HQ.	46 Light Personnel Carries, 12 Trucks
I/361	11 Light Personnel Carriers, 20 Trucks
II/361	11 Light Personnel Carriers, 20 Trucks
361 Art. Bn.	21 Light Personnel Carriers, 20 Trucks

However, III/347th and III/255th battalions did not officially have any vehicles assigned to them at this time.

The 90th Light Division was originally assembled as Afrika-Division z.b.V. (Africa Division for special purposes) in August of 1941. It was composed of new troops brought in from the continent. It first saw serious action during the breakout sortie of the Tobruk garrison on November 21, 1941. On November 28 it was renamed the 90th Light Division, and in March 1942 it was reorganized and redesignated as the 90th Light Africa Division.

21st PANZER DIVISION: January 30, 1942
21. PANZER DIVISION

21st PANZER DIVISION HEADQUARTERS
    200th Motorized Mapping Detachment
    200th Motorized Printing Detachment

5th PANZER REGIMENT
– Panzer Regiment Headquarters
    Armored Signal Platoon
    2 Light Tank Platoons
– 1st Armored Battalion
    Battalion HQ & HQ Company
    3 Light Tank Companies
    1 Medium Tank Company
– 2nd Armored Battalion
    Battalion HQ & HQ Company
    3 Light Tank Companies
    1 Medium Tank Company

104th MOTORIZED INFANTRY REGIMENT
– Regimental HQ & HQ Company
    Signal Platoon
    Anti-Tank Platoon
    Motorcycle Messenger Platoon
    Engineer Platoon
– 11th Motorized Infantry Gun Company
– 1st Motorized Infantry Battalion
    (This infantry battalion went into captivity at
    Halfaya Pass on Jan. 17, 1941)
– 2nd Motorized Infantry Battalion
    Battalion Headquarters
    3 Motorized Infantry Companies
    1 Motorized MG Company
    1 Motorized Heavy Company
      2 Anti-Tank Platoons
      1 Engineer Platoon

8th MOTORIZED MG BATTALION
– Battalion HQ & HQ Company
    Signal Platoon
    2 Motorcycle HMG Platoons
    3 Motorized MG Companies
    1 Motorized Heavy Company
      2 Mortar Platoons
      2 Anti-Tank Platoons
      1 Engineer Platoon
    1 Motorized Anti-Tank Company

3rd ARMORED RECONNAISSANCE BN.
    Battalion HQ & Signal Platoon
    1 Armored Car Company
    1 Motorcycle Company
    1 Motorized Heavy Company
      2 Anti-Tank Platoons
      1 Engineer Platoon

155th MOTORIZED ARTILLERY REGIMENT
    Regiment HQ
– 1st Motorized Artillery Battalion
    Battalion HQ
    3 Motorized Batteries
– 2nd Motorized Artillery Battalion
    Battalion HQ
    3 Motorized Batteries
– 3rd Motorized Artillery Battalion
    Battalion HQ
    3 Motorized Batteries

39th MOTORIZED ANTI-TANK BATTALION
    Battalion HQ & Signal Platoon
    3 Motorized Anti-Tank Companies

200th MOTORIZED ENGINEER BATTALION
    Battalion Headquarters
    3 Motorized Engineer Companies

200th ARMORED SIGNAL BATTALION
    Battalion Headquarters
    1 Armored Radio Company
    1 Armored Telephone Company

15th PANZER DIVISION: January 30, 1942
15. PANZER DIVISION

15th PANZER DIVISION HEADQUARTERS
33rd Motorized Mapping Detachment

8th PANZER REGIMENT
– Panzer Regiment Headquarters
  Armored Signal Platoon
  Light Tank Platoon
– 1st Armored Battalion
  Battalion HQ & HQ Company
  3 Light Tank Companies
  1 Medium Tank Company
– 2nd Armored Battalion
  Battalion HQ & HQ Company
  3 Light Tank Companies
  1 Medium Tank Company

15th MOTORIZED INFANTRY BRIGADE
Brigade Headquarters
– **115th Mot. Infantry Regiment**
  Regiment HQ & HQ Company
    Signal Platoon
    Anti-Tank Platoon
    Motorcycle Messenger Platoon
    Engineer Platoon
  Motorized Infantry Gun Company
– 1st Motorized Infantry Battalion
  Battalion Headquarters
  4 Motorized Infantry Companies
  1 Motorized Heavy Company
  2 Anti-Tank Platoons
  1 Engineer Platoon
– 2nd Motorized Infantry Battalion
  Battalion Headquarters
  4 Motorized Infantry Companies
  1 Motorized Heavy Company
  2 Anti-Tank Platoons
  1 Engineer Platoon

200th Motorized Infantry Regiment
Regiment HQ & HQ Company
  Signal Platoon
  1 Volkswagen Scout Platoon
  1 Motorcycle Scout Platoon

2nd Motorized MG Battalion
Battalion HQ & HQ Company
  Signal Platoon
  2 Motorcycle HMG Platoons
3 Motorized MG Companies
1 Motorized Heavy Company
  1 Motorized Artillery Battery
  1 Engineer Platoon

15th Motorcycle Battalion
  Battalion Headquarters
  3 Motorcycle Companies
  1 Motorcycle MG Company
  1 Motorized Heavy Company
    1 Engineer Platoon

33rd ARMORED RECONNAISSANCE BN.
Battalion HQ & Signal Platoon
1 Armored Car Company
1 Motorcycle Company
1 Motorized Heavy Company
  2 Anti-Tank Platoons
  1 Engineer Platoon

33rd MOTORIZED ARTILLERY REGIMENT
Regiment HQ & HQ Battery
Motorized Observation Battery
– 1st Motorized Artillery Battalion
  Battalion HQ & HQ Battery
  3 Motorized Batteries
– 2nd Motorized Artillery Battalion
  Battalion HQ & HQ Battery
  3 Motorized Batteries
– 3rd Motorized Artillery Battalion
  Battalion HQ & HQ Battery
  3 Motorized Artillery Batteries

33rd MOTORIZED ANTI-TANK BATTALION
Battalion HQ & Signal Platoon
3 Anti-Tank Companies

33rd MOTORIZED ENGINEER BATTALION
Battalion HQ
3 Motorized Engineer Companies

33rd ARMORED SIGNAL BATTALION
Battalion HQ
1 Armored Radio Company
1 Armored Telephone Company

GREIF, ADLER, and IGEL

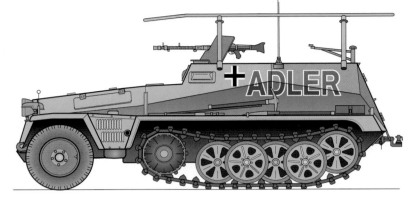

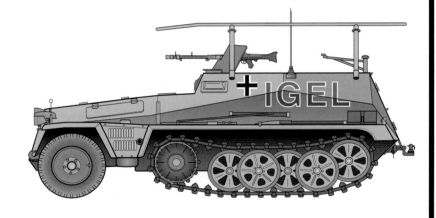

GREIF, ADLER, and IGEL appear to have been the names of some of Rommel's and Crüwell's SdKfz. 250/3 semi-track funkwagens (fitted with radio equipment). However, they pose more questions than answers.

Most of us are familiar with Rommel's early type SdKfz.250/3 leichter Funkpanzerwagen "GREIF" (Griffin), but little has come to light about "ADLER" (Eagle) and "IGEL" (Hedgehog). There are a few photos of these other two vehicles, but nothing confirming who used these vehicles and when. However, IGEL just may have been used by a commander named Keil, and ADLER appears have been one used by Crüwell, but Rommel appears to have used it at times as well, possibly when GREIF was being serviced or was out of reach.

There is also a good chance these questions will never be answered authoritatively.

PzKpfw. II Ausf C

15th Pz. Division,
8th Pz. Regiment,
8th Company

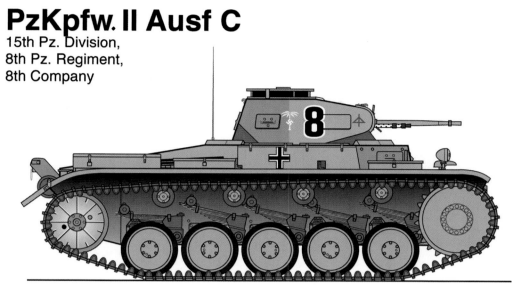

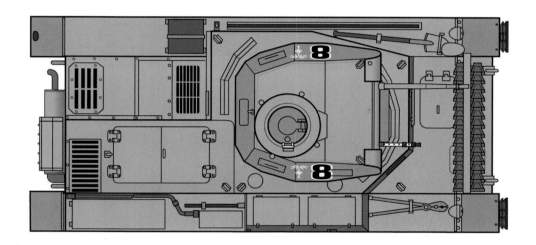

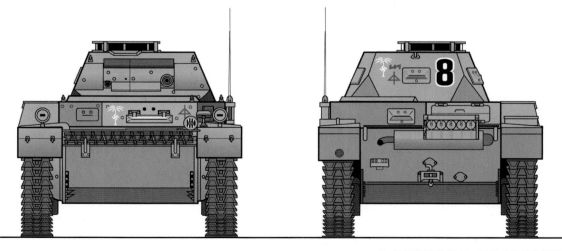

63

PzKpfw. III Ausf J
of 15th Pz. Division, 8th Pz. Regiment, 7th Company, May 1942

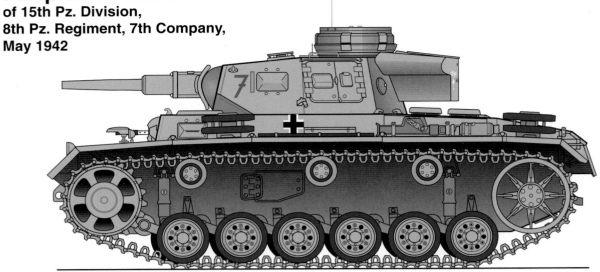

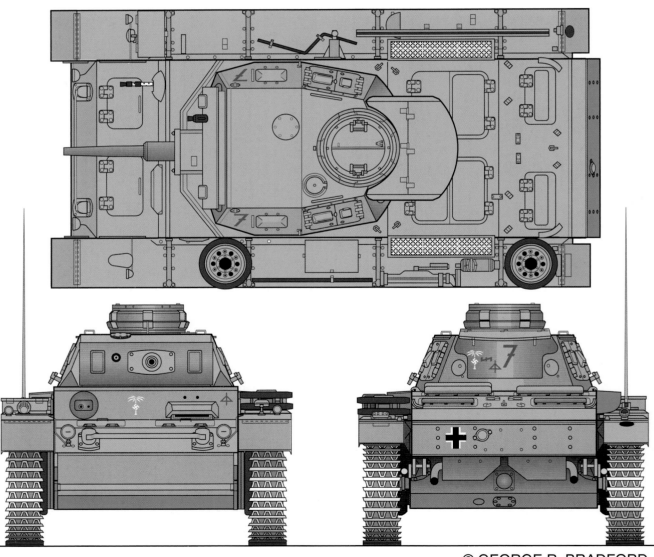

3rd Panzer Division   **15th Panzer Division**   **21st Panzer Division**

PANZER DIVISION TACTICAL SIGNS

Each German armored division had its own tactical marking, and although they are often hard to see, they do show up on many of the photos here. These markings were intended to appear in yellow, but white appears to have been more dominant and in some cases they almost appear to be black on the sand background.

AFRIKA KORPS PALM TREE SYMBOL

The palm/swastika symbol was carried by almost every vehicle, especially softskins and supply trucks, which had them painted prominently on their cab doors. It appeared in numerous variations and often was merely masked over when sand paint was applied, thereby leaving a boxed or irregular shape of the original palm on gray paint. Size varied from about six inches to twelve inches, depending on the location.

65

GAZALA BATTLES

INTO THE CAULDRON

GAZALA BATTLES: INTO THE CAULDRON

The war in North Africa had always depended on resupply by sea, and up to this juncture the British were well ahead. The Axis shipments of tanks and fuel from Italian ports were always at risk, and Armeegruppe Afrika could never be certain that replacement vehicles would arrive as planned. It was now obvious that the war in North Africa was to be won or lost on this point.

Malta was the key to naval superiority in the Mediterranean, and at the end of 1941 Hitler agreed to transfer about two dozen German submarines to the Mediterranean, along with Luftflotte 2, recently arrived from the Russian front. Between them, these forces temporarily neutralized Malta and escorted convoys crossing on the sea lanes to Tripoli, so that Panzergruppe Afrika was able to rebuild itself. Janu-

ary 5 saw the safe arrival in Tripoli of a convoy carrying fifty-five upgraded PzKpfw. III and IV tanks, twenty armored cars, fuel, ammunition, 76.2mm anti-tank guns, and self-propelled Panzerjäger Is mounting 47mm anti-tank guns, complete with crews.

In January 1942 every ship leaving Italy got through, for a total of 43,328 tons of materiel and 22,842 tons of fuel. The Italian Mobile Corps was also upgraded with the arrival of the new Semovente M40 75mm self-propelled guns. Rommel was overjoyed with this turn of events and immediately began planning to go back on the offensive.

Auckinleck, on the other hand, had seen his supplies and reserves drop away drastically because of the entry of Japan into World War II. The British Empire in the Far East was disintegrating rapidly, and Churchill was forced to divert all available troops and resources to halt the rapid expansion of Japanese power in the Pacific. The Axis forces in North Africa appeared to be contained and Auchinleck was now expected to mount Operation Acrobat which was in-

The PzKpfw.III Ausf J model with frontal armor plates increased to 50mm by the addition of bolt-on extra armor. The main gun is still the early short 50mm KwK L/42.

tended to drive the Axis armies back to the Tunisian frontier.

Rommel had lost 386 of his 412 tanks in the battles of attrition that previous fall, but now he could see his Panzerarmee gaining strength again, and from intercepted British wireless messages he knew that Auchinleck was having his problems too. Rommel on the other hand was becoming more and more optimistic about getting the support and supplies he would need for another major offensive. On January 20 Hitler notified Rommel that he had been awarded the Oak Leaves and Swords to the Knight's Cross of the Iron Cross. The following day Rommel went on the offensive once more.

For some time now he had been spreading false rumors about a further withdrawal of his forces, in the hope that the British would drop their guard a bit. On the night before the attack the Germans burned fuel drums and set fires in the town and harbor of Marsa Brega to give the impression that they were pulling back. At the same time, all movement toward the front was prohibited during daylight hours. All the armored units in forward positions were well camouflaged from air reconnaissance, and those in the rear were dummied up to look like transport vehicles.

In the early morning of January 21 the Italian and German artillery opened up on the British positions. German sappers had managed to clear a path through the British minefields and the armor rolled through without a hitch. Since Rommel had made a point of sending no radio signals to anyone outlining his intentions, Ultra

The barren terrain of life in the desert. This scene gives us a glimpse of the everyday lifestyle that frontier troops lived under. Seen here are the basic pots and pans, soap, and wooden stoop. The cammo sheet strung over this Stower Kfz 4 le,E.PKW would be quickly pulled over the vehicles in the event that a British fighter appeared in the sky overhead.

was unable to warn Ritchie of what was coming. As for the Italian *Commando Supremo*, they were furious when they found out that they had not been informed until after the attack was well under way.

The 7th Armoured Division had retired to a refitting area south of Tobruk and had been replaced by part of the inexperienced 1st Armoured Division, with the 4th Indian Division well back and spread out from Benghazi to Tobruk. The stage was set and soon the war in North Africa would flare up again and dominate the news headlines.

Rommel's intention was to entrap 1st Armoured Division with a wide sweep by the DAK through Wadi el Faregh, but the soft terrain slowed them down so much that most of the British armor escaped to a position east of Agedabia. Gruppe Marcks, made up of mobile elements of 90th Light Division and a few tanks from 21st Panzer Division, had attacked deliberately up the Via Balbia in order to pin down the British defenders, while the Afrika Korps made its sweep around their flank. Although the going had been good at first, the DAK soon found itself floundering in huge sand dunes and wasting precious fuel to extricate their vehicles.

The British had similar problems in this area and many of their guns and motor vehicles were

A typical 25-pdr towed field gun crew with gun and limber behind their faithful field artillery tractor.

captured when they bogged down trying to escape the attack.

With no time to wait for his flanking panzers to arrive, Rommel took Gruppe Marcks under his wing and roared up the Via Balbia meeting with only light resistance, entering Agedabia by noon on the twenty-second. He then ordered the spearhead of Gruppe Marcks to continue its drive toward Antelat and Saunnu. They drove on through British supply columns, throwing them into wild confusion and capturing great numbers of trucks and supplies. The spearhead of 15th Panzer Division did not reach Antelat until well after dark, as both panzer divisions were held up by traffic jams everywhere they turned.

On the night of January 22–23 Rommel laid plans that he hoped would nail the coffin shut on 1st Armoured Division, but a gap in the encirclement at Saunnu allowed most of it to escape, and much time was wasted trying to make contact with an enemy which had long since departed. Furious that he had lost them again, on the twenty-fifth Rommel advanced on Msus for one more try.

A spiked 88 being examined by Kiwi gunners of the 4th New Zealand Field Regiment, 2nd New Zealand Division.

The 21st Panzer Division on the right flank met with meager opposition to its advance, but just northwest of Saunnu the 15th Panzer Division ran into a huge force of British tanks. The 8th Panzer Regiment, closely supported by artillery and anti-tank guns, bore down on them and what followed was one of the major routs in the desert war.

Following up hard on their heels, 15th Panzer covered fifty miles in four hours and arrived at

A pair of German PzKpfw.II Ausf C, both fitted with the later-style cupola. The crew has covered the 20mm main gun with a protective sleeve to keep the dust out during travel. Looking closely, you may be able to discern the 15.PD symbol forward of the 8 and a white DAK palm to the rear.

Msus airfield before noon to find twelve transport aircraft waiting to take off. All were captured, along with numerous supply columns, but it was impossible for them to proceed farther since the division was totally out of fuel. A total of 96 tanks, 38 guns, and 190 lorries, plus the aircraft, was their take for the day.

Rommel now ordered his Afrika Korps to make a feint in the direction of Mechili, and Ritchie reacted by concentrating his armor to meet it. Again taking personal command of Gruppe Marcks, Rommel swept towards Benghazi over very difficult ground through a rainstorm to attack Benghazi from the northeast. He entered the city on January 29 after capturing 1,000 prisoners from the 4th Indian Division. This victorious sweep earned Rommel promotion to colonel general.

Ritchie hastily withdrew his forces back to Gazala and willingly gave up the whole of the Cyrenaica bulge. By February 6 Armeegruppe Afrika was facing the Gazala Line and building up its strength for Rommel's next move.

In mid-March Rommel left Africa again and flew to Hitler's Rastenburg headquarters to discuss future operations in the African theater. A total lack of enthusiasm greeted him as the German High Command was totally engrossed in planning the summer offensive in Russia. Hitler was pleasant, but warned Rommel that he could expect only minimal reinforcements for Africa. However, they both agreed that Malta was a thorn in their side and that every effort should be made to neutralize it.

During a meeting between Hitler and Mussolini at Obersalzberg, it was agreed that Rommel should be allowed to go on the offensive and capture Tobruk. However, once that goal was achieved, he was expected to go on the defensive, while the main effort of the Axis forces in the Mediterranean was directed against Malta. This would involve Operation Hercules, the occupation of Malta, to take place during the full-moon period in June.

In preparation for the upcoming offensive an impressive flow of supplies was steadily arriving from Italian ports. On May 2 the SS *Ankara* and SS *Monviso* had arrived in port at Benghazi, and SS *Lerici* and SS *Bixio* reached Tripoli with their four cargoes totalling 4,870 tons of supplies, plus 272 vehicles, 27 field guns, and 20 tanks. Also during late April and early May a total of 5,917 troops were flown to Africa, at a rate of about 200 men a day. May 8 saw the arrival of three ships at Benghazi with a total of 2,400 tons of German supplies and 1,350 tons of fuel.

A good close-up look at the long-barreled 50mm KwK L/60 gun of the new PzKpfw. III Ausf L, which was beginning to arrive in Africa. Readily visible to the left of the MG opening in the bolted-on extra armor plate is the Wolfsangel unit insignia of 8th Panzer Regiment.

On May 12 five ships docked at Tripoli with 1,300 tons of fuel, 1,884 tons of ammunition, 1,625 tons of food, 1,270 tons of other supplies, 540 vehicles, and 14 field guns, followed on the 13th by three ships at Benghazi with another 3,350 tons of supplies, and the tanker SS *Fassio* with 1,400 tons of fuel. May 14 saw the SS *Guiliani* sail into Tripoli with another 950 tons of German supplies. May 17 and 18 saw the SS *Petrarca* with 1,700 tons and the SS *Bixio* and SS *Roselli* with 3,240 tons of supplies reach Benghazi, and SS *Lerici* arrive at Tripoli with 500 tons.

At times there were as many as a dozen ships offloading at Benghazi and the harbor installations were taxed to the limit. With this steady build-up Rommel felt confident that he could successfully engage the Eighth Army and eventually overwhelm the Tobruk defenses.

In effect from X-Day (May 26) on, eight or nine U-boats were to operate in the coastal waters between Tobruk and Alexandria. There were also eight E-boats assembled at Suda Bay, which were assigned to cover Kampfgruppe Hecker's amphibious assault on the beaches east of Gazala and escort their supply transports. Eight minesweepers were also assigned to clear mines and escort vessels involved in this operation. Nine Navy TLCs were to be used to carry supplies and for the landing operation itself.

THE GAZALA LINE BATTLES

The Eighth Army front extended from Gazala to Bir Hacheim and was interlaced with huge minefields of a scale and complexity never encountered before. Behind this line loomed the strongly defended fortresses of Tobruk, Knightsbridge, and El Adem, occupied by experienced desert fighters. Even Rommel underestimated the strength of the forces mustered here, for had he known, it is doubtful he would have embarked on this venture so eagerly. However, within three weeks of opening his offensive, Rommel would reduce this magnificent British army to a state of complete rout.

There is no question that the British infantry divisions were among the finest in the world, and compared to the Italian X and XXI Corps, were far better equipped and superior in numbers. Auchinleck admitted that the British had a superiority in field artillery and tank strength, plus a healthy reserve to draw upon.

Rommel entered this battle with 333 German tanks, plus 228 Italian tanks, while the British had a frontline strength of over 700 tanks, and a superiority in armored cars of about ten times. By this time the American-built M3 Grant medium tank with a sponson-mounted 75mm main gun and turret-mounted 37mm gun had arrived in good numbers. There were now about 200 Grant tanks available to the Eighth Army, and although its main arma-

A pristine PzKpfw. II Ausf F which appears to have been plagued with engine problems.

ment had very limited traverse, it was still a deadly weapon against the lighter German tanks. It was the first tank in service with the British that could reach 1,500 meters and destroy a Panzer III. It was also the first tank in British service that could fire both high-explosive and armor-piercing rounds at will. There were about 144 Grants in British hands by now and they had been distributed among the 4th, 22nd, and 2nd Armoured Brigades.

Of the 220 PzKpfw. IIIs now in the German line-up, only 19 were equipped with the long-barreled 50mm guns which increased range and penetration. The British had by now also received their new 6-pounder anti-tank guns, although Rommel still dominated this arm with his mobile 88s, augmented by the newly arrived 76.2mm anti-tank guns captured from the Russians. Nine of these weapons were mounted on 5-ton half-tracks and supplemented the 605th Panzerjäger Battalion.

Due to their great superiority in armored car numbers and superb radio security, the British were able to mask their positions from German reconnaissance units. Rommel had no idea that the 22nd Armoured Brigade and 32nd Army Tank Brigade were just behind the Gazala Line, nor was he aware of the strength of the Knightsbridge Box and its 201st Guards Brigade. Other surprises would be the 29th Indian Brigade at Bir el Gubi and the 3rd Indian Motor Brigade southwest of Bir Hacheim, along with the extension of the Gazala mine belt as far down as Bir Hacheim.

Rommel's plan of attack, code-named "Case Venezia" (and also referred to as "Theseus"), would once again involve a wide sweep around the British left flank, while the rest of Armeegruppe Afrika applied pressure to the main Gazala Line. Gruppe

A great rear view shot of a fully equipped Honey.

A scene showing a small portion of the thousands of vehicles that would assemble at Rotonda Sagnali for the upcoming attacks south of the Gazala Line. As can be seen, almost every truck shown here are captured British vehicles: Chevrolet, Morris, Norton, BSA, Austin, and Crüwell's captured British AEC Dorchester "Moritz 2", serial no. L4426422.

Crüwell, made up of the German 15th Rifle Brigade and the Italian X and XXI Corps and commanded by General Crüwell, would attack the 1st South African and British 50th Divisions frontally. The main strike force, led by Rommel, would consist of the Afrika Korps (under Gen. Nehring), the Italian XX Corps (Ariete and Trieste), and the 90th Light Division. Moving rapidly by night, this force would advance down beyond the minefields, move south of Bir Hacheim, and sweep northward toward Acroma, hopefully causing chaos in the British rear.

Ariete Armored Division would make an attempt to capture Bir Hacheim, but the Afrika Korps and 90th Light would bypass it well to the south. Events would later prove that the strength and tenacity of the Free French forces in Bir Hacheim had been greatly underestimated. This outpost would remain a kink in Rommel's plan and greatly disrupt his supply lines. In hindsight it would appear that reaching Acroma on the first day of the attack was asking a bit much of his troops, and his decision to send 90th Light and the reconnaissance groups off toward El Adem would achieve very little.

As a point of interest, the British had also been contemplating an amphibious assault behind the German lines during the lull in fighting. The 4th Royal Tank Regiment, commanded by Lt. Col. W. R. Reeves, was being trained for a combined operation which was to be part a new British offensive. 4RTR, now fitted out with Valentines, was to make a seaborne assault from LTCs well behind the German lines in the Gulf of Bomba. They were to land and destroy enemy headquarters and supply dumps well in the rear. Their own supplies would be carried by Lloyd carriers, but no allowance was to be made for carrying extra fuel. As the tanks ran out of fuel they were to be destroyed and the crews would be picked up at pre-arranged rendezvous points by the Long Range Desert Group. The regiment had actually entrained for its embarkation point when the news of Rommel's new offensive came through. The operation was eventually cancelled, but it is interesting to see how both sides had concocted very similar plans over the same stretch of water.

THESEUS: ROMMEL SWINGS SOUTH

Throughout the day on May 26 the Afrika Korps formed up in columns at their concentration area east of Rotonda Segnali in the midst of a persistent dust storm, which helped conceal their movements

from any air reconnaissance. Each column would be headed by about twenty tanks, and well to the front were combat engineers, ready to cut paths through any British minefields they encountered.

The following is a translation from the Italian of the decree: Armata Corazzata Italo Tedesca (Order of the Day of the Army War Zone), May 26, 1942.

"Soldiers! Continuing this year's operation, the African Armored Army is moving today for the decisive attack against the mobile British forces in Libya. Following our deeds of last January and February, we will attack and defeat our enemy everywhere it may show itself.

"To this purpose, outnumbering forces are ready; our equipment and armament has been completed, and a powerful air army will support our soldiers also. The high quality and warlike passion of the Italian and German soldiers, not to mention better weapons, guarantee our victory.

"Therefore, I expect everyone at his place, faithful to the high tradition of his country and army, to do his duty and give of himself completely in an infrangible arms brotherhood. Long live H.M. the King and Emperor of Italy and Ethiopia! Long live the Duce of the Roman Empire! Long live the Führer of Great Germany!

"Your Superior Commander, Rommel."

As darkness fell Rommel placed himself at the head of the Afrika Korps and moved out under a bright moonlit sky. These columns consisted of over 10,000 vehicles of all types which were about to move nearly 50 miles at night, and compass bearings, speeds, and distances had to be meticulously calculated to hold the formation together. Dust raised by the massive columns ahead would be a problem, and each commander was instructed to move at a leisurely pace that would produce the least amount of dust.

This dust problem had nothing to do with being spotted by the British, but was meant to prevent the hordes of vehicles travelling side by side from accidentally colliding with their neighbors in the darkness. Along the route sappers had planted dim lights concealed in empty gasoline tins as marker point references.

As they rolled on toward their first refuelling point southeast of Bir Hacheim, all went well and morale was high. The Afrika Korps was again ready for battle and quite confident of success. Unknown to them, the 4th South African Armored Car Regiment had been keeping their move under close observation and was sending detailed reports back to 7th Armoured Division headquarters.

Fortunately the British thought that this movement was simply a ploy to try to draw their forces south away from the obvious attack to come along the Trigh Capuzzo, and when the Afrika Korps finally swung into battle formation the following morning, there was no organized resistance to be seen.

The Ariete on the left flank plowed through the 3rd Indian Motor Brigade, while on the right, 90th Light and several reconnaissance units swept over the Retma Box. The 90th Light had been supplied with trucks mounting huge fans which could raise enough dust to simulate the movement of a large armored force. This was meant to bait the British ar-

A British recovery crew preparing to tow a captured German PzKpfw III Ausf L off the battlefield. Known to the British as the "Mark III Special," the long 50mm KwK39 L/60 main armament made this a deadly long-range opponent.

mor and draw it away from the main advance of 15th and 21st Panzer Divisions.

The full force of 15th Panzer came to bear upon the 4th Armoured Brigade while it was in the midst of deploying for battle, capturing 7th Armoured Division headquarters and its divisional supply echelons.

However, 15th Panzer suffered severe losses and was relieved to see 21st Panzer come to its assistance. The 8th Hussars was totally destroyed as a fighting force, and 3rd RTR lost sixteen of its Grant tanks. The 7th Armoured Division had been severely mauled and did its best to retire toward Bir el Gubi and El Adem, with 90th Light on its tail.

The newly arrived M3 Grants had been divided fairly evenly among the eighth Army units, with the hope that their presence would boost morale. In the early morning of May 27 the 4th Armoured Brigade was warned about a strong enemy force approaching from the southwest. With a light squadron of M3 Stuarts about 2,000 yards in front, the Grants of B and C squadrons of 3rd RTR moved out in line formation. Within ten minutes they received reports of large dust clouds about three miles ahead. By the time the Grant squadrons had closed ranks with their Stuarts, large formations of PzKpfw. IIIs and IVs had been identified.

These were the forward elements of 8th Panzer Regiment, and when the range closed to about 1,000 yards, the Grants opened fire. For the first time in the desert war the Germans were facing tanks that outranged them. Although suffering heavy losses 15th Panzer Division pressed forward, and by noon the remaining Grants, their ammunition exhausted, were forced to withdraw.

The leader of C squadron had had three different Grants shot out from under him, and B squadron's leader was on his fourth tank. Out of the original 19 tanks making up the Grant squadrons, only seven arrived at their rendezvous point to refuel and rearm. The German tank crews had quickly recognized that the Grants could only fire their main armament on a limited traverse to the front. Therefore, they would encounter these monsters from the front at long range, while a designated portion of their tanks would close in from the flank and knock out the Grants through their weaker side armor.

The fighting continued throughout the afternoon and by the end of the day the 3RTR was down to four Grants mediums and eight Stuarts.

Again the British had failed to concentrate and coordinate their armor and motorized units. The 1st Armoured Division fell prey next, when its 22nd Armoured Brigade, ordered to move south, ran head-

7.62cm FK36(r) auf Panzerjäger Sfl Zgkw 5t (Sd Kfz 6) "Diana"

long into the Afrika Korps. However, as it withdrew, its rearguard of 75mm armed Grants inflicted heavy losses on the German tanks in pursuit. At this point Rommel considered the battle won and congratulated Nehring on their success. Little did he know what was yet to come.

At noon on May 27 the Afrika Korps was engaged by 2nd Armoured Brigade while trying to cross the Trigh Capuzzo east of Knightsbridge. From the west came 1st Army Tank Brigade and between the two of them they caused so much confusion that the German advance came to a halt. The heavy Matildas and Grants tore into the German anti-tank gun positions and killed the crews at close range before they could be stopped. Rifle battalions were overrun and completely destroyed.

At dusk the 15th and 21st Panzer Divisions "hedgehogged" between Rigel Ridge and Bir Lefa, just northwest of Knightsbridge, with a third of their tanks out of action. 15th Panzer was nearly out of fuel and the supply route was in danger of being cut at any point by light forces operating out of Bir Hacheim or Bir el Gubi. The Afrika Korps was now in a desperate position and the Ariete had its hands full with the 1st Free French at Bir Hacheim.

At this point Ritchie might well have regrouped his remaining forces and, with the 100 Matidas of the untouched 32nd Army Tank Brigade, sealed the fate of the overextended Panzerarmee. However, such was not the case, and on the twenty-eighth the British commander decided to do little more than keep an eye on 15th Panzer at Rigel Ridge and probe 90th Light with 4th Armoured Brigade. The 1st Army Tank Brigade and 2nd Armoured Brigade both moved south to confront the Ariete, but the 32nd Tank Brigade stayed put in the rear of the 1st South African Division.

Rommel still had his mind set on cutting the Via Balbia, but with the 15th Panzer out of fuel it was up to 21st Panzer alone to resume the attack, and fierce armor battles raged throughout the twenty-eighth in the area of the Knightsbridge Box. Von Bismarck's tanks managed to reach Point 209 and the escarpment overlooking the Via Balbia, and at the same time Gruppe Crüwell made a concerted attempt to break through the South African front, but failed.

By the morning of the twenty-ninth the position of the Afrika Korps was becoming desperate, so Rommel personally took command of his supply columns and threaded them in through a gap in the minefields that he had found. With 15th Panzer again temporarily resupplied, Rommel struck out at 2nd Armoured Brigade which was trying to drive a wedge between Ariete in the south and his two panzer divisions. His panzers were again confronted by the M3 Grant mediums and their long-range 75mm guns. With the British 22nd Armoured Brigade entering the fray, one of the fiercest battles to date ensued.

In what has come to be known as the "Cauldron" between Sidra and Aslagh Ridges, the tank crews fought through scorching temperatures and swirling sandstorms, and by the evening both sides were content to retire. Even though Rommel's panzer divisions had suffered substantial losses, the chaos of the day had finally reunited the whole Afrika Korps. Heavy losses on the British side had done just the opposite and their tank brigades ended up scattered across the desert.

With his position consolidated, Rommel's biggest problem was his long supply line tailing back around Bir Hacheim. To alleviate this weak link, he decided to strike westward from the "Cauldron" to clear a path through the minefields and regain contact with Gruppe Crüwell. After three days of concentrated effort, he managed to link up with X Italian Corps. The biggest surprise came on May 30 when his forces ran

During a lull in the fighting, Rommel takes a moment to test a can of captured "Empire" peaches. Here again he is seen in his favorite SdKfz.250/3 half-track GREIF.

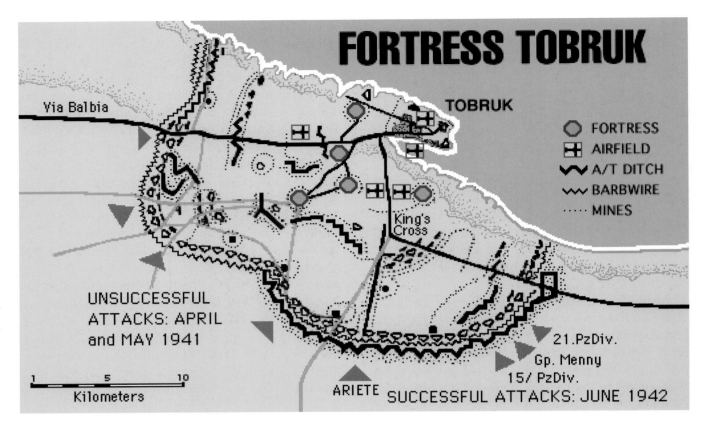

FORTRESS TOBRUK

Via Balbia

TOBRUK

King's
Cross

FORTRESS
AIRFIELD
A/T DITCH
BARBWIRE
MINES

UNSUCCESSFUL
ATTACKS: APRIL
and MAY 1941

1   5   10
Kilometers

21.PzDiv.
Gp. Menny
15/ PzDiv.
ARIETE   SUCCESSFUL ATTACKS: JUNE 1942

head on into the heavily fortified 150th Brigade Box, which German intelligence had failed to uncover.

With Stuka support, Rommel attacked using 90th Light, Trieste, and several kampfgruppes from the DAK, and by noon on June 1 had overrun the box and taken 3,000 prisoners. With 150th Brigade eliminated, his new supply route was now secure.

During all this General Crüwell, who was flying south to X Italian Corps headquarters in a light Storch aircraft, was shot down over British positions and captured. In the interim Generalfeldmarschall Albert Kesselring volunteered his services as a temporary replacement for Crüwell.

Rommel now chose to eliminate the Bir Hacheim strongpoint, and on June 2 the 90th Light and Trieste moved south to challenge the 4,000 Free French and Jewish troops desperately holding out there. The fort was pounded day after day by Stukas and artillery, but the defenders, under Col. Pierre Koenig, refused to surrender. On June 5, 1942, Auchinleck counterattacked, hoping to drive the Afrika Korps out of the "Cauldron" area. His 22nd Armoured Brigade, numbering 156 Grants, Crusaders, and Stuarts, was halted by withering artillery fire, and 32nd Tank Brigade threw away 50 of its 70 Matildas taking on von Bismark's 21st Panzer at Sidra Ridge. They were

caught wallowing in a hidden minefield and were simply shot to pieces by anti-tank fire.

Rommel responded by counterattacking and overrunning 7th Armoured and 5th Indian Division headquarters, and by evening had plowed through 10th Indian Brigade and brushed 9th Indian Brigade aside with the destruction of over 100 British tanks

A British Light AA Mk. I anti-aircraft tank on a transporter. These light AA tanks were based on the Vickers Mk. VI chassis and were assigned to protect their regimental HQ units.

and four regiments of field artillery. On June 8, with the "Cauldron" positions now secure, Rommel sent a strong detachment of 15th Panzer to assist in overpowering Bir Hacheim.

Heavy Stuka bombardment on June 9 followed by a determined assault by infantry of 15th Panzer, finally sealed the fate of the Bir Hacheim defenders, and on the night of June 10 the French garrison finally decided to break out. During the night their fleeing columns were swept by the 606 Flak and 605 Anti-Tank Battalions, but large numbers still managed to break through the Axis encirclement and escape. The following morning the 90th Light Division occupied the fortress and took 500 prisoners, consisting mainly of medics and their wounded.

Most of the 3,000 Free French, Jewish, and British troops managed to reach the British lines after the breakout on the night of June 10–11, although most of their artillery was left behind. Later in the fighting the South Africans would complain about the Ger-mans ranging in on them with captured British 25-pounder field artillery.

A great deal of equipment was destroyed during the Gazala battles, and although the Axis had lost 40% of their infantry and 50% of their tanks halfway through the fighting, they still had 90% of their artillery intact. Thus, with the addition of captured weapons and ammunition, the DAK was now fighting with even more artillery pieces than they had started out with on May 27.

With his southern flank now clear, Rommel once again sent his armor northward for a final confrontation with Ritchie's armor. The Eighth Army still held strong, heavily mined defensive positions north of the "Cauldron," with 201st Guards Brigade within the Knightsbridge Box and 29th Indian Brigade dug in south of El Adem. The British could field 250 cruiser tanks and 80 Matilda infantry tanks, while the 15th and 21st Panzer mustered about 160 tanks between them. Trieste and Ariete added an additional 70 or so

The German 88mm Flak 18 was a massive gun that required careful unloading and an experienced crew to operate it. Here we see the gun in its traveling mode being unloaded at Tripoli. From there it will have to be moved forward roughly 500 miles before it reaches the front.

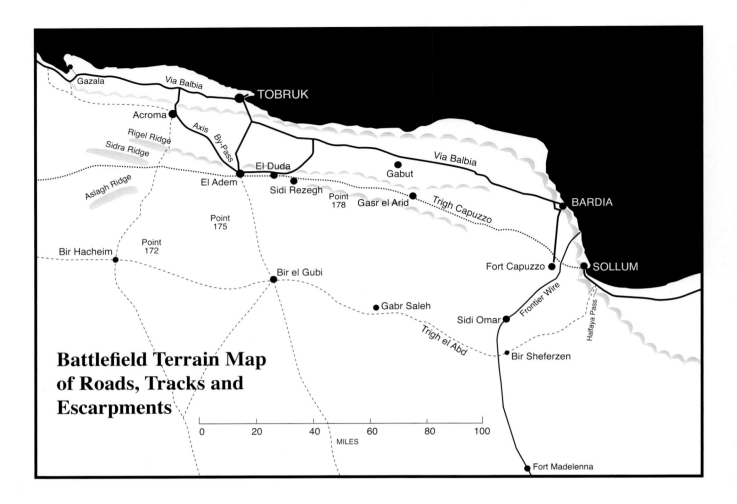

Battlefield Terrain Map of Roads, Tracks and Escarpments

M13/40 or 41s. The 21st Panzer remained in defensive positions along Sidra Ridge, while von Vaerst's 15th Panzer prepared to go on the offensive.

On the afternoon of June 11 the 15th Panzer swept northeast toward El Adem with Trieste on its left and 90th Light guarding its right flank, accompanied by units of 33rd and 3rd Reconnaissance. At this point the 90th Light infantry had been reduced to about 1,000 men. On the morning of June 12 the 15th Panzer readied itself for a British attack, but it never came. General Nehring finally ordered 15th Panzer onto the offensive, and by noon Rommel decided the time was right for 21st Panzer to advance against the open flank of 7th Armoured Division. These moves met with immediate success, and when 22nd Armoured Brigade moved south to try to save the day, they suffered heavy losses from fire by Trieste and 21st Panzer. The retreat of 4th Armoured Brigade eventually became a rout, and 22nd and 2nd Armoured Brigades retired toward the Knightsbridge Box. Heavy fighting continued until dark, but

the British had lost 120 tanks on June 12, and the initiative was now with the DAK.

On June 13 both panzer divisions made a concerted attack against Rigel Ridge, held by the Scots Guards, and after a stubborn defense the ridge was taken. This left the Knightsbridge Box isolated and on the night of June 13–14, the 201st Guards Brigade broke out to the east.

Ritchie now accepted the inevitable and on June 14 ordered a general withdrawal from the Gazala Line. Rommel ordered the DAK to descend the escarpment during the night in an attempt to cut off the South African Division's retreat route, but his orders fell on deaf ears. The fighting of the previous few days had totally exhausted the men, and it was not until the morning of June 15 that forces of 15th Panzer moved down the escarpment and cut off the South African rearguards. 90th Light Division had never found the strength to overpower the El Adem positions, and Rommel now sent 21st Panzer southeast to support them.

Kampfgruppe Hecker: Amphibious Assault, May 27–28, 1942

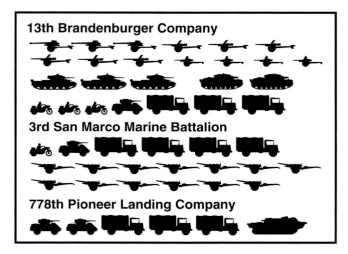

13th Brandenburger Company

3rd San Marco Marine Battalion

778th Pioneer Landing Company

MEDITERRANEAN SEA

Bomba

GAZALA

TOBRUK

Bir Hacheim

WESTERN DESERT

Amphibious landing planned to support Rommel's envelopment of the 8th Army.

May 27th, 1942

13th Company, 800th "Brandenburger" Regiment

The Brandenburger units were special German commando forces fluent in Arabic and English, who were used in long-range reconnaissance missions and raids behind British lines. Rommel frowned on this type of warfare until the British made an attempt on his life and headquarters with similar tactics, and from that point on he was more than happy to employ these units for special missions. They usually used captured British vehicles to penetrate the lines, which at times were in total chaos, and some of these raiders almost reached Cairo.

One of the most daring plans was to be carried out by Kampfgruppe Hecker, made up of the 13th Brandenburger Company, elements of 33rd and 39th Panzerjäger Battalion, 778th Pioneer Landing Company, and accompanied by the Italian 3rd San Marco Marine Battalion, a total of over 700 men. This was an aborted raid to try and cut the Via Balbia supply route by making an amphibious landing 30km east of Tobruk during the attack on the Gazala Line in May 1942. The attacking force would be transported from Bomba to their objective by four self-propelled landing barges and two landing boats. These were to be preceded by four boats from 6th Minesweeper Florilla based at Derna.

To cover this landing force, five boats of the 3rd Torpedo Boat Flotilla from Ras el Hilal were to patrol ahead and attack any enemy ships they encountered. Five German submarines were also on call to support the operation, and the Luftwaffe would supply the crucial air cover. The type of captured British tanks to be used on this mission is far from clear, but the most logical choice appears to be Crusaders, since these would attract the least attention in this time frame. There were also two German S/P guns assigned to this operation and it had been suggested that they might have been the two StuG. IIIs that arrived in Africa with Sonderverband 288, since they reportedly mounted 75mm guns.

One tank was placed on each of three barges, with the Land-Wasser-Schlepper (LWS) on a landing boat. The other equipment was spread among the various crafts and consisted of three 50mm and six 37mm A/T guns; four 2-pdr British A/T guns; ten British trucks; four British armored cars; four motorcycles; three 45mm mortars; over 5000 sandbags; 300 mines; 50 anti-tank charges; plus adequate light and heavy MGs and 10 anti-tank rifles. They were also issued 250 shovels and 250 pickaxes, so they certainly had intentions of filling those sandbags and setting up a determined blocking force. The landing force carried enough ammunition and food for 3 days, and supply by night from the sea would bring additional supplies if they had to hold out longer.

Rommel's orders for the May 26 assault on the Gazala Line close with these lines: "On X+1 Kampfgruppe Hecker will land at Gabr Si. Hameida to block the Via Balbia in the area of Kilometer 136." However, this amphibious operation was never launched, and the reason why seems to have been lost in the annals of time. It is suggested that the required air support was not forthcoming and that one of the barges had sustained damage. It is acknowledged that the vehicles had been loaded and the force was ready to go, but no orders to proceed were given. Seemingly they disembarked, only to be instructed to proceed with the mission again on May 28. Then within 20 minutes another order arrived cancelling the operation again.

Possibly Rommel felt that the British opposition to the DAK sweep was far more intense than anticipated and that Hecker's group would be left stranded. Another suggestion is that the British were warned of the proposed landing, either through air reconnaissance or radio intercept, and Hecker was running into a trap. For now we can only speculate and possibly the whole story will eventually surface.

The Eighth Army was in full retreat and Rommel had no intentions of giving them time to regroup on the Tobruk–El Adem line. Under heavy pressure the 29th Indian Brigade broke out of the El Adem Box on the night of June 16–17. By the evening of the seventeenth von Bismark's 21st Panzer had overrun Sidi Rezegh, but also had their first taste of British fighter-bombers fitted with 40mm cannons. In the early hours of June 18 the 21st Panzer severed the Via Balbia just west of Gambut and followed up by seizing Gambut airfield a few hours later. Tobruk was now isolated, and June 18–19 was spent tightening the noose.

On the evening of June 19 the Afrika Korps moved back from Gambut and formed up in its concentration area southeast of the fortress, ready for the attack on Tobruk. Early the next morning Kesselring's Stukas took off from the Gazala and El Adem airfields and began pounding the outer defenses, while at the same time German and Italian artillery joined in. Gruppe Menny and the Afrika Korps infantry now attacked forward bunkers where they met feeble re-

sistance. The anti-tank ditches were quickly bridged and by 0930 the tanks had crossed the ditches and were fanning out inside the perimeter. In close contact with their forces inside the perimeter were both General Nehring, commander of Afrika Korps, and General von Bismark, with Rommel not far behind, ready to take over if things deteriorated.

By noon both the armored divisions had reached the inner minefields and were meeting solid resistance from both British tanks and artillery. The Afrika Korps reached the escarpment beyond King's Cross at 1400 hours, and Rommel drove forward to direct the next move.

21st Panzer now descended the escarpment and by dusk was entering Tobruk. The tanks of 21st Panzer actually engaged British naval craft trying to make for open water and several were sunk or set ablaze. Meanwhile, 15th Panzer had attacked Pilastrino Ridge where they captured the brigade headquarters

A British officer inspects a disabled German SdKfz. 253 forward observation vehicle.

A close-up look at the turret access door of a PzKpfw.III Ausf J. Note the vision slit in the left half and the pistol port in the right half.

and a large number of prisoners before withdrawing to laager near King's Cross for the night.

On the morning of June 21 General Klopper surrendered the Tobruk garrison of 33,000 men. Although much of the fuel and supplies had been destroyed, there were still great quantities of transport, food, clothing, ammunition, guns, and 2,200,000 gallons of fuel captured intact.

That evening Rommel heard on the radio that at the age of 50 he had been promoted to the rank of field marshal as the crowning glory for a most spectacular series of victories. However, Rommel now had his mind set on rapidly pursuing the Eighth Army into Egypt, even though the Axis leaders had decreed that he set up a defensive line until Malta had been neutralized.

On the afternoon of June 21 he had ordered 21st Panzer to move in haste along the Via Balbia coast road to Gambut. Hearing of this latest move, Field Marshal Kesselring flew to Africa to try to restrain Rommel, warning him that the Luftwaffe must first neutralize Malta to ensure the steady flow of supplies required for a successful advance into Egypt.

Rommel totally disagreed with this approach and stated that the Eighth Army was now in total disarray and that the timing was ideal for a thrust to the Suez Canal. This discussion ended as heatedly as it had started, and Kesselring stated that his air units would not be there to support such a reckless and foolhardy advance. However, Rommel went over his head and sent off a personal liaison officer to to Berlin to present his views to Hitler and Rome. In the end he again managed to get his way, and the Malta attack would be postponed until September.

By the evening of June 23 the advance guard of the Afrika Korps had crossed the Egyptian border and Ritchie hastily withdrew to Mersa Matruh. The morale of the DAK was high, and although the summer heat was devastating, they made a twenty-four-hour march of over 100 miles to reach the coastal road between Mersa Matruh and Sidi Barrani. However, the distance and the rough terrain took a heavy toll on their vehicles and men, and the Afrika Korps entered Egypt with only 44 tanks.

Resistance on the ground was minimal, but now the Desert Air Force pounded them continuously, and without adequate air cover or anti-aircraft defenses of their own, the Axis forces paid a heavy price. From this point on the relentless enemy air bombardments would play an increasingly important role in events to come.

Late on June 25, reconnaissance units of the DAK reached the heavily mined outer defenses of Mersa Matruh. The British Tenth Corps was in Matruh, with the 50th British Division and 10th Indian Division. Also, XIII Corps, with the 2nd New Zealand Division and the 1st Armoured Division, which had just arrived from Syria, were planted south of the Sidi Hamza escarpment. The 1st Armoured Division had been fitted out with 159 tanks, 60 of which were the medium M3 Grants. The space between these two forces was weakly held by two columns, each consisting of two platoons of infantry and a battery of field and anti-tank guns.

Against these forces Rommel could muster only 60 tanks. Striking at this weak center on June 26, the 90th Light Division and 21st Panzer managed to rout the defenders and by the next morning 90th Light overran the 9th Durham Light Infantry south of Matruh. They themselves were then pinned down by heavy artillery fire and Rommel was forced to lead 21st Panzer north, with its 23 remaining tanks and 600 exhausted infantry. This badly separated the two German panzer divisions and 21st Panzer was now threatened by both the Bays and 3rd County of London Yoemanry Armoured Regiments. At the same time, 15th Panzer in the south had been engaged by the 22nd Armoured Brigade and was dangerously low in both ammunition and fuel.

On the afternoon of June 27 Rommel gathered up the 90th Light Division and swept around the southern flank of the British X Corps, and by dark he had managed to cut the coastal road about 20 miles east of Matruh. Although the British still had the upper hand at this point, they failed to play it out. General Gott ordered a withdrawal to the Fuka Line, and once again Rommel had managed to bluff his way out of a major battle that could have destroyed Panzerarmee Afrika.

On June 28 the 90th Light and Italian divisions invested Matruh and made preparations to storm the fortress. In the meantime the rest of the DAK continued eastward toward the Fuka defenses. The British X Corps broke out of Matruh on the night of June 28–29 and chaotic clashes ensued in the darkness as Axis investing troops tried to stop their escape. The bulk of the British columns got through, but several columns ran smack into 21st Panzer near Fuka and 1,600 prisoners were taken. The following morning the 90th Light Division entered Mersa Matruh, the battle having netted them 8,000 prisoners and numerous guns, vehicles, other war materiel, foodstuffs, and fuel.

Unfortunately these rather fragile victories had raised Rommel's hopes of penetrating through to the Suez Canal even higher. His forces were now in a state of total exhaustion from continuous pursuit, with no air cover to speak of, and would soon be facing fresh troops waiting for them in the Alamein positions.

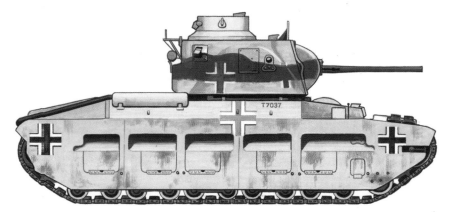

A captured British Matilda infantry tank as it appeared in service with the DAK forces. Captured enemy tanks like this were referred to as beutepanzers *and heavily decorated with crosses so there would be no mistakes.*

605th Self-Propelled Anti-Tank Battalion: May 27, 1942

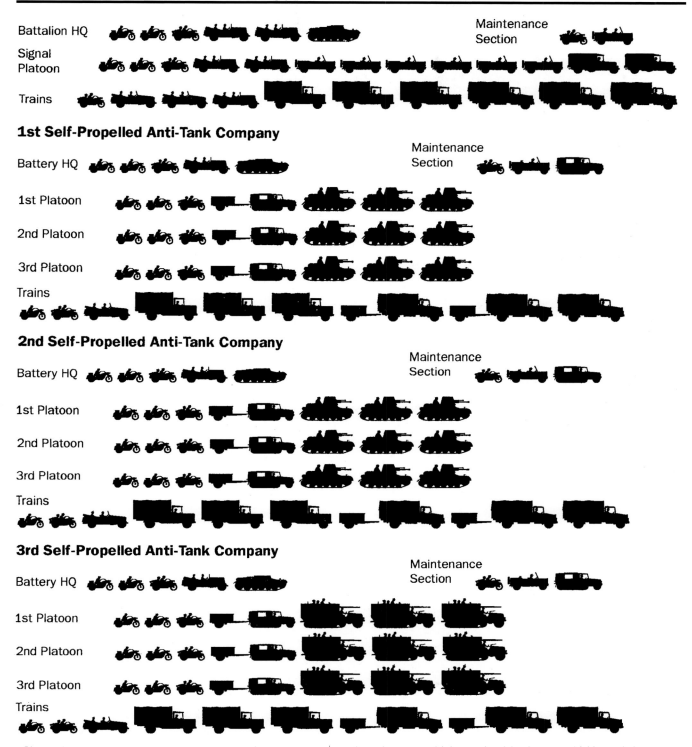

Shown here is the suggested composition of the independent 605. PzJäg-Abt. at the outset of Rommel's attack on the Gazala Line in late May. Its anti-tank capability has been strengthened by the arrival of the 7.62 "Diana" mounts. Six of these vehicles arrived in January 1942 and

three more in February. Their German crews nicknamed these self-propelled guns "Diana." They managed to make themselves felt during the heavy fighting against the new British Grants and at the assault on Bir Hacheim.

15th Panzer Division: May 27, 1942
15. Panzer Division

15th PANZER DIVISION HQ
– 33rd Motorized Mapping Detachment
– Armored Command Detachment (Tropical)
– Motorized Military Police Detachment "b"
– Motorized Army Post Office

8th PANZER REGIMENT
– Panzer Regiment Headquarters
    Armor Maintenance Company
– Panzer Battalion Headquarters
    Armored Signal Platoon
    Light Tank Platoon

1st Armored Battalion
–Battalion HQ & HQ Company
    3 Light Tank Companies
    1 Medium Tank Company

2nd Armored Battalion
–Battalion HQ & HQ Company
    3 Light Tank Companies
    1 Medium Tank Company

115th MOTORIZED INFANTRY REGT.
– Regiment HQ & HQ Company
    Signal Platoon
    Anti-Tank Platoon
    Motorcycle Messenger Platoon
    Engineer Platoon
– Infantry Gun Company (motorized)
– Motorized Combat Engineer Co. (Africa)

– 1st Motorized Infantry Battalion
    Battalion Headquarters
    4 Motorized Infantry Co. (Africa)

–2nd Motorized Infantry Battalion
Battalion Headquarters
    4 Motorized Infantry Co. (Africa)
– 3rd Motorized Infantry Battalion
    Battalion Headquarters
    4 Motorized Infantry Co. (Africa)

33rd MOTORIZED RECON. BATTALION
– Battalion HQ & Signal Platoon

1 Armored Car Company
1 Motorized Recon Company (Africa)
1 Motorized Heavy Company
1 Motorized Light Recon Column

33rd MOTORIZED ARTILLERY REGT.
– Regiment HQ & HQ Battery
    Armored Calibration Battery

1st Motorized Artillery Battalion
– Battalion HQ & HQ Battery
    3 Motorized Batteries

2nd Motorized Artillery Battalion
– Battalion HQ & HQ Battery
    3 Motorized Batteries

3rd Motorized Artillery Battalion
– Battalion HQ & HQ Battery
    3 Motorized Batteries

78th MOTORIZED ANTI-TANK BN.
– Battalion HQ & Signal Platoon
    1 Motorized Anti-Tank Company
    1 Self-Propelled Anti-Tank Company

33rd MOTORIZED COMBAT ENGINEER BN.
– Battalion HQ
    3 Motorized Combat Eng. Co. (Africa)
    1 Motorized Light Engineer Company

33rd ARMORED SIGNAL BN.
– Battalion HQ
    1 Armored Radio Co. (Tropical)
    1 Motorized Telephone Company
    1 Motorized Light Signal Column "a"

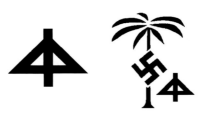 

21st Panzer Division: May 27, 1942
21. Panzer Division

21st PANZER DIVISION HEADQUARTERS
– 200th Motorized Mapping Detachment
– Armored Command Detachment (Tropical)
– 200th Mot. Military Police Detachment "b"
– Motorized Army Post Office

5th PANZER REGIMENT
– Panzer Regiment Headquarters
     Armor Maintenance Company
– Panzer Battalion Headquarters
     Armored Signal Platoon
     Light Tank Platoon
1st Armored Battalion
     Battalion HQ & HQ Company
     3 Light Tank Companies
     1 Medium Tank Company
2nd Armored Battalion
     Battalion HQ & HQ Company
     3 Light Tank Companies
     1 Medium Tank Company

104th MOTORIZED INFANTRY REGIMENT
Regiment HQ & HQ Company
     Signal Platoon
     Anti-Tank Platoon
     Motorcycle Messenger Platoon
     Engineer Platoon
– Infantry Gun Company (motorized)
– Motorized Combat Engineer Co. (Africa)

1st Motorized Infantry Battalion
     Battalion Headquarters
     4 Motorized Infantry Companies (Africa)
2nd Motorized Infantry Battalion
     Battalion Headquarters
     4 Motorized Infantry Companies (Africa)

3rd Motorized Infantry Battalion
     Battalion Headquarters
     4 Motorized Infantry Companies (Africa)

3rd MOTORIZED RECON. BATTALION
     Battalion HQ & Signal Platoon
     1 Armored Car Company
     1 Motorized Recon Company (Africa)

     1 Motorized Heavy Company
     1 Motorized Light Recon Column

155th MOTORIZED ARTILLERY REGIMENT
     Regiment HQ & HQ Battery
     Armored Calibration Battery

1st Motorized Artillery Battalion
     Battalion HQ & HQ Battery
     3 Motorized Batteries
2nd Motorized Artillery Battalion
     Battalion HQ & HQ Battery
     3 Motorized Batteries
3rd Motorized Artillery Battalion
     Battalion HQ & HQ Battery
     3 Motorized Batteries

39th MOTORIZED ANTI-TANK BATTALION
     Battalion HQ & Signal Platoon
     1 Motorized Anti-Tank Company
     1 Self-Propelled Anti-Tank Company

200th MOTORIZED COMBAT ENGINEER BN.
     Battalion HQ
     3 Motorized Combat Eng. Companies (Africa)
     1 Motorized Light Engineer Company

200th ARMORED SIGNAL BATTALION
     Battalion HQ
     1 Armored Radio Company (Tropical)
     1 Motorized Telephone Company
     1 Motorized Light Signal Column "a"

87

90th Light Motorized Africa Division: May 27, 1942

90. Leichte-Afrika-Division

DIVISION HEADQUARTERS
259th Motorized Mapping Detachment
190th Motorized Signal Company
190th Motorized Army Post Office

155th MOTORIZED INFANTRY REGIMENT
Regiment HQ & Motorized HQ Company
Motorized Signal Platoon
Motorized Anti-Tank Platoon
Motorcycle Platoon
– Infantry Gun Company (self-propelled)

1st Motorized Infantry Battalion
Battalion Headquarters
4 Motorized Infantry Companies (Africa)

2nd Motorized Infantry Battalion
Battalion Headquarters
4 Motorized Infantry Companies (Africa)

1st Battalion/190th MOTORIZED ARTILLERY REGIMENT
– Battalion HQ & HQ Battery
Motorized Signal Platoon
Calibration Section
– 2 Motorized Light Field Howitzer Batteries
– 1 Motorized Gun Battery

900th MOTORIZED COMBAT ENGINEER BN.
–Battalion Headquarters
2 Motorized Combat Eng. Co. (Africa)
1 Motorized Light Engineer Column

580th MOTORIZED MIXED RECON COMPANY
–Company Headquarters
– 1 Motorized Mixed Recon Company
Recon Platoon
Armored Car Platoon
Anti-Tank Platoon
Anti-Aircraft Platoon

190th MOTORIZED ANTI-TANK BN.
– Battalion Headquarters
1 Motorized Anti-Tank Company
1 Motorized Anti-Aircraft Company

2nd Company/190th ARMORED SIGNAL BATTALION
1 Armored Radio Company (Tropical)

288th Special Services Unit: May 27, 1942
5th (Infantry Anti-Tank) Company (motorized)
5. (Panzerjäger-Kompanie) (motorisiert)

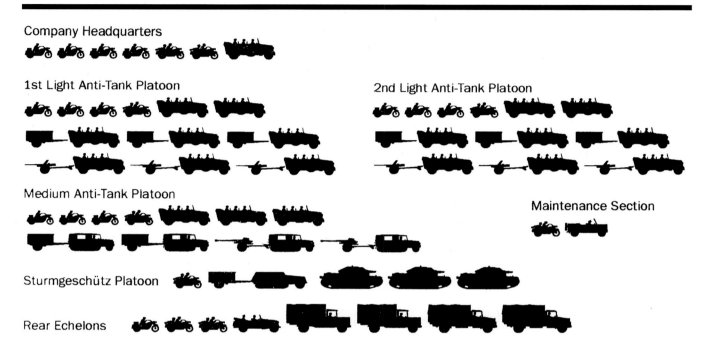

Company Headquarters

1st Light Anti-Tank Platoon

2nd Light Anti-Tank Platoon

Medium Anti-Tank Platoon

Maintenance Section

Sturmgeschütz Platoon

Rear Echelons

*Oberst Hecker receiving instructions while one of their
StuG.IIIs sits in the background.*

288th Special Services Unit: May 27, 1942

Sonderverband 288

HEADQUARTERS
288th SPECIAL SERVICE UNIT
– Unit Headquarters

HQ COMPANY,
288th SPECIAL SERVICE UNIT
– Company Headquarters
    Armored Car Section
    Scout Platoon
    Printing Section
    Maintenance Section

2nd (Mountain Infantry) COMPANY (mot)
– Company Headquarters
    Anti-Tank Section
    Mortar Section
    3 Infantry Platoons
    Maintenance Section

3rd (Infantry) COMPANY (mot)
– Company Headquarters
    Anti-Tank Section
    Mortar Section
    3 Infantry Platoons
    Maintenance Section

4th (Machine Gun) COMPANY (mot)
– Company Headquarters
    2 Machinegun Platoons
    Mortar Platoon
    Maintenance Section

5th (Infantry Anti-Tank) COMPANY (mot)
– Company Headquarters
    2 Light Anti-Tank Platoons
    1 Medium Anti-Tank Platoon
    1 Sturmgeschütz Platoon
    Maintenance Section

6th (Anti-Aircraft) COMPANY (mot)
– Company Headquarters
    Signal Detachment
    3 Anti-Aircraft Platoons
    Maintenance Section

7th (Combat Engineer) COMPANY (mot)
– Company Headquarters
    3 Combat Engineer Platoons
    Maintenance Section

288th MOTORIZED SIGNAL COMPANY /
288th SPECIAL SERVICE UNIT
– Company Headquarters
    2 Radio Platoons
    2 Telephone Platoons
    Maintenance Section

288th LIGHT INFANTRY COLUMN (mot)
– Column Headquarters
    Transport Platoon

288th MEDICAL DETACHMENT (mot) /
288th SPECIAL SERVICE UNIT

288th Motor Maintenance Platoon (mot)

288th P.O.L. Inspection Detachment (mot)

The Sonderverband 288 was raised on July 1, 1941, at Potsdam (near Berlin). It was composed of units from all over Germany. The 1st Company was the former 13th Company/Lehr Regiment Brandenburg zur besonder Verwendung 800, an OKW unit of the Amt Ausländischer Abwehr (Foreign Intelligence Department). It did not have an Army KStN (T/O), and normally operated independently from the 288th Special Service Unit. According to the book *Die Brandenburger* by Helmuth Spaeter, this company had the following organization by mid-June 1942.

COMPANY: One 1st Lieutenant and one 2nd Lieuteneant; one Sergeant;
    – 102 enlisted men
    – 3 Detachments (each lead by one of the above)
    – 12 captured British vehicles
    – 12 captured British S/P 40mm A/T guns
    – 1 captured "stationwagon"
    – 4 jeeps with heavy machineguns
    – 1 radio van
    – "various" cars
    – 1 water tanker
    – fuel tanker
    – 1 Maintenance Section
    – 1 Spitfire (flown by a Brandenburg Captain)

The Sonderverband 288 was eventually redesignated as Panzergrenadier-Regiment Afrika on October 31, 1942, and was reorganized at that time.

132nd "ARIETE" Armored Division: May 27, 1942

132ª Divisione Corazzata "ARIETE"

DIVISION HEADQUARTERS
– Headquarters Detachment

Tactical Command Unit
– (Divisional HQ close defense)

BRIGADE HEADQUARTERS
– Headquarters Company

132nd TANK REGIMENT
– Regiment Headquarters & HQ Company
    Regimental Tank Reserve

VIII Tank Battalion
– Battalion Headquarters & HQ Company
– 1st Tank Company
    3 Tank Platoons
– 2nd Tank Company
    3 Tank Platoons
– 3rd Tank Company
    3 Tank Platoons

IX Tank Battalion
– Battalion Headquarters & HQ Company
– 1st Tank Company
    3 Tank Platoons
– 2nd Tank Company
    3 Tank Platoons
– 3rd Tank Company
    3 Tank Platoons

X Tank Battalion
–Battalion Headquarters & HQ Company
– 1st Tank Company
    3 Tank Platoons
– 2nd Tank Company
    3 Tank Platoons
– 3rd Tank Company
    3 Tank Platoons
– Anti-Aircraft Company
– Recovery & Repair Section

8th BERSAGLIERI MOTORIZED INFANTRY REGIMENT
– Regiment Headquarters
– Machinegun Company

V Bersaglieri Battalion
– Battalion Headquarters & HQ Company
    Bersaglieri Anti-Tank Company
    Bersaglieri Infantry Company
XII Bersaglieri Battalion
– Battalion Headquarters & HQ Company
    Bersaglieri Anti-Tank Company
    Bersaglieri Infantry Company

ANTI-AIRCRAFT & Support Weapons Bn.
– Headquarters Platoon
    Anti-Aircraft Company
    Machinegun Company
    Mortar Company
    Motor Reserve Section

132nd ARTILLERY REGIMENT
– I Artillery Group
    (75/27 mod. 906 T.M.)
– II Artillery Group
    (75/27 mod. 906 T.M.)
– V Semovente Group
    (75/18 M40)
– VI Semovente Group
    (75/18 M40)
– DI Auto Cannoni Group
    (90/53-Lancia 3/RO)
– XXXI 88/55 Group
    (A/T & A/A)

As always, these units were in a state of flux and it is difficult to know for certain which elements were up to full strength at any given time. Listed here are the elements that supposedly made up the "Ariete" at this time, and in his book, Major Rizzo, then assistant chief of staff for "Ariete," stated that "the unit would be completed by the end of May".

EL ALAMEIN
THE FINAL GAMBIT

EL ALAMEIN: THE FINAL GAMBIT

Thirty-eight miles south of the small railway station known as El Alamein lies the Qattara Depression. At this point the desert terrain drops away many hundreds of feet to the ancient salt marshes below. Rommel visited the rim of this great canyon numerous times in July 1942, and he knew that this time there would be no wide flanking attack made well to the south of the British lines.

The DAK troops that had arrived in front of the El Alamein positions were exhausted and in no shape to launch a concerted attack. Rommel had surged forward after his victory at Mersa Matruh in an attempt to cut off the withdrawing British forces before they could link up with the fresh troops on the Alamein Line. Although there was a slight brush with the 1st Armoured Division that evening, little was accomplished by this desperate thrust forward and all it did was stretch his fuel and supply problem to the limit.

During the afternoon of June 29 the 90 Light Division had moved along the coast road from Matruh to El Duda at the head of the DAK with the Italian XXI Corps and the Littorio Armored Division, now equipped with the moderately improved M.14-41 medium tanks and Semovente da 75/18 assault guns. However, the smooth approach of 90th Light along

A view of the Qattara Depression looking westward along the precipitous drop-off slopes leading down to the almost impassible salt marshes below.

the coast road came to a sudden end when Rommel ordered them south through rough desert toward El Quseir on the rim of the Qattara Depression. This southern sweep simply increased the wear and tear on their vehicles, used up precious fuel, and netted nothing. By that evening they had swung north again and camped fifteen miles west of the Alamein Box.

The Alamein Line was never really a continuous line of fortifications, but rather a series of fortified boxes that extended from El Alamein to the Qattara Depression. On June 30 Rommel decided to move under cover of darkness to penetrate between the boxes at Alamein and Deir el Abyad to a position about 10 miles south of El Alamein station. However, Rommel thought that the XIII Corps was well to the south with 1st Armoured Division, 2nd New Zealand Division, and 5th Indian Division. The 90th Light Division was chosen for the task and was ordered to sweep in south of the Alamein Box and then upward to sever the coastal road that ran behind it.

THE INITIAL EL ALAMEIN BATTLES

The tally for the Afrika Korps on that evening was a total of 55 tanks in running condition. Once the 90th Light had penetrated the line, the DAK armor would move forward to link up and support it. However, the supporting DAK was held up by rough terrain and the box at Deir el Shein.

The 90th Light had moved out in a swirling sandstorm and raced for the gap, only to stumble on unknown strongpoints manned by the 1st South African Division. The artillery fire from these boxes was so heavy that they were stopped dead in their tracks. To the south the German armor also ran into a hidden surprise at Deir el Shein in the form of an unknown fortified box held by the 18th Indian Brigade. Neither Rommel nor Nehring had any idea that these boxes existed when they laid out their plan of attack. By the afternoon of July 1 the 104th Rifle Regiment supporting the 21st Panzer had driven the Indians out of their positions, losing 18 of their 55 tanks, but the main attack had been halted and lost its impetus. Another 18 tanks were burning wrecks, and very little had been achieved.

Rommel and Bayerlein, while trying to get things moving again, found themselves under such heavy artillery fire that they were forced to scatter their vehicles and ended up lying flat on the ground for two hours until it subsided. Here for the first time the Afrika Korps had been drawn into a strong defen-

An Italian Autoblinda 41 armored car under field repair and maintenance, August 21, 1942. The vehicle in the distance to the left is a Fiat S.P.A.38 workshop truck.

sive position and reduced by attrition, much the way Rommel had so often defeated the British armored thrusts.

By July 2 the British 1st Armoured Division had strongly implanted itself on Ruweisat Ridge, and the South African positions were strengthened considerably. Even more disturbing was the fact that from this point on the Desert Air Force would give the British commanding control of the skies over the region.

On the morning of July 3 the New Zealanders attacked from their box at Qaret el Abd and surprised the Ariete Division, capturing all their artillery. However, the main attack still went in that afternoon with heavy artillery support and the Afrika Korps gained a bit of ground on Ruweisat Ridge, but by that evening it was obvious that it was a stalemate.

At this point his Panzerarmee had been ground down to a mere shadow of its former strength, and Rommel knew that he would have to suspend further attacks until his forces could be rebuilt. The Afrika

Korps now had only 36 tanks in good running order, and a mere fraction of its infantry remaining. The artillery, including a large number of captured British guns, was in good shape but dangerously low in shells. At this point the eighth Army had a perfect opportunity to break the back of the DAK, but although Auchinleck had ordered such an attack, his commanders were hesitant to carry it off. Minor skirmishes took place on July 5, and the New Zealand 4th Infantry Brigade was badly mauled by attacking Stuka dive bombers, but on the whole the

4th New Zealand Field Regiment firing their 25-pdr guns from prepared positions on the Alamein Line.

front had stabilized. The 15th Panzer Division on Ruweisat Ridge was now down to fifteen tanks, to hold back the 1st Armoured Division with over one hundred, but no attack ensued.

By July 6 huge stocks of mines had arrived, along with a few reinforcements which brought the total tank strength of the Afrika Korps to about forty-four, with a small mobile reserve. During the morning of July 9 the 6th New Zealand Brigade quietly left their box at Qaret el Abd and moved back, shortly to have their fortified position occupied by Littorio and 21st Panzer. Rommel was jubilant about such an easy gain and spent the night far to the south in the Qaret el Abd Box assessing the situation.

However, the morning of July 10 opened in the north with heavy bombardment of the Sabratha Division and a violent attack by the 9th Australian Division along the coastal road. The Italian division was in full retreat when the Germans finally realized just how serious the situation was along the coast road. The Panzerarmee HQ was only a few miles behind the front at this point and came under severe pressure to withdraw. Only by throwing everything they had together did they manage to stop the Australians at their doorstep. That same day Infantry Regiment 382 arrived on their long trip from Europe to reinforce the German 164th Infantry Division.

By July 11 the Australians were on the move again and this time they ravaged the Trieste Division, and it was now obvious that the Italian troops could not withstand these onslaughts. The attack was halted by heavy artillery fire, and by July 12 the Australians had dug into their new positions. Rommel was still certain that he could destroy the El Alamein Box with a direct attack and thereby isolate the Australian positions at Tel el Eisa.

He therefore brought 21st Panzer Division north and called for every gun and aircraft available to be targeted on Alamein. The 21st Panzer, supported by Stukas, went in around noon on the thirteenth with heavy artillery support. However, their infantry was too far to their rear and was unable to take advantage of the initial gains. It then came under heavy artillery and machine-gun fire from the box just as it reached the wire. The Luftwaffe attacked again, trying to silence the fire from the 3rd South African Brigade, but to no avail. The tanks of 21st Panzer pounded the concrete defenses inside the box, but by the end of the day the attack had failed.

The following day Rommel sent 21st Panzer northwest to try to cut through the rear of the Australian position at Tel el Eisa and gain the coast road. They reached the rail line, but the flanking fire from the Alamein Box and the stubborn fighting of the

This concealed firing position at El Alamein shows the Q.F. 25-pdr Mk. 2 gun to good advantage. The standard circular turntable firing platform under the gun can be readily seen.

Two German tanks of 21st Panzer Division that were knocked out by Australian gunners during the battles for Tel el Eisa in mid-July 1942. Shown above is a PzKpfw.III Ausf J, and below, exuding smoke from a burning interior, is a PzKpfw.IV with its 75mm gun traversed to the rear.

Australian infantry made it a tenuous gain at best. Before the attack could be resumed on July 15 the 2nd New Zealand Division, supported by 5th Indian Brigade, had swept through the Italian Brescia Division on Ruweisat Ridge and threatened to break the Axis lines. Again they were halted by the infusion of German units brought from the central sector, but it was becoming clear that without German stiffening the Italian units were getting more and more demoralized.

The supply question was also starting to haunt the Afrika Korps again, and when Kesselring and Cavallero visited the front on July 17, Rommel made it quite clear that he would never be able to withhold a concerted British attack if things carried on the way they were.

Auchinleck was preparing for just that, and on the night of July 21–22 they attacked along Ruweisat Ridge and eventually reached the depression at El Mireir after stiff fighting. However, the supporting armor for 6th New Zealand Brigade did not arrive

A PzKpfw IV/F2 knocked out during the Alam Halfa battles. This was the latest version of the PzKpfw IV referred to by the British as a Mark IV Special.

on time and 15th Panzer was able to crush them, taking several hundred prisoners. A German dispatch of July 25 mentions that since the initial attack on May 27 the 15th Panzer Division had destroyed 650 enemy tanks and armored vehicles, and 21st Panzer Division had destroyed 658.

The freshly arrived 23rd Armoured Brigade was now sent forward and made a frontal attack on the German positions, with a creeping barrage ahead of them. With all the dust raised the first half dozen Valentines managed to sail past the German anti-tank positions without even being spotted. However, they were actually in the midst of heavy minefields and the 76.2 Russian anti-tank guns of 104th Panzer Grenadier Regiment.

As the dust cleared, the young Gunther Halm and the other anti-tank gunners, who had dug their guns into the rocky desert with pickaxes as best they could, peeked out to see endless rows of British tanks moving toward their position. About 50 Valentines of the newly arrived 23rd Armoured Brigade were advancing toward them from the southeast. Most of these were from 40th RTR, and their commanding officer's tank was one of the first to be destroyed, leaving the unit with next to no effective command.

THE BATTLE OF ALAM HALFA: Aug. 31–Sept. 5, 1942

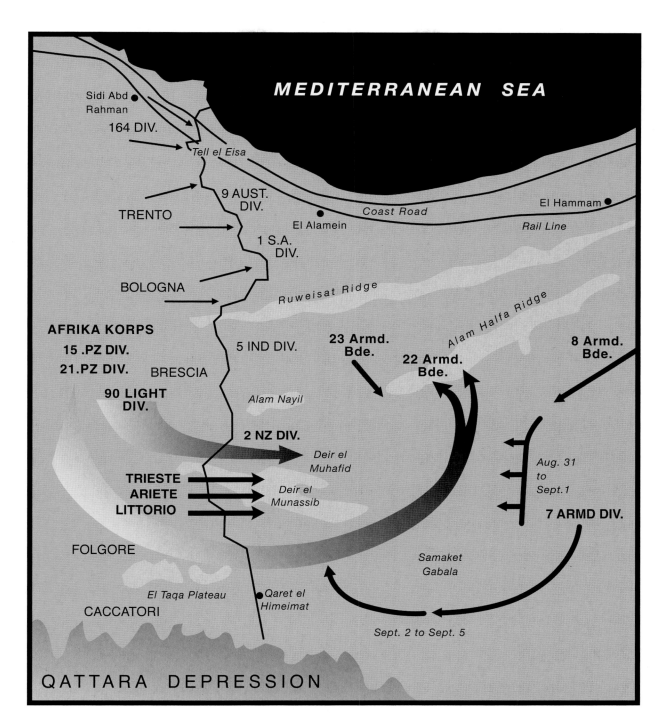

The Battle of Alam Halfa would so deteriorate Rommel's forces that they would never fully recover. With the help of Ultra intercepts the British were able to prepare heavily defended positions on Alam Halfa Ridge and await the attack. Their well-prepared minefields channeled the DAK to within range of their guns, with the RAF pounding them during their approach. Here, for the first time, Rommel himself was lured into a trap where his armor was systematically destroyed by well-emplaced anti-tank guns, while the British tanks fired from hulldown positions.

The German gunners had trouble swinging their guns around to face the enemy, more to the south, and thereby lost all their prepared protection, but managed to get their first few shots off successfully before fighting with the heavy trails of their gun to roll it back into a proper firing position again. The gun was prone to creeping steadily rearward with every shot fired, since the trails could not bite into the hard ground surface. Unseen by the advancing tanks, they were able to stop one after the other, and Halm's gun alone accounted for nine of them. The Valentines were shot to pieces by strong anti-tank fire and well-placed minefields, and the ones that had managed to roll through in the clouds of dust were also shot up and captured when they ran into the strongly defended 15th Panzer HQ positions in the rear.

Eventually, the 21st Panzer was directed forward and pounced on the remnants in what became a killing ground, so that by the end of the day 23rd Armoured Brigade had lost 96 tanks. Thus, in the central sector the British had lost well over 100 tanks along with 1,400 prisoners and high numbers of casualties.

In the north the South Africans and Australians had fared a bit better but failed to make a breakthrough. In the end, July 22 had gone quite well for Rommel, although the German infantry had suffered heavy losses. The Afrika Korps had again managed to hold the line and inflict heavy damage on a superior enemy force. The rest of the month was quiet, except for a daring attack made by the Australians on the night of July 26–27. They had attempted to clear a path through the minefields for the advance of the British 169th Infantry Brigade and 1st Armoured Division, but it was snuffed out with heavy losses to the 169th.

Fighting now dropped off all along the front while both sides licked their wounds, but although the Panzerarmee had failed to break through to the Nile, it had still inflicted heavy losses on the eighth Army and swung the balance of power in their favor.

During this lull the troops on both sides were forced to sweat it out in hastily built trenches and dugouts. Above and beyond the torment of the sweltering heat were the swarms of flies that assaulted the troops every morning. In search of any form of moisture these flies were attracted to the eyes, mouth, and

The 15cm sFH13/1 (Sf) auf Geschützwagen Lorraine Schlepper (f) shown here was captured by the British during the August–September 1942 Alam Halfa battles. Based on a captured French chassis, it served with the German 155th Motorized Artillery Regiment of 21st Panzer Division in the final battles at El Alamein.

An 88mm gun being towed into position by a Zgkw 8-ton SdKfz.7 semi-tracked prime mover.

nostrils, swarming over both the men and their food. Sleep during the day was made impossible since the flies continually tried to crawl into the nostrils, and headnets, although available, were in short supply. When darkness came and the temperature dropped, the flies would let up a bit, but come morning, they were back again by the thousands.

Often during this period, the nights were spent laying mines, resupplying, or going on patrol. Since the temperature from midday to late evening could record a 60-degree drop, this was the time when most of the strenuous activity took place, such as unloading trucks and digging emplacements.

A knocked-out Diana self-propelled 76.2mm gun from the 605th Panzerjäger Abteilung. With the side blown off, the wheeled carriage of this boxed-in gun is readily visible.

THE BATTLE OF ALAM HALFA

The German threat to the Middle East had caused a great stir in the British camp, and convoy after convoy was now heading for the Suez Canal to try to ward off any further advances. These were just the prelude to an immense influx of troops and equipment, which by September would give the eighth Army overwhelming superiority. Finally, to start with a clean slate, on August 13 Montgomery would replace Auchinleck as commander of this revitalized eighth Army.

Rommel was well aware of the British build-up and was determined to launch a major offensive that would break through to the Suez Canal and checkmate any future British offensives. His plan was to use head-on attacks by the Italian XXI and X Corps in the north to hold the enemy's attention, while his DAK, including the Italian XX Corps, swung south to break through the British defenses and then sweep north to the coast road behind the eighth Army. If this attack was successful, a threefold pursuit of the enemy would ensue. Gruppe Bismark, made up of 21st Panzer Division and 164th Light Division, would strike out for Alexandria. The Afrika Korps, led by 15th Panzer and the 90th Light, would cross the Nile at Cairo and strike out immediately for the Suez Canal. The Italian XX Corps, with Ariete and Littorio Armored Divisions and Trieste Motorized Division, would clean up any British resistance still existing in the rear areas.

Rommel had used this southern sweep approach in most of his earlier attacks, and the British had always responded by sending their armor to intercept him. However, their new commander, Montgomery, would have none of it and insisted that in the event of this type of attack the British armor would take up defensive hulldown positions, and the artillery, anti-tank guns, and the RAF would take on the German armor.

While Ultra fed Montgomery any information it could glean from the German radio intercepts, the British were planting false information of their own. A phoney map, developed by Brig. Francis de Guingand, was planted in a damaged armored car which had to be left behind, with the hope that the Germans would find it. Col. Fritz Bayerlein confirmed that indeed the Germans did find it and treated it as authentic. The map supposedly showed the minefield positions, soft sand areas, and the condition of the various desert tracks in the XIII Corps sector. Undoubtedly, it added to the confusion of the battles to follow.

Rommel was ready to strike with the full moon on the night of August 26, but supply difficulties forced him to postpone until the thirtieth. At 0200 hours on the thirty-first the DAK reached the British minefields. The 15th and 21st Panzer Divisions were in the lead, followed by the Italian XX Corps and 90th Light in the rear. Their total tank strength was 515, of which 234 were German and included 26 of the newly arrived PzKpfw. IV/F2 models with the long 75mm gun. The towed artillery included 72 mobile 88mm guns, but these would find few suitable targets, since Horrock's XIII Corps had been warned not to play into Rommel's hand by engaging him with their armor.

From the start, things went badly, as Rommel received reports that his armor had come up against unmarked minefields or was bogged down in bad terrain. The anticipated thirty-mile penetration by daybreak had dissolved to a mere ten miles, and his sweep north would now lead him under the guns on the crest of Alam el Halfa Ridge. To add to his problems, he learned that Maj. Gen. Georg von Bismark, commander of 21st Panzer Division, had been killed by a mine explosion and Lt. Gen. Walther Nehring, commanding the Afrika Korps, had been badly wounded during an air attack. An assault on the highest point of Alam Halfa Ridge was repulsed and the Italian XX Corps on the left was halted in its tracks. Maj. Gen. Kleemann, commanding the 90th Light Division opposite the New Zealand Division was also seriously wounded in an air attack, and on September 1 Rommel himself barely escaped another British bombing raid.

The RAF continued to pound the Axis forces at every opportunity, and on September 3 Rommel de-

A pair of Italian M. 14-41s end up as smoldering wrecks after the early fighting.

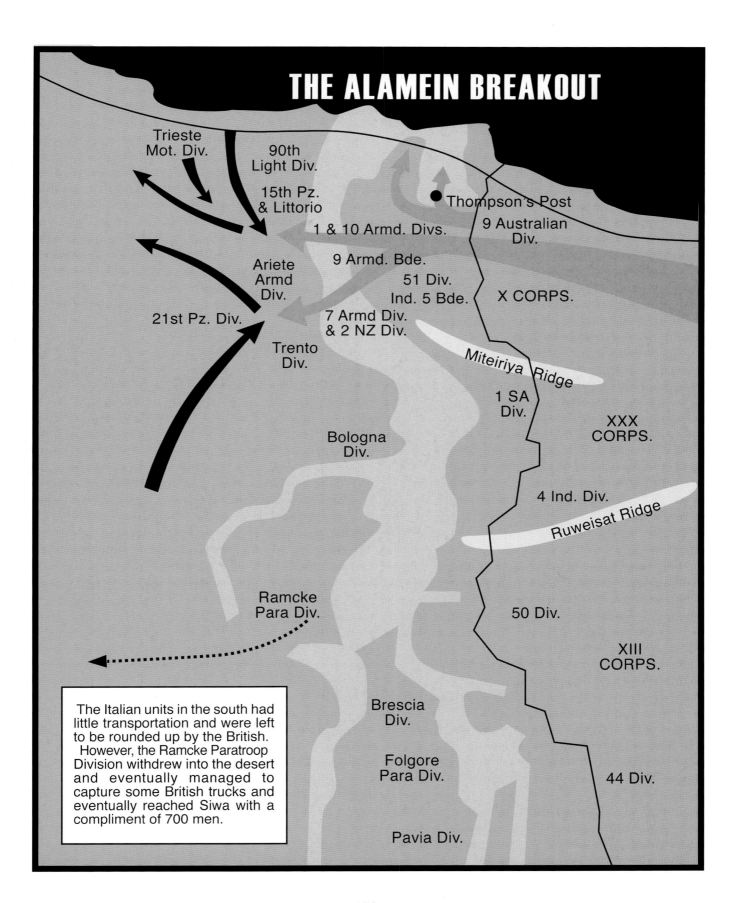

THE ALAMEIN BREAKOUT

Trieste Mot. Div.

90th Light Div.

15th Pz. & Littorio

1 & 10 Armd. Divs.

Thompson's Post

9 Australian Div.

Ariete Armd Div.

9 Armd. Bde.

51 Div.

Ind. 5 Bde.

X CORPS.

21st Pz. Div.

7 Armd Div. & 2 NZ Div.

Trento Div.

Miteiriya Ridge

1 SA Div.

XXX CORPS.

Bologna Div.

4 Ind. Div.

Ruweisat Ridge

Ramcke Para Div.

50 Div.

XIII CORPS.

Brescia Div.

Folgore Para Div.

44 Div.

Pavia Div.

The Italian units in the south had little transportation and were left to be rounded up by the British. However, the Ramcke Paratroop Division withdrew into the desert and eventually managed to capture some British trucks and eventually reached Siwa with a compliment of 700 men.

cided to withdraw. Axis losses were 536 dead, 1,760 wounded, and 569 missing, along with 49 tanks, 55 guns, and 395 trucks captured or destroyed. The great dream of a quick thrust to the Nile was now extinguished.

Rommel's health had been failing for some time and on September 19, Gen. Georg Stumme arrived to act as a temporary replacement. On the twenty-third Rommel flew from Derna to Rome, then on to Germany for public appearances and medical treatment.

THE ALAMEIN BUILD-UP

Since the fall of Tobruk and President Roosevelt's decision to supply aid to the faltering British forces in Egypt, every effort was made to get as many of the new M4A1 and M4A2 Sherman tanks as possible to the eighth Army. The original plan was to send the complete U.S. 2nd Armored Division to Egypt, but since this would take until October or November to complete, it was decided to skim off about 300 new Shermans from training troops and send them off to Egypt immediately, along with 100 of the new M7 "Priest" self-propelled 105mm howitzers.

A special convoy of six ships was assembled and sailed on July 15, accompanied by three U.S. destroyers. On the second day out the *Fairport*, with a cargo of 8,000 tons, was torpedoed by the German sub *U-161* and sunk 500 miles north of the Virgin Islands. Another fast ship with 52 more Shermans set sail to fill the loss.

By September 11 a total of 318 Shermans had reached the Middle East, most of which were the cast-hull M4A1s, with a few M4A2 diesel models thrown in. These were the first Shermans to arrive in quantity, but a single M4A1 had arrived earlier in Au-

gust so that the ordnance and armored troops could familiarize themselves with the vehicle. The Sherman at this time was almost classified as a secret weapon, and its arrival stirred many a tank crewman's heart. These new American medium tanks had until now been referred to by their codename, "Swallow," in an attempt to hide their true identity from any German radio intercepts. However, once in hand in Egypt, Churchill suggested that these new tanks be referred to as the "General Sherman," and the Sherman name would stick forever. The British tactically referred to them as Cruiser tanks: Sherman II for the M4A1 and Sherman III for the M4A2. For the next few months the Shermans would rule the battlefield, and the British would finally have a tank with a turret mounted 75mm gun that fired both AP and HE.

Immediately upon their arrival at Port Tewfik, they began being modified for desert conditions, plus the addition of sandshields and side rails to support sunshields and stowage items. Bags of gear would readily be stored along the sunshield rails long after the need for sunshields ended. They also had stowage bin "blanket boxes" attached to the rear turret bustle. British-style radios were fitted, and a number of minor items, like extra water bottles, were added to the interior.

They were then repainted and passed on to the training centers. When the battle of Alamein began on the night of October 23 there were 252 Shermans with the forward elements of the eighth Army. However, the 36 Shermans of 9th Armoured Brigade had only arrived that same day, and there was little time to check them over before the great barrage began.

The Sherman II (M4A1) featured a cast hull and was driven by a Wright Continental 9-cylinder air-

RELATIVE STRENGTHS AT EL ALAMEIN

Recorded by C. E. Lucas Philips, quoting figures from the Historical Branch of the British War Office.

	PANZERARMEE AFRIKA	EIGHTH ARMY
Men:	108,000 (53,736 Germans)	220,476 (in fighting state)
18,000 German reinforcements landed just before the and during the battle. A further 77,000 Italians were in rear areas.		including 20,000 non-effective
Guns: field and medium (in action)	552	892
Tanks: (fit for action)	548 (249 German)	939 (in forward areas)
Guns: anti-tank	1,063	1,451
Mines: (serviceable)	460,000	--
Aircraft: (serviceable)	350	530
Excluding long-range in Greece, Crete and Sicily.		

cooled engine which ran on high-octane aircraft fuel, much the same as used in the Grant. The Sherman III (M4A2) on the other hand was powered by a 12-cylinder General Motors liquid-cooled diesel engine. Where possible, units were outfitted with one type or the other, since mixing them together would further complicate logistics.

OPERATION LIGHTFOOT

Montgomery had put great effort into concealing his build-up in the north, and at the same time he had dummy tank parks and refuelling depots set up in the south, in the hope that he could keep much of Rommel's armor guarding the southern flank.

In the early hours of October 23, 1942, the British artillery illuminated the night sky with one of the heaviest bombardments to date. The main impact was felt from the coast to Ruweisat Ridge, but in the south, XII Corps also joined in with diversionary fire. The artillery barrage lasted 15 minutes and severely disrupt-

More than likely left behind for lack of fuel or mechanical reasons, and with its muzzle dust cover still in place, this PzKpfw IV/F2 was the best tank that the DAK could field during the Alamein battles.

ed the enemy's communication lines and destroyed artillery batteries and minefield emplacements. This was the beginning of twelve days of battle which would see the Axis line falter and then fall under the enormous pressure applied by the eighth Army.

Sappers now moved forward using the first mine-detectors to see service in World War II, followed by unique "Scorpion" mine clearing tanks, lashing the sand with huge chain flails to clear paths through the minefields. Two main corridors were to be opened up: the upper corridor being given to the 9th Australian and 51st (Highland) Divisions and the lower one to the 2nd New Zealand Division. Both attacks fell somewhat short of their objectives, but the attrition on the enemy infantry positions had begun. The Italian Trento Division had been very badly mauled and the German 164th Division had two battalions almost wiped out. A further attempt to break through met even stiffer resistance with considerable loss of men and machines.

On the twenty-fourth, after taking time to organize and assess the situation, 15th Panzer and Littorio Armored Divisions were ordered to regain the lost positions. The IV Battalion and DLIV Group of

A command Crusader II of the 9th Australian Division's Cavalry Regiment in a hulldown position at El Alamein. It is interesting to note that it is still fitted with a flimsy rack below the extra petrol drum.

Littorio, reinforced with elements of 15th Panzer, attacked and drove the British back until German infantry was able to take over the old positions. In the south, detachments of 21st Panzer, V Semoventi Group, and some ardent Italian infantry using grenades counterattacked and stopped the attack there.

During these battles, General Stumme, commander of the DAK, suffered a heart attack while moving across the battlefield and fell from his vehicle without his driver noticing the mishap. It was then several days before his body was found. To fill the vital position until Rommel's return, Lt. Gen. Ritter von Thoma assumed command on the evening of October 24.

On the twenty-fifth General Montgomery again ordered XIII and XXX Corps to advance, but both met stiff resistance and failed to gain their objectives. This was the situation on October 26 when Rommel arrived back at his headquarters from Austria. Since the 15th Panzer Division was now down to its last 39 tanks and Littorio Armored Division had only 69, he was forced to bring northward the 106 tanks of 21st Panzer.

These forces were ordered to counterattack and regain the old positions, but the British were waiting with their new 6-pounder anti-tank guns, and

a heavy toll was taken. The RAF also pounded the Axis armor from the air and by the end of the day the battlefield was littered with wrecked vehicles.

The 9th Australian Division now struck northward and sliced into the German 164th Division, trapping the greater part of it against the sea. The 1st South African and 4th Indian Divisions joined up to punch a hole in the Bologna Division positions, and now Rommel ordered his last armor reserves, the Ariete Armored reserves, and the Ariete Armored Division to move north.

A typical 88mm anti-tank gun emplacement dug in on the open desert, showing the size of the 88 round.

WOODCOCK AND SNIPE

Kidney Ridge would prove to be a pivotal point for the final breakout at El Alamein, and to further expand its potential, two rarely heard of missions were assigned to two infantry units and their accompanying anti-tank guns. Their missions were to take and occupy two positions on the Axis anti-tank screen, one code-named "Woodcock" north of Kidney Ridge and the other named "Snipe" to the south of the ridge.

On the evening of October 26, 1942 these two probes were launched by 7th Motor Brigade, which had just been supplied with plenty of the new 6-pounder anti-tank guns. They had a 30-gun, half-hour barrage layed down ahead of them. Due to a navigational error 60th Rifles stumbled into the German line way too soon, while the infantry was still aboard their trucks, and recklessly made a mad dash

ahead to get out of the line of fire of the Axis anti-tank guns. They captured about 100 stunned German soldiers plus six anti-tank guns and settled into their new positions at "Woodcock.

At "Snipe" a few miles to the south, the 2nd Battalion's Rifle Brigade under Lieutenant Colonel Turner was also having navigational problems caused by faulty maps. By 0200 he had led his battalion about 2,000 yards from the start line to a small-oval shaped depression that he assumed was "Snipe." They set up a 19-gun defense all around the perimeter and dug in where necessary with little difficulty. The depression was fringed with tamarisk bushes and camel thorn which helped conceal the guns and infantry firing positions. They had captured a dozen German sappers as they took the position and found a ten-foot-square-roofed dug-out where Turner was quick to set up his battalion HQ.

Gen. Sir Bernard L. Montgomery atop his personal M3 Grant command tank. This photo was taken in late December 1942 while he was inspecting the British forward positions in Libya.

This structure was used as the control tower of the Driving and Maintenance Section of the Middle East Training Centre Repair Depot near Heliopolos, Egypt.

Meanwhile, several of the Bren gun carriers, feeling their way through a minefield, raced off to attack a German-Italian refuelling depot about a mile distant, setting several trucks and a fuel tanker aflame. They lost one carrier and set the night sky ablaze. Upon returning with a dozen prisoners they were told that about twenty German tanks were now encircling their position.

Heading the attack was a Mark IV Special with the long 75mm gun. It was followed by an Italian Semovente da 75/18. Both sides now opened up, but at 30 yards a 6-pdr stopped the Mark IV and several more rounds set it on fire, which lit up the Semovente some 200 yards behind it. That was also swiftly destroyed, and at that point the other tanks began to back off. Obviously, there was something deadly out there!

When dawn came, the battalion began to realize from distant landmarks that they had plunged themselves right into the gap between 15th Panzer to the north and the Littorio Armored Division to the south. All they could see for miles was Axis vehicles and tanks. They had plowed through to the rear echelons, where softskins scurried about making early-morning deliveries.

The gunners decided that this was the time to find out if their new 6-pdrs were as good as they were cracked up to be and began picking off tanks as fast as they could find them in their sights. In this first exchange they destroyed fourteen tanks, several SP guns, some trucks, an 88mm gun, and a staff car.

It wasn't long before they were under heavy shelling, which took its toll among gunners trying to move their guns to better field-of-fire positions, and infantry trying to hunker down. The battalion was virtually cut off from the British lines to the east but somehow expected the 24th Armoured Brigade to show up at any moment. Unfortunately, when the Shermans of the 24th crested Kidney Ridge, all they could see was German vehicles and they had no idea that the "Snipe" position was now buried in the Axis lines. They began merrily bombarding the whole area.

Unable to warn off the tanks because they were on different radio frequencies, Turner decided to send his intelligence officer off in a Bren gun carrier to try

Two British officers examine the results of of a trial firing at 1,000 yards with a German 50mm anti-tank gun on a newly arrived American M3 Lee tank. Suez Road, October 1942.

A British Grant medium tank being worked on at the repair depot near Heliopolis, Egypt. October 1942.

to make contact with the 24th and stop this friendly fire. Eventually, the firing on Snipe ceased, and the Shermans moved forward. German tanks that swung to face this new threat were now taken broadside by the 6-pdrs again. When the Shermans did reach Snipe, their high silhouettes brought in devastating fire from German anti-tank guns and soon seven were ablaze. Soon after arrival the remaining Shermans withdrew east behind Kidney Ridge again.

Turner's men were on their own again, and it was obvious that the cavalry was not going to come and save them. A number of the guns were hit and others broke down. Ammunition was getting desperately low, and by midday there were only 13 guns left in action. The infantry was picking off any enemy infantry that ventured too close. Six of the Bren gun carriers were set ablaze by enemy fire, sending up columns of black smoke.

At about one o'clock that afternoon, nine Italian M.14-41 tanks from Littorio, supported by several Semoventes, approached their flank. Unfortunately, only one gun could be brought to bear on this group. Pulling together a full crew of volunteers, they held their fire until the tanks were within 600 yards and then dispatched six of them in a row. They had three rounds left! The accompanying Semoventes continued to lob 75mm rounds into their position, but the shallow depression was a perfect spot for the low-profile 6-pounder.

More 6-pdr rounds were found elsewhere and dragged to this lone gun, which then took out three more M.14s at about 300 yards and under. This gave

the Italians pause and they withdrew. However, later that afternoon they again came under friendly fire, this time from the 105mm guns of the brand-new Priests of 2nd Armoured Brigade who were in combat for the first time. This was devastating to the men, and they began to pray for darkness and escape from this mess.

Then, at about 5 p.m., with maybe two hours of good light left, they saw about 70 enemy tanks, in two groups, assembling to attack the British armor beyond Snipe. This was one of the attacks for which 21st Panzer had been brought up from the south. For some reason it seems that the newly arrived 21st Panzer had not been informed of the nasty group of enemy anti-tank guns hidden at Snipe. As the German attack moved forward, the nearest tanks were well within 200 yards range of the four guns that had seen the least action that day and were manned by Royal Artillery gunners rather than infantry gunners.

Within minutes they took out nine panzers, and as others turned head on to deal with these guns, the Shermans had broadside targets in abundance. Gradually, the German tanks drew back, but soon fifteen Mark IIIs approached from the west. There were still two guns in action that could take them on and four panzers were soon disabled. Others swept around to a different approach and the available guns were now down to about six. Two more Mark IIIs were knocked out, the last for the day, and then darkness set in.

Their casualties included about seventy dead or wounded, including ten officers. They buried their dead in the slit trenches they had occupied and then withdrew from Snipe. Only one gun was retrieved, as they had lost all their transport but for one truck.

It was only some days later, when battalion had a chance to visit Snipe, that the full impact of their 24-hour battle was revealed. A conservative estimate concluded that they alone had destroyed or disabled 33 tanks, 5 SP guns, several artillery pieces and trucks, and a staff car. They had possibly damaged another 20 tanks which had been forced out of combat for repairs.

Snipe was obviously one of the turning points of the Second Battle of El Alamein, and Rommel had lost irreplaceable armor to a small group of British anti-tank guns that had accidentally embedded themselves in the Axis lines.

OPERATION SUPERCHARGE

Although Churchill was totally disappointed with Monty's failure to break through during the initial battles, the general stuck to his plans for a decisive breakthrough. On November 2 Supercharge was unleashed and the fiercest fighting to date ensued. General Freyberg's 9th Armored Brigade lost 70 of its 94 tanks, with Italian anti-tank gunners engaging targets at ranges as short as 20 yards in a swirling nightmare of dust and destruction. At the end of the day, the Axis front was a shambles and Rommel knew it was time to withdraw to new positions 20 kilometers to their rear if he hoped to save the Afrika Korps from a complete rout.

This movement had just begun on November 3 when a message from Hitler insisted that the Afrika Korps hold its ground to the last man. Rommel hesitated and then finally cancelled his orders to withdraw. Fortunately for the DAK, Montgomery failed to exploit this opportunity of indecision.

The Ariete moved in on the right flank of 15th Panzer on the morning of November 4 and soon found itself under heavy attack from the south and rear by armored elements of the British X Corps. The Italian armor was hopelessly outclassed and almost completely surrounded but fought on heroically until the following dawn. The Italian XX Corps was almost completely destroyed, and the last message from Ariete gave its position as 5 kilometers northwest of Bir el Abd.

By that afternoon the eighth Army had opened a 15-mile breech in the Axis lines, but what remained of the mechanized units of Rommel's Panzerarmee managed to escape to the west. However, the non-motorized Italian Trento, Bologna, Brescia, Pavia, and Folgore infantry divisions were left stranded.

During this breakthrough, the commander of the DAK, General von Thoma, was also captured as he leapt from his burning vehicle. The German Ramcke

The second-to-last remaining StuG. III Ausf D of Kampfgruppe Menton, which apparently broke down somewhere short of Tobruk while taking part in the rearguard actions along with 90th Light Division.

Parachute Brigade managed to withdraw on foot into the desert wastes and was able to capture some British transport with which to make its way west. On November 7 they were spotted by German reconnaissance vehicles north of Siwa, and General Ramcke and 700 of his men were brought in.

The following 15th Panzer Division reports during the stages of their withdrawal give us a good insight into how it was carried out. On November 4 they moved back into defensive positions around Sidi Hamid and waited as the remnants of 2nd Battalion, 115th Panzer Grenadier Regiment, continued to come in. Movement westward had to be timed so that their transport, supply services, and regular units could move smoothly through the various defiles open to them.

On November 5 the division moved off at 0400 hours toward their new positions in an area 50 kilometer south of Fuka. The rearguard was formed of the remaining few tanks, as about 200 British tanks and carriers followed up from the southwest. They reached the specified area in the vicinity of Bir Abdalla around 0900 hours and organized for defense. Lack of fuel was always a problem at this time. During the day enemy tanks and armored cars felt their way forward and attempted to outflank them to the south but were driven off by artillery and anti-tank fire. Their next objective was the area south of Mersa Matruh, and the required fuel arrived in the nick of time. During the night they withdrew to the eastern limits of the Mersa Matruh minefields, arriving in the early hours of November 6.

Kampfgruppe Menton (Sonderverband 288) under Colonel Menton was already located on the southeastern edge of the minefields. The lanes through these extensive minefields were largely unknown now and 15th Panzer was forced to squeeze through the only known gap east of the Siwa track. In this new position they were somewhat protected by the minefields but had no freedom of movement. Both fuel and water were in short supply.

On November 7 a detachment from 33rd Panzer Engineer Bn. was sent out to reconnoitre routes of withdrawal through the minefields to the southwest and northwest. Both proved impassable and they were finally ordered to move westward along the congested coastal road by night to Sidi Barani, despite the risk of air attack. Shortly after moving out, their armored spearhead was engaged by gunners of Kampfgruppe Menton, which in the darkness mistook them for the advancing British armor. Two tanks were knocked out and the division was delayed for two hours.

On November 8, with the British continuing to follow cautiously, 15th Panzer managed to withdraw to Bug-Bug with only two minor skirmishes. On November 9 they passed through Halfaya Pass to the Capuzzo area. During November 11 they moved along the Trigh Capuzzo to El Duda. On November 12 they reached El Adem, and on the thirteenth passed through the Gazala minefields on the Acroma track to reach Bir Temrad. On November 14 they moved along the Martuba route and Via Balbia to Maraua. November 15 saw them move from Barce to El Abjar. On November 17 they passed through Benghazi, Ghemines, and Magrun. By November 19 they were just north of Agedabia, and by the twenty-fifth were in positions east of El Agheila. The long retreat from Alamein was over.

British 1st Armoured Division: Oct. 23, 1942

2nd ARMOURED BRIGADE:
The Queen's Bays (Regiment)

Regiment HQ Troop

"A" SQUADRON
Squadron HQ and
5 Troops of three each

"B" SQUADRON
Squadron HQ and
4 Troops of three each

"C" SQUADRON
Squadron HQ and
4 Troops of three each

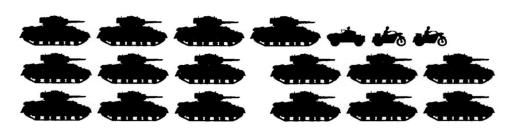

The above T/O&E of the Bays is representative of the composition of the Sherman- and Crusader-equipped regiments at the time of the Alamein breakout. The following list reflects the make-up of many of the other armored units of the eighth Army at this date and gives us an idea of the number of Grants, Valentines, and Stuarts involved as well.

GHQ: EIGHTH ARMY - 1 Grant
B Squadron, 6 RTR - 12 Grants
1st Army Tank Brigade - Matilda Scorpion Flails
42nd & 44th RTR (Det.) -
      6 Matilda Scorpion Flails each

XXX CORPS
4/6 SA A/Car Regt. - 55 Marmon-Herringtons
23 Armoured Brigade HQ - Valentines and
6 Matildas
      40th RTR - 42 Valentines
      46th RTR - 49 Valentines
      50th RTR - 44 Valentines
      8th RTR - 51 Valentines
2 New Zealand Division - Stuart command tank
9 Armored Brigade HQ - 1 Sherman, 3 Crusaders
3 Hussars - 9 Grants, 12 Shermans, 16 Crusaders
Royal Wilts. Yeo. - 14 Grants, 10 Shermans, 13 Crusaders

Warwicks Yeo. - 14 Grants, 13 Shermans, 17 Crusaders
2 NZ Div. Cav. Regt. - 29 Stuarts, 44 Bren Carriers
3rd South African A/Car Regt. -
     55 Marmon-Herringtons
9th Aust. Div. Cav. Regt. -
     15 Crusaders, 52 Bren Carriers

XIII CORPS - 13 A/Cars in Corps HQ
7th Armoured Div. - 7 Crusaders, 5 A/Cars in HQ
4th (Lt) Armoured Bde. - 9 Armored Cars
Royal Scots Greys - 19 Stuarts (A), 14 Grants (B & C)
4th/8th Hussars - 48 Stuarts
22nd Armoured Bde. - 4 Crusaders in Bde. HQ
     1st RTR - 19 Stuarts, 24 Grants
     5th RTR - 18 Crusaders, 25 Grants
     4th C.L.Y. - 28 Crusaders (A & B), 9 Grants (C)
Household Cavalry Regiment - 53 Armored Cars
11 Hussars - 61 Humber Mk.III Armored Cars
2nd Derbyshire Yeomany - 50 Humber Mk.III A/Cars

X CORPS - 2 Grants in Corps HQ
1st Armoured Div. - 8 Crusaders in Division HQ
2nd Arm'd Bde. - 1 Grant, 92 Shermans, 68 Crusaders
The Queen's Bays - Crusaders (A), Shermans (B & C)
9th Lancers - Crusaders (A), Shermans (B & C)
10th Hussars - Crusaders (B), Shermans (A & C)
7th Motor Bde. - 6 Churchill Mk. IIIs (Kingforce)
12 Lancers - 55 Humber Armored Cars

10th Armoured Div. - 7 Crusaders in Division HQ
8th Arm'd Bde. - 57 Grants, 31 Shermans, 45 Crusaders
3rd RTR - Crusaders (A), Shermans (B), Grants (C)
Nottingham. Yeo. Crusaders (A), Shermans (B), Grants (C)
Staffordsh. Yeo. - Crusaders (A), Shermans (B), Grants (C)
24th Arm'd. Bde. - 2 Grants, 93 Shermans, 45 Crusaders
     41st RTR - Crusaders (A), Shermans (B & C)
     45th RTR - Crusaders (A), Shermans (C & C)
     47th RTR - Crusaders (A), Shermans (B & C)
1st Dragoons (Royals) - 46 Armored Cars.

A destroyed Sherman of the 2nd New Zealand Division, 9th Armoured Brigade, 3rd Hussars, knocked out by a German anti-tank gun during the fighting around the Sidi Rahman track in early November 1942.

21st Panzer Division: October 27, 1942
21. Panzer Division

21st PANZER DIVISION HEADQUARTERS
– 200th Motorized Mapping Detachment
– 200th Motorized Printing Detachment
– Armored Command Detachment

5th PANZER REGIMENT
– Panzer Regiment Headquarters
    Armored Signal Platoon
    2 Light Tank Platoons
1st Armored Battalion
    Battalion HQ & HQ Company
    3 Light Tank Companies
    1 Medium Tank Company
2nd Armored Battalion
    Battalion HQ & HQ Company
    3 Light Tank Companies
    1 Medium Tank Company

104th MOTORIZED INFANTRY REGIMENT
Regiment HQ & HQ Company
    Motorized Signal Platoon
    Motorized Anti-Tank Platoon
    Motorcycle Platoon
    Motorized Engineer Platoon (50mm)
– 13th S/P (Inf. Gun) Company 150mm)
– 14th Motorized (Eng.) Co.

1st Motorized Infantry Battalion
– Battalion Headquarters
    4 Motorized Infantry Companies
2nd Motorized Infantry Battalion
– Battalion Headquarters
    4 Motorized Infantry Companies
3rd Motorized Infantry Battalion
– Battalion Headquarters
    4 Motorized Infantry Companies

3rd MOTORIZED RECON. BATTALION
– Battalion HQ & Signal Platoon
    Heavy Armored Car Platoon (75mm)
    Armored Car Company
    Armored Recon Co. (75mm & 76.2mm)
    Heavy Reconnaissance Company
    – Engineer Platoon
    – A/T Platoon (75mm & 76.2mm)

– Signal Platoon
Motorized Artillery Battery (105mm)

155th MOTORIZED ARTILLERY REGIMENT
– Regiment HQ & HQ Battery
    115th Artillery Obsevation Battery
    724th Artillery Calibration Detatchment

1st Motorized Artillery Battalion
    Battalion HQ & HQ Battery
    3 Motorized Batteries (105mm)
2nd Motorized Artillery Battalion
    Battalion HQ & HQ Battery
    3 Motorized Batteries (105mm)
3rd Motorized Artillery Battalion
    Battalion HQ & HQ Battery
    3 Motorized Batteries (105mm)

3rd ARMORED RECON BATTALION
– Battalion HQ & Signal Platoon
    Heavy Armored Car Platoon (75mm)
    Armored Car Company
    Armored Recon Co. (75mm & 76.2mm)
    Heavy Reconnaissance Company
    – Engineer Platoon
    – A/T Platoon (75mm or 76.2mm)
    – Signal Platoon
    Motorized Artillery Battery (105mm)

200th MOTORIZED ENGINEER BATTALION
– Battalion Headquarters
    3 Motorized Engineer Companies

200th ARMORED SIGNAL BATTALION
– Battalion HQ & Signal Platoon
    1 Motorized Anti-Tank Company (50mm)
    1 S/P Anti-Tank Company (75mm/76.2mm)

200th ARMORED SIGNAL BATTALION
– Battalion Headquarters
    Armored Radio Company
    Armored Telephone Company
    Support Troops

155th MOTORIZED ARTILLERY REGIMENT
155. ARTILLERIE-REGIMENT (motorisiert)

IIIrd MOTORIZED ARTILLERY BATTALION

Battalion Headquarters

Signal Platoon

Motorized Calibration Detachment

1st Armored Heavy Field Howitzer Battery

Battery Headquarters

Signal Detachment

Gun Platoon

2nd Armored Heavy Field Howitzer Battery

Battery Headquarters

Signal Detachment

Gun Platoon

Motorized 105mm Gun Battery

Battery Headquarters

Signal Detachment

Gun Platoon

Following the German invasion of France, many of the captured French vehicles were converted to suit German military needs. Among these were more that 300 French "Tracteur Blindé 38L", which had been stockpiled for future use as Panzerjäger chassis. In May 1942, with Rommel pressuring him for mobile heavy artillery, Hitler ordered that 40 of them be fitted with the 15cm sFH and shipped to North Africa. By late July a total of 94 conversions had been completed, a dozen or more of which had been shipped to the D.A.K. Thus the 155th Motorized Artillery Regiment of 21st Panzer Division was the first unit to take the "Lorraine Schlepper" (Sd Kfz 135/1) into action. These self-propelled heavy field howitzers were issued to the IIIrd Motorized Heavy Artillery Battalion sometime around October 1942, and required a five man crew.

Although there was certainly a need for the firepower these vehicles could deliver, reports from that time period suggest that the gun mounting was quite unstable and had to be attended to constantly. In the end, British photos show row upon row of these S/P guns which were captured during the Alamein breakout.

90th Light Motorized Africa Division: Oct. 27, 1942
90. Leichte-Afrika-Division

DIVISION HEADQUARTERS
    259th Motorized Mapping Detachment

155th MOTORIZED INFANTRY REGIMENT
– Regiment HQ & HQ Company
    Motorized Signal Platoon
    Motorized Engineer Platoon
    Motorcycle Platoon
– 13th Motorized (Inf.Gun) Co.
    (75mm & 150mm)

1st Motorized Infantry Battalion
    Battalion Headquarters
    4 Motorized Infantry Companies (Africa)
2nd Motorized Infantry Battalion
    Battalion Headquarters
    4 Motorized Infantry Companies (Africa)

200th MOTORIZED INFANTRY REGT.
– Regiment HQ & HQ Company
    Motorized Signal Platoon
    Motorized Engineer Platoon
    Motorcycle Platoon
    13th Motorized (Inf. Gun) Co.
    (50mm & 150mm)
1st Motorized Infantry Battalion
– Battalion Headquarters
    4 Motorized Infantry Co.
    (75mm or 76.2mm)
2nd Motorized Infantry Battaion
– Battalion Headquarters
    4 Motorized Infantry Co.
    (75mm or 76.2mm)

190th MOTORIZED ARTILLERY REGT.
– Regiment Headquarters and HQ Battery
    724th Artillery Calibration Detachment
    190th Motorized A/Aircraft Co. (20mm)
1st Motorized Artillery Battalion

– Battalion HQ & HQ Battery
    2 Mot. Light Field Howitzer Batteries
    1 Motorized Battery (105mm)
2nd Motorized Artillery Battalion
– Battalion HQ & HQ Battery
    2 Mot. Light Field Howitzer Batteries
    1 Motorized Battery (105mm)

580th ARMORED RECON BATTALION
– Battalion HQ & Signal Platoon
– 1 Heavy Armored Car Platoon (75mm)
    Armored Car Company
    Armored Recon Co. (75mm or 76.2mm)
    Heavy Reconnaissance Company
    Engineer Platoon
    A/T Platoon (75mm or 76.2mm)
    Signal Platoon
– Motorized Artillery Battery (105mm)

109th ARMORED BATTALION
– Battalion HQ & HQ Company
    3 Light Tank Companies
    1 Medium Tank Company

900th MOTORIZED ENGINEER BN.
–Battalion Headquarters
    2 Motorized Eng. Co. (50mm)
    1 Motorized Assault Engineer Co.

190th MOTORIZED ANTI-TANK BN.
– Battalion HQ & Signal Platoon
    2 Motorized Anti-Tank Co. (37mm)
    Recon Platoon

190th ARMORED SIGNAL BATTALION
– Battalion Headquarters
– Armored Radio Company
– Armored Telephone Company

90th Light Africa Division: October 27, 1942

580th ARMORED RECONNAISSANCE BATTALION

AUFKLÄRUNGS-ABTEILUNG 580

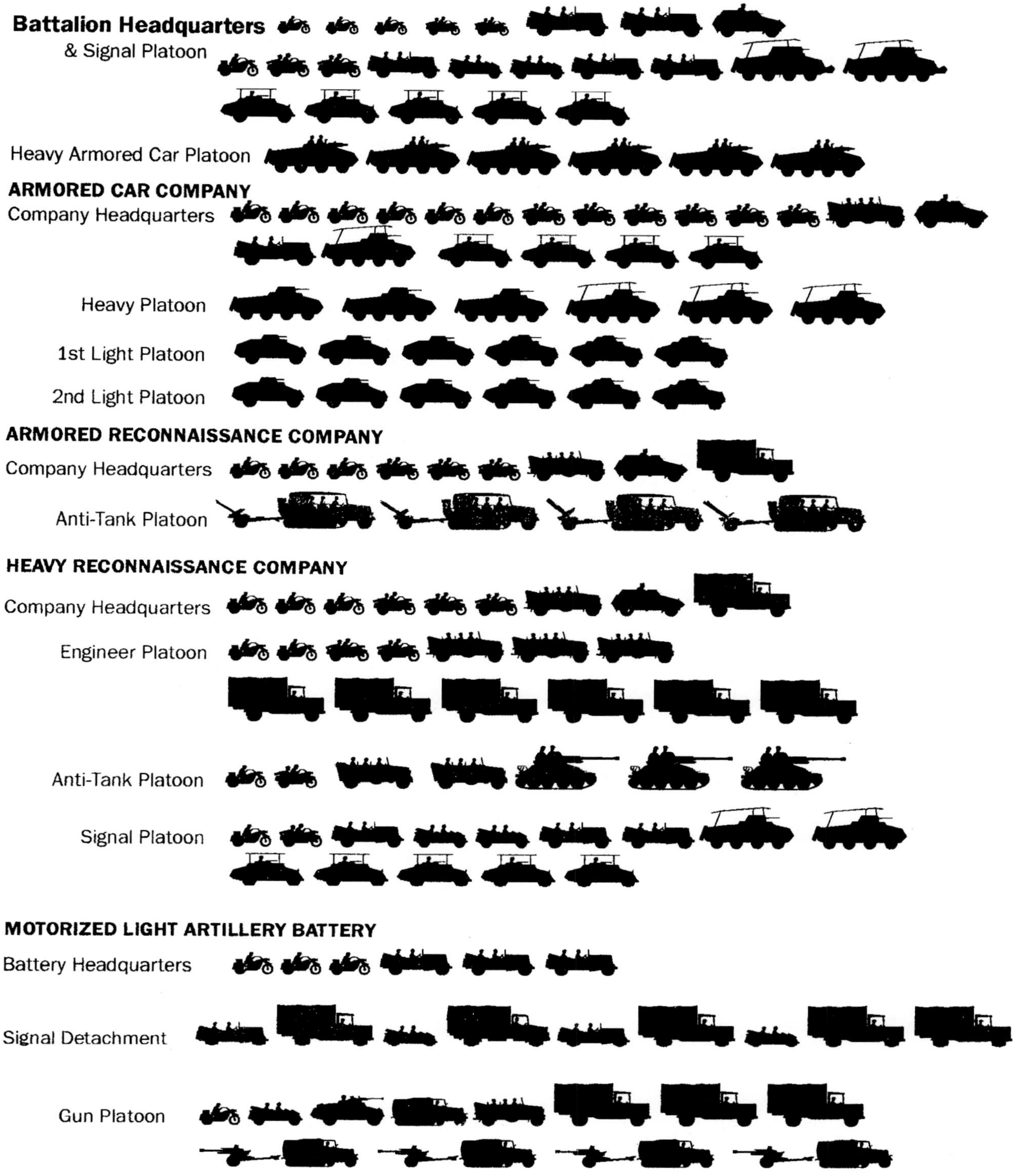

Battalion Headquarters
& Signal Platoon
Heavy Armored Car Platoon
ARMORED CAR COMPANY
Company Headquarters
Heavy Platoon
1st Light Platoon
2nd Light Platoon
ARMORED RECONNAISSANCE COMPANY
Company Headquarters
Anti-Tank Platoon
HEAVY RECONNAISSANCE COMPANY
Company Headquarters
Engineer Platoon
Anti-Tank Platoon
Signal Platoon
MOTORIZED LIGHT ARTILLERY BATTERY
Battery Headquarters
Signal Detachment
Gun Platoon

15th Panzer Division: October 27, 1942

15. Panzer Division

15th PANZER DIVISION HQ
– 33rd Motorized Mapping Detachment
– Armored Command Detachment (Tropical)

8th PANZER REGIMENT
– Panzer Regiment Headquarters
    Armored Signal Platoon
    1 Light Tank Platoon

1st Armored Battalion
– Battalion HQ & HQ Company
    3 Light Tank Companies
    1 Medium Tank Company

2nd Armored Battalion
– Battalion HQ & HQ Company
    3 Light Tank Companies
    1 Medium Tank Company

115th MOTORIZED INFANTRY REGT.
– Regiment HQ & HQ Company
    Motorized Signal Platoon
    Motorized Anti-Tank Platoon (37mm)
    Motorcycle Messenger Platoon
    Motorized Engineer Platoon
– 13th S/P (Inf. Gun) Company (150mm)
– 14th Motorized Combat Engineer Co.
– 1st Motorized Infantry Battalion
    Battalion Headquarters
    4 Motorized Infantry Co. (Africa)
– 2nd Motorized Infantry Battalion
    B attalion Headquarters
    4 Motorized Infantry Companies
– 3rd Motorized Infantry Battalion
    Battalion Headquarters
    4 Motorized Infantry Companies

33rd MOTORIZED ARTILLERY REGT.
– Regiment HQ & HQ Battery
– 33rd Artillery Observation Battery
– 723rd Artillery Calibration Detachment
1st Motorized Artillery Battalion
– Battalion HQ & HQ Battery
    3 Motorized Batteries (105mm)
2nd Motorized Artillery Battalion

– Battalion HQ & HQ Battery
    3 Motorized Batteries (105mm)
3rd Motorized Artillery Battalion
– Battalion HQ & HQ Battery
    3 Motorized Batteries (105mm)

33rd ARMORED RECON. BATTALION
– Battalion HQ & Signal Platoon
    1 Heavy Armored Car Platoon (75)
    1 Armored Car Company
    1 Armored Recon Co. (75mm)
    1 Heavy Recon Company
    Engineer Platoon
    A/T Platoon (75mm or 76.2mm)
    Signal Platoon
    Motorized Artillery Battery (105mm)

33rd MOTORIZED ENGINEER BN.
– Battalion HQ
    3 Motorized Combat Engineer Co.

33rd ARMORED SIGNAL BN.
– Battalion HQ & Signal Platoon
    1 Motorized Anti-Tank Company (50mm)
    1 S/P Anti-Tank Company (75mm/76.2mm)

78th ARMORED SIGNAL BATTALION
– Battalion Headquarters
    Armored Radio Company
    Armored Telephone Company
    Support Troops

164th Light Africa Division: Oct. 27, 1942
164. Leichte Afrika Division

164th LIGHT DIVISION HEADQUARTERS
– 220th Motorized Mapping Detachment

125th MOTORIZED INFANTRY REGIMENT
– Regiment Headquarters & HQ Company
    Motorized Signal Platoon
    Motorized Engineer Platoon
    Motorcycle Platoon
– 13th Motorized (Inf. Gun) Co. (150mm)
– 14th Engineer Company

1st Motorized Infantry Battalion
– Battalion Headquarters
    4 Motorized Infantry Companies
2nd Motorized Infantry Battalion
– Battalion Headquarters
    4 Motorized Infantry Companies

382nd MOTORIZED INFANTRY REGIMENT
Regiment HQ & HQ Company
    Motorized Signal Platoon
    Motorized Engineer Platoon
    Motorcycle Platoon
– 13th Motorized (Inf. Gun) Co. (150mm)

1st Motorized Infantry Battalion
– Battalion Headquarters
    4 Motorized Infantry Companies
2nd Motorized Infantry Battalion
– Battalion Headquarters
    4 Motorized Infantry Companies
3rd Motorized Infantry Battalion
– Battalion Headquarters
    4 Motorized Infantry Companies

433rd MOTORIZED INFANTRY REGIMENT
– Regiment HQ & Signal Platoon
    Motorized Signal Platoon
    Motorized Engineer Platoon
    Motorcycle Platoon
– 13th Motorized (Inf. Gun) Co. (150mm)
1st Motorized Infantry Battalion
– Battalion Headquarters
    4 Motorized Infantry Companies
2nd Motorized Infantry Battalion
– Battalion Headquarters
    4 Motorized Infantry Companies

220th ARMORED RECON BATTALION
– Battalion HQ & Signal Platoon
– Heavy Armored Car Platoon (75mm)
– Armored Car Company
– Armored Recon Co. (75mm or 76.2mm)
– Heavy Reconnaissance Company
    Engineer Platoon
    A/T Platoon (75mm or 76.2mm)
    Signal Platoon
– Motorized Artillery Battery (105mm)

220th ARTILLERY REGIMENT
– Regiment HQ & HQ Battery
1st Artillery Battalion
    3 Motorized Batteries (105mm)
2nd Artillery Battalion
    2 Mountain Batteries (75mm)

220th MOTORIZED ENGINEER BATTALION
– Battalion Headquarters
– 3 Motorized Engineer Companies (50mm)

220th MOTORIZED ANTI-TANK BATTALION
– Battalion HQ & Signal Platoon
    2 Motorized Anti-Tank Companies (50mm)
– Support Troops

   This division was flown from Crete to Africa in early July 1942, but without its vehicles, which put quite a strain on logistics. On arrival they were immediately moved to the front to relieve the 90th Light Africa Division units. Shortly after this they were renamed as 164th Light Africa Division and saw their first action on August 30 against Australian positions at El Alamein, with heavy losses. Although vehicles and anti-tank guns were promised for this division, very few were shipped across, and Rommel was continually reminding Berlin of this fact in his communiqués.
   Their first major engagement was during the British offensive on October 23. During the Axis withdrawal the 164th and others acted as the rear guard units, and during the retreat the surviving units of the division were distributed between the Panzer Divisions to rebuild their infantry strength.

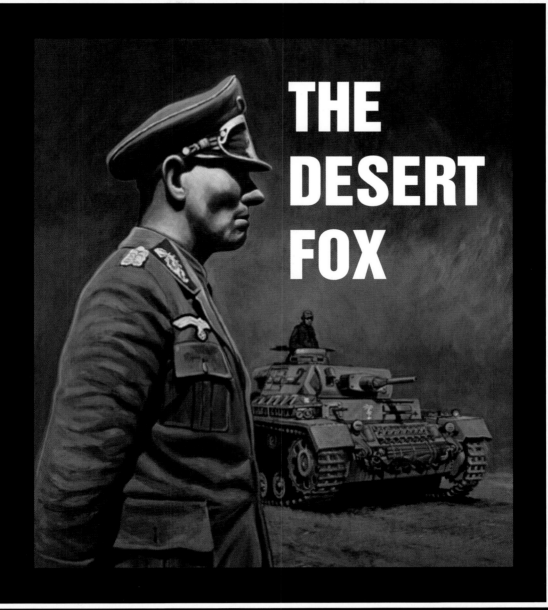

THE DESERT FOX

1891–1944

A SHORT BIOGRAPHY OF
The Desert Fox

Driving along the quiet river valley road leading into Herrlingen on the outskirts of Ulm, I wondered if Rommel had ever come and gone by this route as he rushed back to the Western Front in June 1944. I was touring Germany in 1985 and had made a point of visiting Rommel's grave on our way from Stuttgart to Munich.

In a small, treed graveyard, with curbed walkways, I finally approached a simple wooden grave marker surmounted by a carved Iron Cross. Here then lay the ashes of one of the most respected generals of World War II, admired by both friend and foe alike. The simple message below the cross reads: GENERALFELDMARSCHALL ERWIN ROMMEL 1891-1944. It is embellished with carved representations of his medals.

It should be noted that this cross was altered sometime in the postwar period. Originally, it carried a swastika at the center of the cross and the date 1939 in the bottom arm of the cross. Both of these items were removed, the center of the cross recessed, and the outer edge painted white.

Upon inquiring about his home, we were informed that it was several blocks away but was now being used as a nursery school. This revelation disturbed me so much that I chose not to do more than glance at the house from a distance and try to picture that fateful day when he donned his Afrika Korps uniform for the last time and walked out to the waiting staff car.

Born on November 15, 1891, in the small Württemberg town of Heidenheim near Ulm, the son of a local schoolmaster, Erwin Johannes Eugen Rommel was destined to become one of the most respected military men of his time. He was one of five, although his one brother, Manfred, died early in life. His father, who was also named Erwin Rommel, died suddenly in 1913, and his mother Helena lived on until

Rommel's grave at Herrlingen. This is how it appeared in 1985, but earlier photos show that it originally featured a Nazi swastika in the center of the cross and 1939 in the bottom arm. This alteration involved routing out the inner portion of the cross to remove the Nazi aspects and then adding a white border to the cross.

1940, just long enough to see her second son become a major general.

There was no military tradition in the family, and they were simply a respectable Swabian family of average income, with no obvious influential friends in military circles. Since most of the high-ranking officers in the German military would flow from the Prussian officer class and aristocratic families, Rommel would later be considered a misfit by many of these career officers. At the age of 19 he joined the 124th Infantry Regiment at Weingarten and in March 1911 was posted to the War Academy in Danzig. It was in Danzig that he would meet his future wife, Lucie Mollin, and with a pleasant mixture of courtship and studies, he earned his commission as a second lieutenant in early 1912 and returned to his regiment.

Rommel was not a big man, but his physical stamina made up for any lack of size. He neither drank nor smoked, and the local nightlife was not part of his lifestyle. He approached everything very seriously and chose to absorb discussions rather than enter into them. In March 1914 he was attached to the Field Artillery Regiment in Ulm, but on July 31 he was recalled to the 124th and went off to war the following day.

His record in France during World War I was exemplary, and his eagerness to use surprise and bold moves to overcome the enemy would groom him for ever-greater achievements. Wounded several times, he was soon promoted to first lieutenant and eventually found himself posted to Austria for intensive training in mountain warfare and then off to the Rumanian front. During this period he had slipped off to Danzig in November 1916 to get married.

He was soon back into the thick of things, probing the Italian and Rumanian positions and leading skillful attacks through the enemy lines. His reputation was known throughout the division and his men looked up to him, even though he was still a 25-year-old who looked even younger because of his stature. For his achievements at Monte Matajur he was awarded the Pour le Mérite, comparable to the Victoria Cross and usually only awarded to senior generals. On this occasion he had scaled 7,000 feet up the rear of the mountain, leading only six companies, and had captured 150 Italian officers, 9,000 enemy soldiers, and 81 guns.

Promoted to captain, he was now given a staff position and sent on leave, much to his disappointment. He was in this position when the war came to an end. All of these early experiences would indelibly leave their mark on Rommel's mind, and when war again beckoned, he would eagerly seek out the enemy's weak points with that same "sixth sense" that he always seemed to possess. However, by 1920 he was posted in Stuttgart, commanding a company

of Infantry Regiment 13, and here he would remain for the next nine years. He and Lucie embarked on a pastime of canoeing, mountain treks, and skiing, and in December 1928 their only child, Manfred, was born.

The young captain had also caught the attention of his battalion commander and was soon posted as a junior instructor at the Dresden School of Infantry. He was finally promoted to major in April 1932 and in October 1933 became a battalion commander with 17th Infantry Regiment at Goslar in the Harz Mountains district.

When Hitler came to power, he demanded a personal oath of allegiance from the military, and henceforth the Führer's decisions would rule the course of events. Rommel first came to Hitler's attention in 1934 during his visit to review the troops at Goslar. In 1935 he was posted as the War Ministry's special liaison officer to Baldur von Schirach's Hitler Youth Organization. He soon realized that he had no use for the young von Schirach's methods, and Rommel's heavy Swabian accent did not sit well with the Hitler Youth leader's expectations. They soon parted ways, but while in Potsdam Rommel had managed to complete his brilliant book on infantry tactics *Infantry Attacks* and get it published. This book obviously came to Hitler's attention and apparently he was very impressed by it.

In 1938 when Hitler decided to visit his newly acquired Sudetenland, he chose Rommel as the commandant for his escort battalion. This single appointment immediately propelled Rommel into the spotlight, where he would remain for many years to come. In November of that very same year he was posted as commandant of the officer cadet school at Wiener-Neustadt, near Vienna. These would be some of the happiest years for his little family, and they would live in comfortable surroundings.

Then again, in March 1939 Hitler chose Rommel to command his mobile headquarters during the occupation of Prague. With the invasion plans for Poland well under way, Rommel learned that he was to be promoted to major general, and he was subsequently made responsible for Hitler's safety during his numerous visits to the front. During the invasion Rommel was well aware of the German panzer units and the blending of artillery and air support, along with motorized infantry to achieve the desired blitzkrieg results.

Following the cessation of hostilities in Poland, Rommel was again thrust back into the mundane duties of everyday routine. Counting on his close connections with Hitler and realizing that the invasion of France and the Low Countries was inevitable, he decided to ask for a fighting command. In February 1940 his request was granted and Rommel assumed command of 7th Panzer Division. At this point the Army High Command objected strenuously, stating that he had not enough experience with armored troops, but Hitler was adamant and brushed aside their complaints.

The western offensive opened on May 10 and 7th Panzer Division crossed the frontier into Belgium at first light and had reached the Meuse River by May 12. After establishing a bridgehead across the Meuse, Rommel prepared to concentrate his 25th Panzer Regiment and break through on a narrow front, then drive west without regard for his flanks. By May 18, the 7th Panzer Division spearhead had reached Cambrai, but the rest of his forces were strung out precariously behind him. Strong French armored forces on both flanks threatened the operation, but never intervened. On May 21 at Vailly, southwest of Arras, Rommel ran into the heavily armored Matildas of the British 1st Tank Brigade. The standard 37mm German anti-tank guns could not penetrate the thick-skinned Matildas and Rommel was forced to hold them off with 105mm field guns and a few 88mm anti-aircraft guns

With the situation again in hand, Rommel's 7th Panzer rolled south of Arras, but on May 24 a halt was ordered by OKW to allow the infantry to move up to protect the exposed armored spearheads. On the twenty-sixth they were on the move again with Rommel commanding both 7th and 5th Panzer Divisions for the attack on Lille. On June 2 Hitler requested Rommel's attendance at a conference in Charleville, where he was greeted enthusiastically by the Führer. Returning to the front, Rommel's 7th Panzer struck out for the channel, sweeping aside any resistance they encountered.

On June 8 they reached the coast at Les Petites Dalles, destroying an enemy motorized column on the way. Turning north, they then focused their attention on the British and French forces holed up in St. Valéry, surrounding the town on June 11. Late the following evening, the defenders capitulated and Rommel had bagged a dozen generals and almost 13,000 prisoners. The French had referred to Rommel's fast-moving 7th Panzer Division as the "Ghost Division," and the term stuck.

With the major fighting over, Rommel's unit took several days for rest and reorganization. However, on June 17 the Ghost Division was off again with orders to capture the deep-water seaport of Cherbourg. Advancing a record 200 miles the first day, Rommel attacked Cherbourg fortress on June 18 with heavy Stuka support, and by the time it surrendered, the 7th Panzer had captured another 30,000 prisoners.

With an armistice signed on June 21, 1940, Rommel again returned to Wiener-Neustadt for rest and relaxation with his wife and son. During the final months of 1940 Rommel and his 7th Panzer Division did exhaustive training preparing for the invasion of England. Operation Sealion required trials of loading and offloading from the converted river barges which would ferry the division to the British coast. This invasion was finally postponed and then cancelled completely, in favor of air attacks by the Luftwaffe to first control the air over the channel.

This then was the man Hitler would choose to lead his German troops to North Africa, and Rommel would continue to employ his fast-movement tactics throughout the desert war. When the end was in sight in Tunisia, Rommel flew to Hitler's headquarters in the Ukraine to plead for a timely withdrawal of his forces from Africa, but to no avail. He was then ordered to take his long-delayed sick leave, and his faithful Afrika Korps was left to face its fate on Cap Bon.

It was not until July 23, 1943, that he received orders from Hitler to go to Saloniki to assess the situation in Greece. At the same time he was told to prepare to take command of an army group north of the Alps, which would ensure the security of German troops in Italy. During this period, he and Kesselring were at odds over how best to defend Italy, and by November 5 he and his staff had been commissioned to examine the defenses of the Atlantic Wall.

On December 31 he was named commander of Army Group B and proceeded to instill an air of confidence into the troops defending the coastal areas by installing numerous beach obstacles and an additional four million mines. Rommel's plan had always been to stop the invasion on the beaches, before the Allies could establish a foothold on the continent. Hitler was convinced that the Pas de Calais area in the north would be the obvious invasion site, and most of the available armor had been positioned to suit his whims. When the weather turned stormy in early June, Rommel felt confident that the invasion would not take place for several weeks. On June 5 he left his headquarters at La Roche–Guyon by car for a quick visit with his family in Herrlingen. The following morning he learned of the invasion and by noon on D-Day he was speeding back to France.

We all know of the indecision that followed which allowed the Allies to gain a firm beachhead in Normandy, and by June 11 it was clear to Rommel that Normandy was lost and that a withdrawal to the Orne was their only hope. However, Hitler would not hear of this and Rommel had no choice but to do his best to shore up the sagging German defenses, hoping that Hitler would release some of the armored units still waiting for the nonexistent landing at Calais.

On July 17, during a return trip to La Roche–Guyon from the front, Rommel's staff car was spotted by two enemy attack planes near Livarot. They tried to drive for cover, but the driver was severely wounded and the Horch staff car swerved into the ditch out of control, throwing the field marshal onto the roadway. Rommel sustained severe head injuries and was eventually moved to a Luftwaffe hospital at Bernay, where he gradually recovered. On August 8 he was allowed to return to his home in Herrlingen, and the following day the German press announced simply that he had been wounded in action.

By this point in time Rommel was accused of having conspired in the July 20 attempt on Hitler's life. During September he learned of the numerous arrests being made to round up conspirators and began to suspect that he too was under suspicion. When requested by phone to come to Berlin on October 7 he declined the offer, suspecting that his life was in danger. A week later, another call from Berlin simply stated that two officers from Berlin would be arriving at his home on October 14.

At precisely noon on the fourteenth the two generals arrived and presented Rommel with a protocol which gave him the choice of facing these charges in court or taking poison to save himself and his family from disgrace. He chose the latter, and the German people were then informed that Rommel had finally succumbed to his severe head injuries and that a state funeral, to be held in Ulm, had been ordered.

Afrika Korps Order of Battle, 1941 and 1942

On JUNE 27, 1941
Deutsches Afrika Korps (Rommel)
– 5th Light Division (Streich)
– 15th Panzer Division (von Esebeck)

From AUGUST 15, 1941
Panzergruppe Afrika (Rommel)
Afrika Korps (Crüwell)
– 15th Panzer Division (Neumann-Silkow)
– 21st Panzer Division (von Ravenstein)
– "Afrika" Division (Sümmermann)
– 55th Savona Infantry Division (Giorgis)

Italian XXI Army Corps (Navarrini)
– 17th Pavia Infantry Division (Franceschini)
– 27th Brescia Infantry Division (Zambon)
– 25th Bologna Infantry Division (Gloria)
– 102nd Trento Mot. Infantry Div. (de Stefanis)

Italian XX Corps (Gambarra)
– 132nsd Ariete Armored Division (Balotta)
– 101st Trieste Mot. Infantry Division (Piazzoni)

On APRIL 22, 1942
Armeegruppe Afrika (Rommel)
Panzerarmee Afrika (Crüwell)
– Reserve: "Afrika" Division (Sümmermann)
                     25th Bologna Inf. Div. (Gloria)
                     60th Sabrath Infantry Division

Deutsches Afrika Korps (Nehring)
– 15th Panzer Division (von Vaerst)
– 21st Panzer Division (von Bismark)

Italian X Army Corps (Gioda)
– 27th Brescia Infantry Division (Zambon)
– 17th Pavia Infantry Division (Franceschini)

Italian XX Army Corps (Baldassare)
– 132nd Ariete Armored Division (Balotta)
– 101st Trieste Mot. Infantry Division (Piazzoni)

Italian XXI Army Corps (Navarrini)
–102nd Trento Mot. Infantry Div. (de Stefanis)
– 60th Sabratha Infantry Division

On MAY 26, 1942
Armeegruppe Afrika (Rommel)
Panzerarmee Afrika (Crüwell)
Deutsches Afrika Korps (Nehring)
– 15th Panzer Division (von Vaerst)
– 21st Panzer Division (von Bismark)
– 90th Light Division (Kleemann)

Italian X Army Corps (Gioda)
– 27th Brescia Infantry Division (Zambon)
– 17th Pavia Infantry Division (Franceschini)

Italian XX Army Corps (Baldassare)
– 132nd Ariete Armored Division (Balotta)
– 101st Trieste Mot. Infantry Division (Piazzoni)

Italian XXI Army Corps (Navarrini)
– 102nd Trento Mot. Infantry Div. (de Stefanis)
– 60th Sabratha Infantry Division

On OCTOBER 23, 1942
Armeegruppe Afrika (Rommel)
Panzerarmee Afrika (von Thoma)
Deutsches Afrika Korps (Stumme)
– 15th Panzer Division (von Vaerst)
– 21st Panzer Division (von Randow)
– 90th Light "Afrika" Division (Graf Sponeck)
– 164th Light "Afrika" Division (Lungershausen)
– "Ramcke" Parachute Brigade (Ramcke)
– Giovani Fascisti Infantry Division

Italian X Army Corps (Gioda)
– 27th Brescia Infantry Division (Predieri)
– 17th Pavia Infantry Division (Lombardi)
– 185th Folgore Parachute Division (Frattini)

Italian XX Army Corps (Zingales de Stefanis)
– 132nd Ariete Armored Division (Baldassare)
– 133rd Littorio Armored Division (Azzi, Bitossi)
– 101st Trieste Mot. Infantry Division (La Feria)

Italian XXI Army Corps (Navarrini, Berardi)
– 102nd Trento Infantry Division (de Stefanis)
– 25th Bologna Infantry Division (Gloria)

Chronology of Afrika Korps, 1941–42

1941

Feb. 6: Rommel appointed as commander of the German Forces in North Africa.

Feb. 13: Rommel arrives in Tripoli.

Feb. 15: 5th Light Division starts arriving.

Feb. 19: Hitler names "Deutsches Afrika Korps."

Feb. 24: First exchange of fire between DAK and British recon units.

Mar. 4: 15th Panzer Division starts arriving.

Mar. 18: Rommel flies to Hitler's Wolf's Lair HQ.

Mar. 19: Rommel receives Oak Leaves to Knight's Cross.

Mar. 24: DAK captures El Agheila.

Mar. 30: Cyrenaica offensive begins.

Apr. 2: DAK captures Agedabia.

Apr. 3: Recon group reaches Benghazi.

Apr. 4: Capture of Benghazi and Msus.

Apr. 5: The 15th Motorcycle Battalion begins to arrive in Tripoli.

Apr. 7: Capture of Derna.

Apr. 10: Capture of Bardia.

Apr. 13: Rommel encircles Tobruk.

Apr. 14: Capture of Fort Capuzzo.

Apr. 14: First Tobruk attack repulsed.

Apr. 18: First Bf109 E fighters arrive at Gazala airfield.

Apr. 19: Heavy company of 8th Panzer Regiment reaches Tobruk front.

Apr. 25: Capture of Halfaya Pass.

Apr. 28: Capture of Sollum.

May 1: Second Tobrul attack repulsed.

May 15: British retake Sollum and Halfaya.

May 27: Germans retake Sollum and Halfaya Pass.

June 14: British Operation Battleaxe begins.

June 15: British attack Sollum and Ft. Capuzzo.

June 17: British retire toward Egypt.

June 21: Auchinleck replaces Wavell.

Aug. 15: Panzergruppe Afrika formed.

Sep. 14: "Midsummer Night's Dream" probe begins.

Nov. 13: Rommel leaves for Rome again.

Nov. 15: Rommel, his wife, and the von Ravenstein's celebrate his 50th birthday in Rome.

Nov. 17: British commando raid to kill Rommel.

Nov. 18: Rommel returns from Rome.

Nov. 18: British Operation Crusader begins.

Nov. 19: British reach Sidi Rezegh.

Nov. 19: Ariete holds off 22nd Armoured Division.

Nov. 20: Tank battle at Sidi Rezegh.

Nov. 21: New Zealanders capture Capuzzo.

Nov. 22: DAK recaptures Sidi Rezegh.

Nov. 23: DAK destroys S.African 5th Brigade.

Nov. 24: Rommel's "dash for the wire" begins.

Nov. 25: Rommel swings toward Bardia and the coast.

Nov. 27: Rommel heads back toward Tobruk.

Nov. 29: Rommel counterattacks the New Zealanders.

Nov. 30: Tobruk-Sidi Rezegh corridor battles.

Dec. 1: Rommel tries to liberate his garrisons.

Dec. 4: El Duda recaptured by DAK.

Dec. 6: Neumann-Silkow killed by artillery fire.

Dec. 12: Rommel withdraws to Gazala Line.

Dec. 15: Rommel decides to evacuate Cyrenaica.

Dec. 19: New tank shipment reaches Benghazi.

Dec. 27: Crüwell wins Agedabia tank battle.

Dec. 31: Bardia pounded with heaviest barrage yet.

1942

Jan. 2: Rommel moves back to Marsa Brega.

Jan. 2: Bardia garrison capitulates to 2nd South African Division.

Jan. 5: British attack Halfaya Pass.

Jan. 5: Huge Axis convoy arrives in Tripoli.

Jan. 11: South Africans recapture Sollum.

Jan. 17: Halfaya Pass falls to 2nd South African Division.

Jan. 20: Rommel awarded Oakleaves and Swords to the Knight's Cross.

Jan. 21: Rommel's second Cyrenaican offensive begins.

Jan. 22: Group Marcks with Rommel at its head enters Agedabia.

Jan. 24: DAK wastes its time sweeping an empty battlefield.

Jan. 25: British supply dumps at Msus fall into German hands.

Jan. 27: A reinforced Group Marcks moves on Benghazi from Msus positions.

Jan. 28: 33rd Recce reaches the sea at Coefia, north of Benghazi.

Jan. 29: Rommel enters Benghazi.

Jan. 30:	Panzergruppe Afrika now becomes the Panzerarmee Afrika.
Feb. 1:	Rommel promoted to Colonel General.
Feb. 3:	33rd Recce recaptures Derna.
Feb. 5:	Rommel halts before the Gazala Line.
Mar. 15:	Rommel flies to Rastenburg to see Hitler.
May 26:	Rommel launches Case Venezia south of the Gazala Line.
May 27:	The DAK and Ariete overrun 3rd Indian Motor Bde. and turn north to confront the British armor.
May 28:	Tank battles at Bir Hacheim.
May 28:	Rommel falls back into the "Cauldron."
May 29:	The "Cauldron" battles continue.
May 29:	General Crüwell captured by the British.
May 30:	Both sides fight to a bloody stalemate.
May 31:	Rommel leads breakout that overwhelms 150th Brigade.
June 1:	New supply line finally opened to DAK.
June 2:	90th Light & Trieste sent to subdue forces at Bir Hacheim.
June 4:	Ritchie opens attack on the "Cauldron".
June 5:	British attack against Ariete hits open desert but is pounded by artillery and 88s, with 200 tanks disabled and 5th Indian Division decimated.
June 6:	Rommel mops up the remaining British infantry and artillery.
June 8:	Group Hecker assaults Bir Hacheim and takes forward posts.
June 9:	Rommel ready to call it off, but Group Hecker drives even deeper.
June 10:	Bir Hacheim finally falls, as Gen. Koenig's Free French breakout during the night.
June 11:	Rommel goes back on the offensive and drives north.
June 12:	Closing on Knightsbridge, Rommel disables over 100 enemy tanks.
June 13:	British armor now reduced to about 70 tanks.
June 14:	The Guards withdraw from Knightsbridge.
June 15:	British begin to withdraw but the exhausted DAK is unable to bag them.
June 16:	British begin to evacuate El Adem.
June 17:	DAK cuts the Via Balbia east of Tobruk.
June 19:	Bardia occupied by 90th Light.
June 18:	Rommel pursues British armor.
June 20:	Rommel launches all out assault on Tobruk.
June 21:	The Tobruk garrison surrenders.
June 22:	Rommel promoted to Field Marshal.
June 24:	DAK advances beyond Sidi Barrani.
June 25:	Auchinleck comes out to relieve Ritchie.
June 27:	DAK advances to Mersa Matruh.
June 29:	90th Light reaches El Daba.
June 30:	Rommel reaches the El Alamein Line.
July 1:	Initial Alamein battle begins.
July 2:	Rommel halted at El Alamein Line.
July 3:	DAK stalemate at Ruweisat Ridge.
July 9:	New Zealanders retire from Qaret el Abd Box.
July 10:	9th Australian Division attack along the coastal road halted.
July 12:	Germans begin attacks on Tel el Eisa salient.
July 14:	Eighth Army attacks at Ruweisat Ridge.
July 18:	Rommel begins to concentrate on regrouping and to strengthening his minefields.
July 21:	Auchinleck renews Ruweisat attacks.
Aug. 13:	Montgomery takes command of the eighth Army.
Aug. 31:	Battle of Alam Halfa begins.
Sept. 1:	New Zealanders attack at Alam Halfa.
Sept. 3:	Rommel withdraws from Alam Halfa battles.
Sep. 19:	Stumme arrives to temporarily relieve Rommel.
Sep. 23:	Rommel flies from Derna to Rome, then on to Germany for medical treatment.
Sep. 30:	Eighth Army offensive probes begin.
Oct. 23:	Battle of Alamein opens.
Oct. 24:	Stumme dies at the front from an unexpected heart attack.
Oct. 25:	Alamein battle intensifies.
Oct. 25:	Rommel returns to Africa via Crete.
Oct. 27:	Eighth Army regroups for breakout.
Oct. 28:	RAF strikes German tank formations.
Oct. 29:	Eighth Army strikes on northern flank.
Oct. 29:	Australians drive for the sea.
Nov. 1:	Operation Supercharge begins.
Nov. 4:	Rommel begins to withdraw from his El Alamein positions.

Desert Armor Color Profiles, 1941–42

GERMAN:
PzKpfw. I, Ausf B (SdKfz 101)

A good number of PzKpfw Is arrived with the 5th Panzer Regiment in early 1941, but were soon found to be far too lightly armed, with only a pair of 7.92mm MGs, to survive on the open desert. Originally incorporated into the early light platoons of the DAK, it was eventually replaced by the more robust PzKpfw. II. North Africa was about the last campaign in which the PzKpfw I would appear in significant numbers.

Battalion Commander's PzKpfw. I Ausf B of 5th Light Division, April 1941.

GERMAN:
PzKpfw. II, Ausf F (SdKfz 121)

The PzKpfw II mounted a 20mm cannon and filled out the better part of 5th Light Division's light tank platoons. Its main armament still left much to be desired, and eventually, it was relegated mainly to reconnaissance duties. They were also prominent in headquarters light platoons and engineer platoons. Vehicle production was finally terminated in late 1942 and the PzKpfw II chassis was then chosen as the basis for a number of self-propelled guns.

Headquarters PzKpfw.II of 5th Pz.Regt., 5th Light Division, May 1941.

GERMAN:
Kleiner Panzerbefehlswagen (SdKfz 265)

Developed as an armored command vehicle, this version of the PzKpfw. I also saw a very short service life. Until 1940 it was issued to company, battalion, regimental, and brigade headquarters, but by 1941 it only remained in service with higher headquarters. Its superstructure was modified to accommodate a small map table and two wireless sets, an FU2 and FU6, plus a power generator to keep the radio batteries constantly charged. These vehicles were gradually replaced by the larger Panzerbefehlswagen III command vehicles.

A Regimental kl PzBef. command vehicle of 8th Panzer Regiment, March 1942.

BRITISH:
Cruiser Tank, Mark I (A9)

At the outbreak of hostilities with Italy, the A9 and A10 cruisers made up the bulk of the gun-armed tanks available to the British. The A9 had lighter armor, a 2-pdr gun, plus three MGs, two of which were mounted in separate turrets at the front. It was gradually phased out by mid-1941, but many were also lost from mechanical failures.

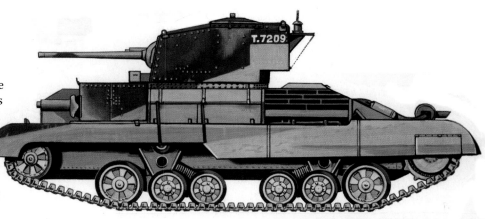

A Cruiser Tank Mk. I of the British 7th Armoured Division, April 1941.

BRITISH:
Cruiser Tank, Mark II (A10)

The A10 cruisers were more heavily armored but slower than the A9 and it was eventually classified as a "heavy cruiser." It mounted the normal 2-pdr and coaxial MG as main armament. The A10 had a very short production run and the A13 soon began to replace it. Features of the A10 would be incorporated into the later Valentine tank.

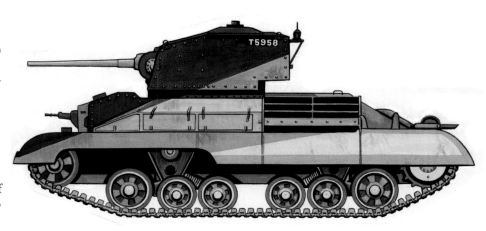

A Cruiser Tank Mk. II of the British 7th Armoured Division, June 1941.

BRITISH:
Cruiser Tank, Mark IVA (A13 Mk. II)

The A13 was the best of the British cruisers in 1940–41 but was in short supply in North Africa. Although prone to mechanical breakdowns, their speed gave them maneuverability in the desert skirmishes. They were gradually replaced by early Crusaders, but some A13s were still fighting with the 9th Lancers as late as April 1942.

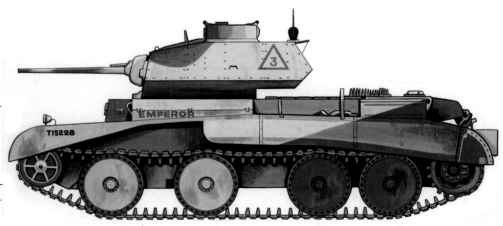

A Cruiser Tank Mk. IVA of the British 7th Armoured Division, 1941. The blue triangular marking stands for A Squadron, tank 3, junior regiment.

BRITISH:
Morris CS9 LAC (Light Armored Car)

The Morris CS9 LAC saw service with the 11th Hussars during Operation Compass in December 1940 as reconnaissance vehicles for 7th Armoured Division. The vehicle mixture of 11th Hussars was about 20 Morris LAC and 40 Rolls-Royce armored cars. The vehicle is shown here in the three-tone Caunter banded pattern of the early period.

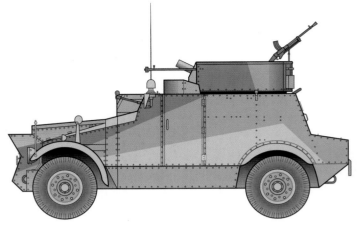

A Morris CS9 LAC scout car fitted with Boys anti-tank rifle and Bren machine gun.

BRITISH:
Vickers Light Tank Mark VI/B

The 7th Armoured Division was using the little Mk.VI/B light tank in Egypt and they were used in the early stages of the campaign in Libya against the Italians. It also features the Caunter striped pattern common during the 1940 and early 1941 period. This vehicle carries the red open diamond marking of a regimental HQ tank of 3rd Hussars, 7th Armoured Division.

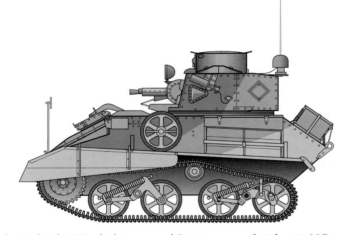

A Vickers Light Tank Mk VI/B of 7th Armoured Division, armed with twin MGs.

ITALIAN:
Carro Armato M. 11-39

These Italian medium tanks were armed with two Breda MGs in the turret and a 37mm cannon in the right hand sponson, in a similar manner to the American M3 Mediums. Only about 100 were produced and most were shipped to Libya, where they were lost to the British at the Sidi Barani and Bardia battles. This chassis would become the basis for their improved medium tank, the Carro Armato M. 13-40.

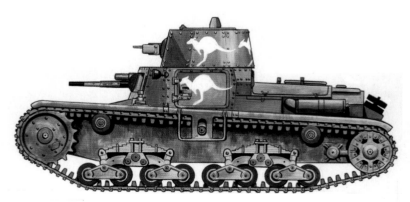

A captured Italian M. 11-39 in service with the Australian 6th Armoured Cavalry, 1941.

ITALIAN:
Carro Armato M. 13-40

The Italian M. 13-40 medium tank appeared in impressive numbers during the desert war, and its 47mm gun could hold its own against the British cruiser tanks of the period. However, it also suffered from frequent mechanical breakdowns, overheated engines, and its riveted armor plate had a bad habit of cracking under impact by HE fire from the British 25-pdr field guns. In the later fighting they were completely outclassed by the 75mm guns of the M3 Grant and later the M4 Sherman.

An M. 13-40 of X Tank Battalion, 132nd "Ariete" Armored Division, March 1942.

GERMAN:
PzKpfw. III, Ausf F (SdKfz 141)

The PzKpfw. III was the backbone of the Afrika Korps panzer regiments' light tank companies, and as such was in the forefront of every major action. Eventually, additional face-hardened plates were added to the original design to up-armor the driver's plate and gun mantlet. The majority of PzKpfw. III/F models in North Africa mounted the 50mm KwK L/42 gun and outranged the British tanks they encountered.

A PzKpfw.III Ausf F from the 8th Panzer Regiment, 15th Panzer Division, June 1941.

GERMAN:
PzKpfw. IV, Ausf E (SdKfz 161)

The PzKpfw. IV made up the bulk of the medium tank companies of 5th and 8th Panzer Regiments. Their short-barreled 75mm gun fired both HE and AP type ammunition, making them a formidable weapon against both armor and gun emplacements. The Ausf E featured 30mm spaced armor on the front plate and additional 20mm armor bolted to the sides of the superstructure.

A PzKpfw.IV Ausf E of 5th Panzer Regiment, 21st Panzer Division, November 1941.

BRITISH:
Infantry Tank, Mk. II
Matilda II (A12)

In Libya from 1940 to mid-1941 the heavy armor of the British Matilda made it virtually immune to all anti-tank fire. Only with the arrival of the German 88 in the anti-tank role could its armor be penetrated at long range. With a maximum speed of 15 mph, it was not ideally suited for the fast moving battles of the Western Desert, and Rommel took full advantage of this limitation.

A Matilda II of the 42nd Royal Tank Regt. with Operation Crusader markings, Nov. 1941.

BRITISH:
Light Tank, General Stuart Mk.I (Honey)

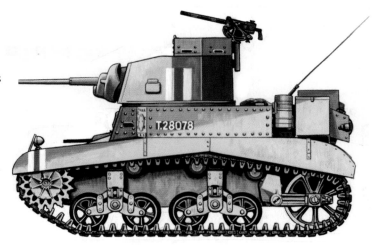

The first shipment of American-built M3 Light Tanks reached the eighth Army in July 1941 and played an important role in the British offensives of that fall. Its 37mm gun was not much better than the British 2-pdr, but it had speed and mechanical reliability which earned it the nickname of "Honey" from its British crewmen. Stuarts were heavily involved in the ranging battles for Sidi Rezegh airfield during Operation Crusader. It was powered by a Pratt & Whitney radial aero-engine and required special aviation fuel, which further complicated refueling operations.

A "Honey" with markings of the 3rd Royal Tank Regiment, November 1941.

BRITISH:
Infantry Tank, Mk. III
Valentine

Although designed as an infantry tank, in North Africa the Valentine was pressed into service as a heavy cruiser tank and was rather slow for this function. It was mechanically reliable and logged enormous distances without problems. One drawback was the 3-man crew, which forced the commander to act as loader and wireless operator on top of his other duties.

A Valentine infantry tank of 8th Royal Tank Regiment near Bardia, January 1942.

GERMAN:
4.7 cm PaK(t) (Sf) auf Panzerkampfwagen I, Ausf B

Serving as a self-propelled anti-tank gun, this vehicle was also referred to as the Panzerjäger I/B. The merging of the Czech-built Skoda 47mm anti-tank gun with the obsolete PzKpfw. I/B chassis resulted in Germany's first mobile tank destroyer. Although ineffective against the Matilda infantry tanks, it was quite capable of dealing with the British Cruiser tanks and armored cars and made itself felt in many of the early battles. It saw service with the 605th Heavy Anti-Tank Battalion of 5th Light Division.

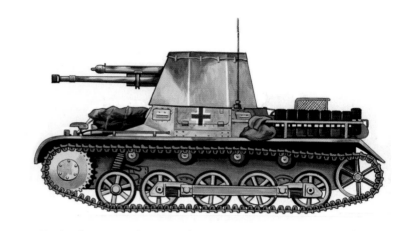

A PzJag.I/B of 39th Motorized Anti-Tank Bn., 21st Panzer Division, March 1941.

ITALIAN:
Semovente M. 40 da 75/18

This Italian self-propelled gun/howitzer first saw action with the two artillery groups of Ariete's 132nd Artillery Regiment in early 1942. Although designed for the artillery role, they were often pressed into service as anti-tank weapons. The effectiveness of their 75mm gun was further enhanced by the use of shaped-charge ammunition, and at the time of their introduction they were a formidable weapon against most British tanks.

Semovente M. 40 of 132nd Artillery Regt, 132nd "Ariete" Armored Div., June 1942.

GERMAN:
15cm sFH13/1(Sf) auf Geschützwagen Lorraine Schlepper (f) (Sd Kfz 135/1)

The GW Lorraine Schlepper was a captured French armored tractor chassis converted to mount the German 15cm sFH heavy field howitzer. The first dozen to see action were issued to 21st Panzer Division and served with the 155th Motorized Artillery Regiment in the closing months of 1942.

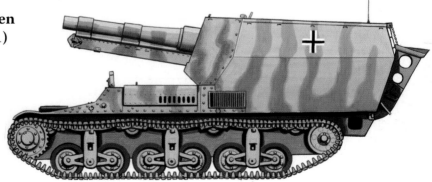

Lorraine Schlepper of the 155th Mot. Artillery Regt., 21st Pz.Div., October 1942.

BRITISH: Armored Car, Marmon-Herrington Mk. II

Serving as a self-propelled anti-tank gun, these South African–built armored cars were heavily involved in the early skirmishing with German advance units. Mounting only a Boys anti-tank rifle and Browning MG, they were hard pressed to hold their ground when confronted with the heavier armed German 8-wheelers. However, a good number of them were field-modified to mount captured Breda 20mm or 47mm guns.

Marmon-Herrington of 1st King's Dragoon Guards, 3rd Armoured Brigade, March 1941.

ITALIAN: Autoblinda AB.40/AB.41 Armored Car

The original AB. 40 mounted only machine guns but was eventually fitted with a turret mounting a 20mm Breda cannon as well, and finally evolved into the AB. 41 model. These armored cars were employed in the Italian Army reconnaissance units to search out and make contact with the enemy. They would also carry out routine patrols along the front and on the flanks to repel British scout vehicles that were trying to ascertain where the enemy forces were deployed.

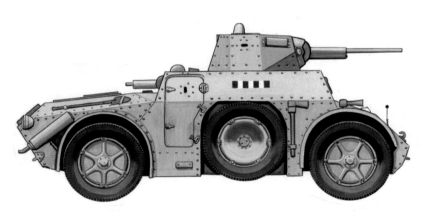

AB. 41 of an Italian Gruppo di Cavaleria reconnaissance unit, September 1941.

GERMAN: Schwerer Panzerspähwagen (SdKfz 231) 8-Rad

The SdKfz 231 armored car was faster and better armed that its British counterparts and could usually dominate the battlefield. These fast 8-wheelers were issued to the heavy platoons of German recon units and were often doled out to support the smaller 4-wheeled armored cars. The space behind the armored shield on the front was often used for stowing gear.

SdKfz 231 of 580th Armored Recon Bn., 90th Light Afrika Division, September 1942.

GERMAN:
Panzerfunkwagen
(SdKfz 263) 8-Rad

The SdKfz 263 armored car was only armed with a single 7.92mm MG34 and was not meant as a fighting vehicle. They were employed as mobile communications vehicles for staff, and as such made up the bulk of armored radio companies. The national flag draped across the rear of the aerial was to ensure friendly recognition from the air while in forward areas.

An SdKfz. 263 of 3rd Signal Company, 5th Light Mechanized Division, June 1941.

GERMAN:
PzKpfw. III, Ausf L (SdKfz 141/1)

This version of the PzKpfw. III, known by the British as the "Mark III Special," mounted the long-barrelled 50mm KwK 39 L/60 gun with spaced armor on the gun mantlet. Always in short supply in North Africa, these tanks were the only ones able to reach British Grant medium tanks at a stand-off range. They were first introduced in Africa during the Gazala Line battles in May 1942.

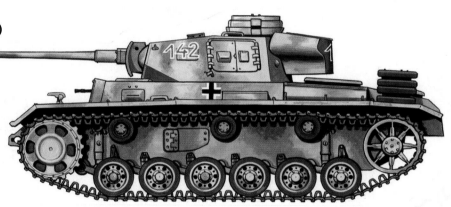

A PzKpfw. III Ausf L of 5th Panzer Regiment, 21st Panzer Division, June 1942.

GERMAN:
Panzerkampfwagen IV, Ausf F2
(SdKfz 161/1)

This upgunned verion of the PzKpfw. IV was armed with the long 75mm KwK L/43 and began to arrive in North Africa around June 1942. It was known by the British as the "Mark IV Special" and was only available in limited numbers. They were issued to 15th and 21st Panzer Divisions and used in action during the Alam Halfa and El Alamein battles.

A PzKpfw. IV Ausf F2 of 15th Panzer Division at Alam Halfa, September 1942.

BRITISH:
Cruiser Tank, Mark VI,
Crusader II (A15)

To fill the dire needs of the eighth Army for replacement tanks, the Crusader was rushed into production and suffered from track and breakdown problems from the start. It first went into action with 6 RTR near Capuzzo in mid-June 1941 and was prominent in all the major desert actions that followed.

A Crusader Mk. II of 9th Lancers, 2nd Armoured Brigade, December 1941.

BRITISH:
Cruiser Tank,
General Grant I

The Grant was an American M3 medium tank, built to British specifications, with a specially designed turret to house the radio equipment, rather than its normal location in the hull. It first went into action with the 7th Armoured Division during the Gazala Line battles, where its powerful dual-purpose 75mm gun allowed the British gunners to outrange their opponents for the first time in the desert war.

A Grant from 1st Royal Tank Regiment, 22nd Armoured Brigade, October 1942.

BRITISH:
Cruiser Tank,
General Sherman II

The Sherman was destined to become the most important tank in British service, but at this time it was almost classified as a secret weapon. Its 76mm frontal armor, speed, and turret-mounted 75mm gun made it the most deadly tank on the battlefield. The first shipment of Shermans was almost all the cast-hull M4A1 model and was designated as Sherman II.

An M4A1 Sherman II of the 9th Lancers, 2nd Armoured Brigade, October 1942.

GERMAN RECOGNITION SYMBOLS

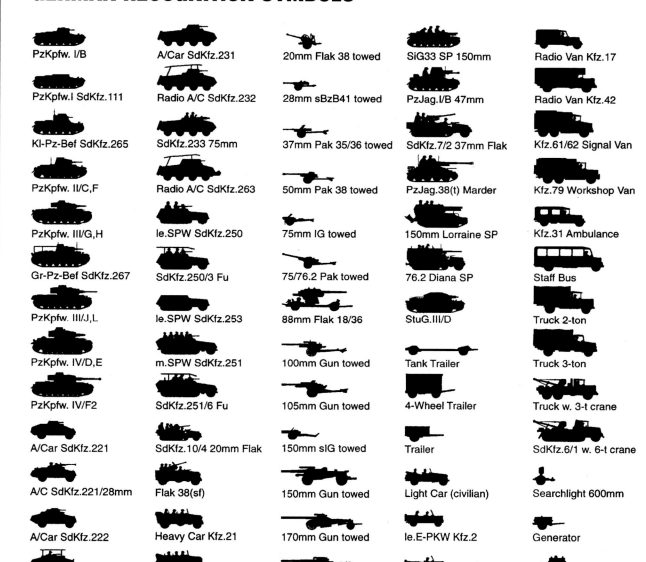

PzKpfw. I/B	A/Car SdKfz.231	20mm Flak 38 towed	SiG33 SP 150mm	Radio Van Kfz.17
PzKpfw.I SdKfz.111	Radio A/C SdKfz.232	28mm sBzB41 towed	PzJag.I/B 47mm	Radio Van Kfz.42
Kl-Pz-Bef SdKfz.265	SdKfz.233 75mm	37mm Pak 35/36 towed	SdKfz.7/2 37mm Flak	Kfz.61/62 Signal Van
PzKpfw. II/C,F	Radio A/C SdKfz.263	50mm Pak 38 towed	PzJag.38(t) Marder	Kfz.79 Workshop Van
PzKpfw. III/G,H	le.SPW SdKfz.250	75mm IG towed	150mm Lorraine SP	Kfz.31 Ambulance
Gr-Pz-Bef SdKfz.267	SdKfz.250/3 Fu	75/76.2 Pak towed	76.2 Diana SP	Staff Bus
PzKpfw. III/J,L	le.SPW SdKfz.253	88mm Flak 18/36	StuG.III/D	Truck 2-ton
PzKpfw. IV/D,E	m.SPW SdKfz.251	100mm Gun towed	Tank Trailer	Truck 3-ton
PzKpfw. IV/F2	SdKfz.251/6 Fu	105mm Gun towed	4-Wheel Trailer	Truck w. 3-t crane
A/Car SdKfz.221	SdKfz.10/4 20mm Flak	150mm sIG towed	Trailer	SdKfz.6/1 w. 6-t crane
A/C SdKfz.221/28mm	Flak 38(sf)	150mm Gun towed	Light Car (civilian)	Searchlight 600mm
A/Car SdKfz.222	Heavy Car Kfz.21	170mm Gun towed	le.E-PKW Kfz.2	Generator
Radio A/C SdKfz.223	s.E-PKW (Kfz.18)	210mm Mrs.18 towed	le.E-PKW Kfz.2/40	Generator Trailer
A/Car SdKfz.247	Zgkw 1-t SdKfz.10	Horch Kfz.15		
Radio A/C SdKfz.260	Zgkw 3-t SdKfz.11	s.E-PKW Kfz.70		
Motorcycle	Zgkw 5-t SdKfz.6/1	Flak Car Kfz.4		
With Sidecar	Zgkw 8-t SdKfz.7			
VW Kfz.1	Zgkw 18-t SdKfz.9	LWS Amphibious		

Since German vehicles make up the greater part of the T/O&E's featured in this book, they are given more prominence. Every effort has been made to keep the proportion and scale of these vehicle icons in reasonable size relationship to each other, and at the same time hold the finer detail. Their names in some cases have been abbreviated slightly to fit the space limitations.

ITALIAN SYMBOLS

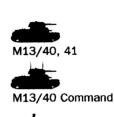
M13/40, 41

M13/40 Command

Semovente 75/18

Semovente Command

Autoblinda 41

Motorcycle

With Sidecar

3-Wheeler

T.L.37 Tractor

Pickup Truck

"Vender" Tractor

Dovunque

A.S.37 Truck

Lancia 3RO

Lancia 3RO+

Workshop Truck

47mm A/T Gun

65mm Gun

75mm TL35 Gun

Tank Trailer

Fuel Tanker

Lancia 90/53 SP

Staff Car

L6/40

Trailered M13/40

Large Truck

BRITISH SYMBOLS

Mk.VI Light

A9/A10 Cruiser

A9CS Cruiser

A13 Cruiser

A13CS Cruiser

Matilda II Infantry

Matilda IIICS Infantry

M3 Stuart Light

Crusader I & II Cruiser

Valentine II Infantry

Crusader III Cruiser

M3 Grant Medium

M4 Sherman Medium

Marmon-Herrington A/C

M-H w. Breda 20mm gun

Daimler Scout Car

Indian Carrier APC

Humber A/Car

Universal Carrier

Motorcycle

Austin 2 seater

Truck

Ford Utility

Wireless Truck

Mk I, Light AA Tank

Shown on these two pages are the icon symbols which represent the different vehicles, guns, trailers, etc. that appear on the illustrated Table of Organization and Equipment pages throughout this book. These icons are an attempt to give as graphic a representation as possible of the T/O&Es and other charts.

The names assigned to the icons are simplified but should be adequate to identify the vehicle. Some vehicles show only subtle differences, and in other cases the same icon is used to represent two very similar models. More than likely some vehicles will have been overlooked, partly because of lack of research facts, and partly because of oversight. The many support units have been played down because of the endless series of vehicles they encompassed.

5th Light Mechanized Division: March 15, 1941
5. LEICHTE DIVISION (motorisiert)

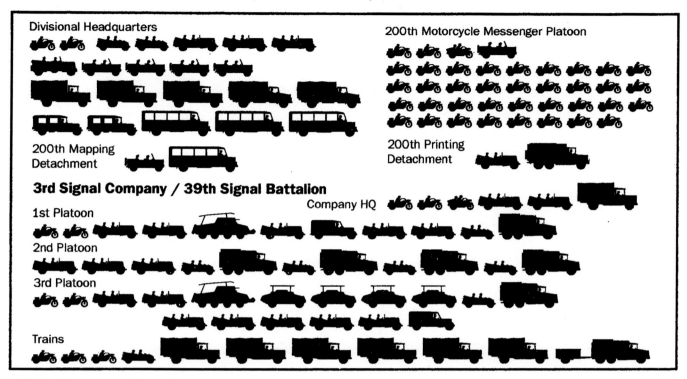

Divisional Headquarters

200th Motorcycle Messenger Platoon

200th Mapping Detachment

200th Printing Detachment

3rd Signal Company / 39th Signal Battalion

Company HQ

1st Platoon

2nd Platoon

3rd Platoon

Trains

5th Panzer Regiment

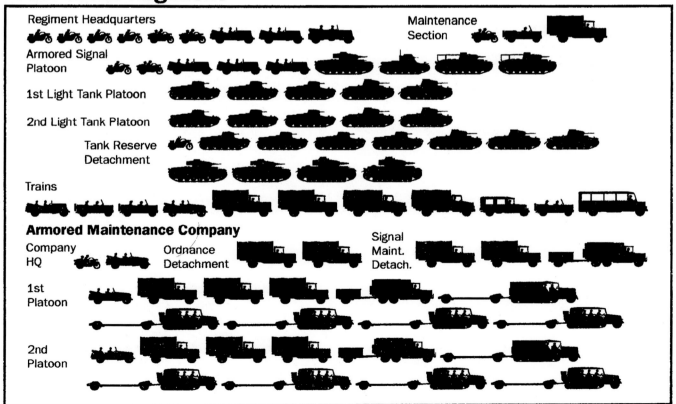

Regiment Headquarters

Maintenance Section

Armored Signal Platoon

1st Light Tank Platoon

2nd Light Tank Platoon

Tank Reserve Detachment

Trains

Armored Maintenance Company

Company HQ

Ordnance Detachment

Signal Maint. Detach.

1st Platoon

2nd Platoon

5th Light Mechanized Division (cont'd)
5th Panzer Regiment (cont'd)

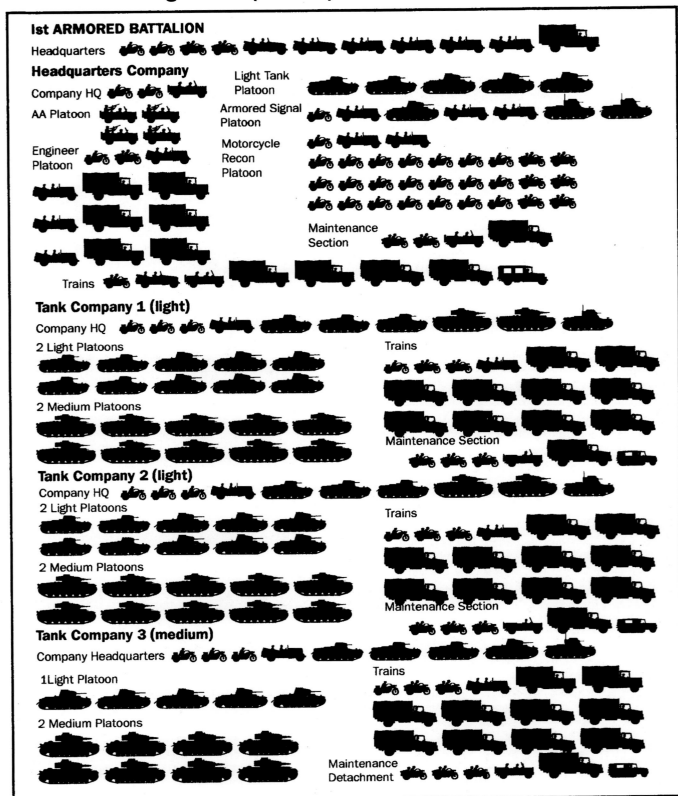

1st ARMORED BATTALION

Headquarters

Headquarters Company

Company HQ

AA Platoon

Engineer Platoon

Trains

Light Tank Platoon

Armored Signal Platoon

Motorcycle Recon Platoon

Maintenance Section

Tank Company 1 (light)

Company HQ

2 Light Platoons

2 Medium Platoons

Trains

Maintenance Section

Tank Company 2 (light)

Company HQ

2 Light Platoons

2 Medium Platoons

Trains

Maintenance Section

Tank Company 3 (medium)

Company Headquarters

1 Light Platoon

2 Medium Platoons

Trains

Maintenance Detachment

5th Light Mechanized Division (cont'd)
5th Panzer Regiment (cont'd)

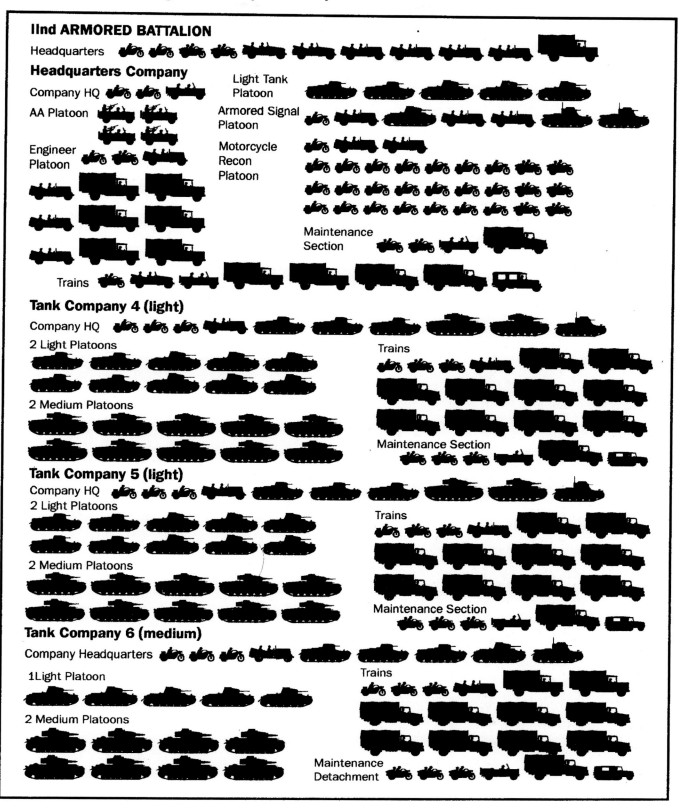

IInd ARMORED BATTALION

Headquarters

Headquarters Company

Company HQ

AA Platoon

Engineer Platoon

Light Tank Platoon

Armored Signal Platoon

Motorcycle Recon Platoon

Maintenance Section

Trains

Tank Company 4 (light)

Company HQ

2 Light Platoons

2 Medium Platoons

Trains

Maintenance Section

Tank Company 5 (light)

Company HQ

2 Light Platoons

2 Medium Platoons

Trains

Maintenance Section

Tank Company 6 (medium)

Company Headquarters

1 Light Platoon

2 Medium Platoons

Trains

Maintenance Detachment

5th Light Mechanized Division (cont'd)
200th Infantry Regiment HQ (motorized) special purpose

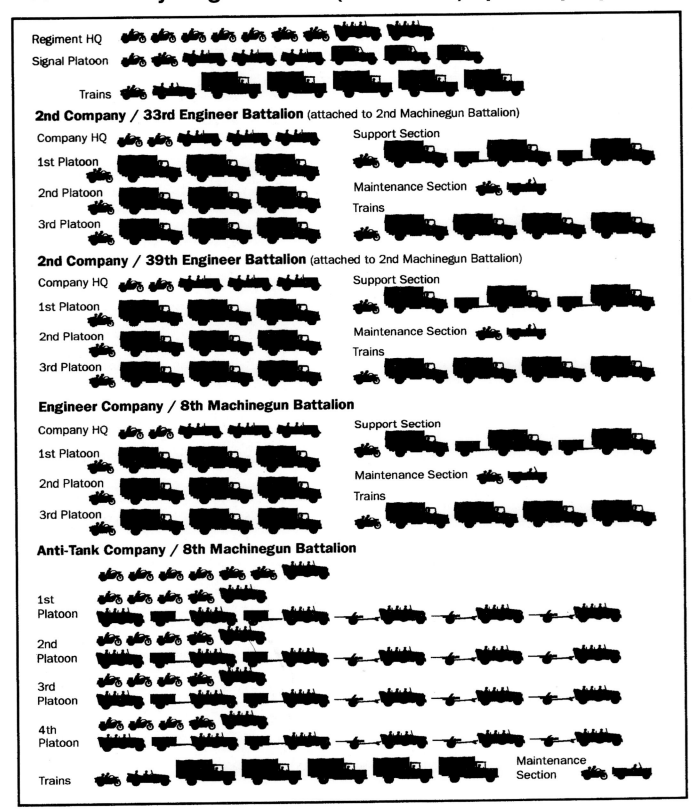

Regiment HQ

Signal Platoon

Trains

2nd Company / 33rd Engineer Battalion (attached to 2nd Machinegun Battalion)

Company HQ

1st Platoon

2nd Platoon

3rd Platoon

Support Section

Maintenance Section

Trains

2nd Company / 39th Engineer Battalion (attached to 2nd Machinegun Battalion)

Company HQ

1st Platoon

2nd Platoon

3rd Platoon

Support Section

Maintenance Section

Trains

Engineer Company / 8th Machinegun Battalion

Company HQ

1st Platoon

2nd Platoon

3rd Platoon

Support Section

Maintenance Section

Trains

Anti-Tank Company / 8th Machinegun Battalion

1st Platoon

2nd Platoon

3rd Platoon

4th Platoon

Trains

Maintenance Section

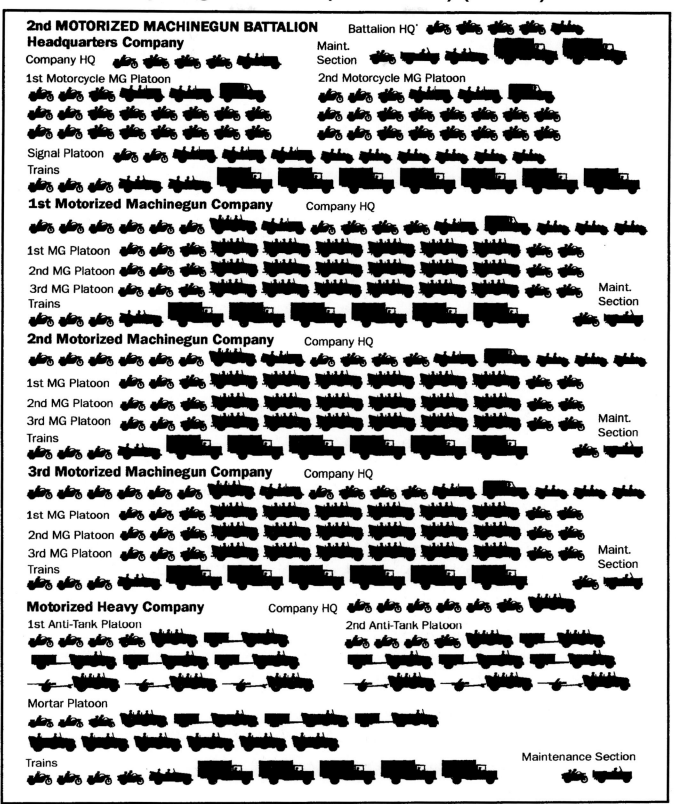

2nd MOTORIZED MACHINEGUN BATTALION — Battalion HQ

Headquarters Company — Maint. Section

Company HQ

1st Motorcycle MG Platoon — 2nd Motorcycle MG Platoon

Signal Platoon

Trains

1st Motorized Machinegun Company — Company HQ

1st MG Platoon

2nd MG Platoon

3rd MG Platoon — Maint. Section

Trains

2nd Motorized Machinegun Company — Company HQ

1st MG Platoon

2nd MG Platoon

3rd MG Platoon — Maint. Section

Trains

3rd Motorized Machinegun Company — Company HQ

1st MG Platoon

2nd MG Platoon

3rd MG Platoon — Maint. Section

Trains

Motorized Heavy Company — Company HQ

1st Anti-Tank Platoon — 2nd Anti-Tank Platoon

Mortar Platoon

Maintenance Section

Trains

5th Light Mechanized Division (cont'd)
200th Infantry Regiment HQ (motorized) (cont'd)

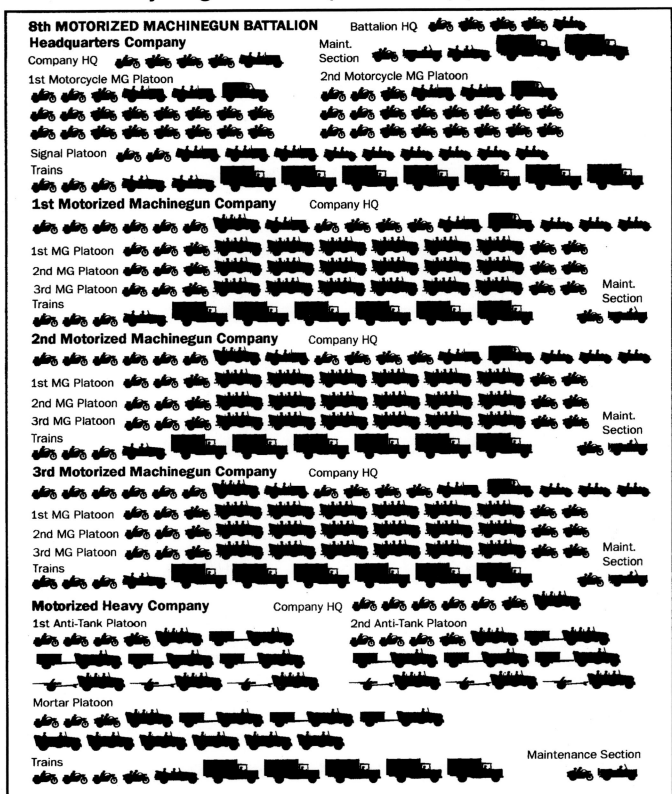

8th MOTORIZED MACHINEGUN BATTALION Battalion HQ

Headquarters Company Maint. Section

Company HQ

1st Motorcycle MG Platoon / 2nd Motorcycle MG Platoon

Signal Platoon

Trains

1st Motorized Machinegun Company Company HQ

1st MG Platoon
2nd MG Platoon
3rd MG Platoon — Maint. Section
Trains

2nd Motorized Machinegun Company Company HQ

1st MG Platoon
2nd MG Platoon
3rd MG Platoon — Maint. Section
Trains

3rd Motorized Machinegun Company Company HQ

1st MG Platoon
2nd MG Platoon
3rd MG Platoon — Maint. Section
Trains

Motorized Heavy Company Company HQ

1st Anti-Tank Platoon / 2nd Anti-Tank Platoon

Mortar Platoon

Trains — Maintenance Section

5th Light Mechanized Division (cont'd)
39th Motorized Anti-Tank Battalion

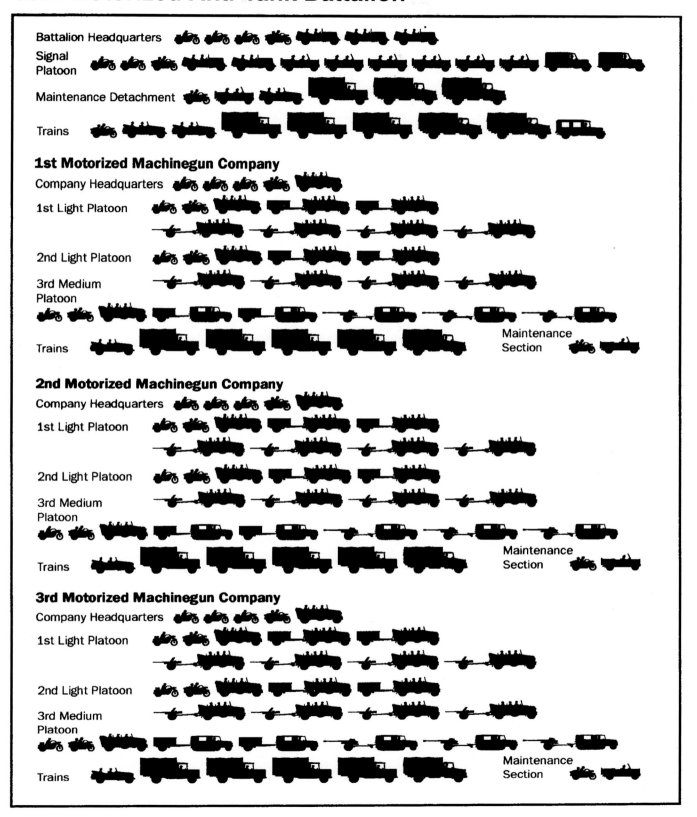

5th Light Mechanized Division (cont'd)
3rd Armored Reconnaissance Battalion

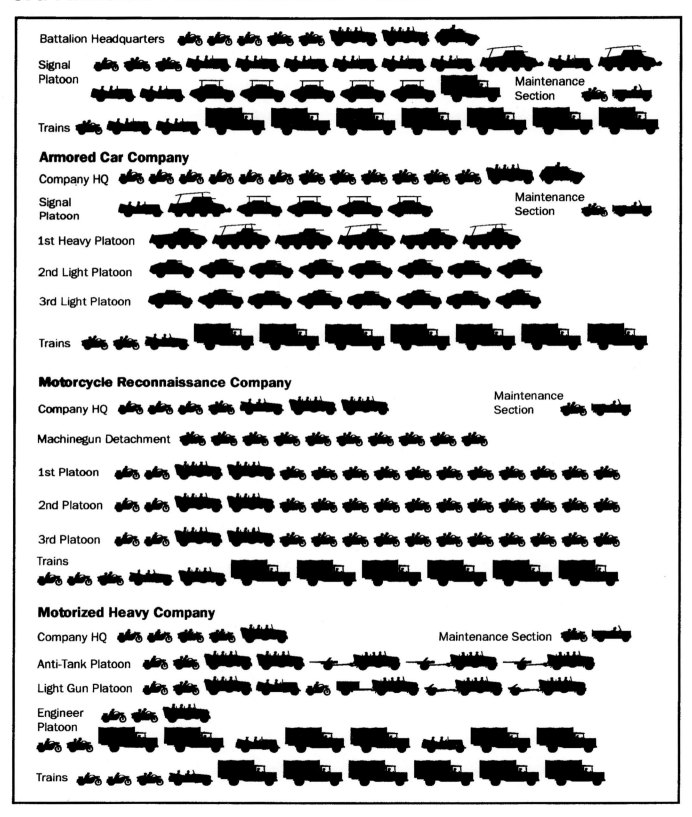

5th Light Mechanized Division (cont'd)
1st Battalion/75th Motorized Artillery Regiment

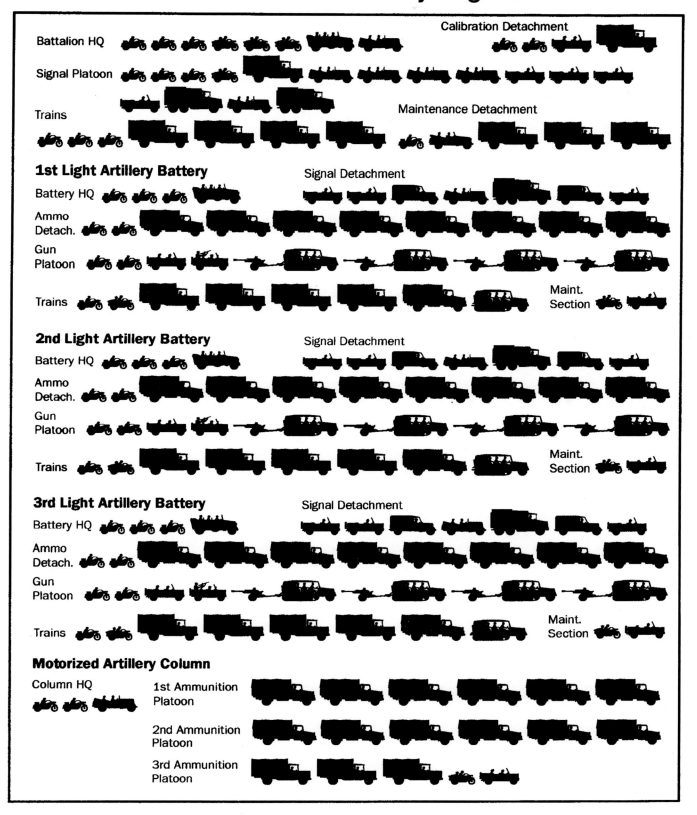

5th Light Mechanized Division (cont'd)
605th Self-Propelled Anti-Tank Battalion

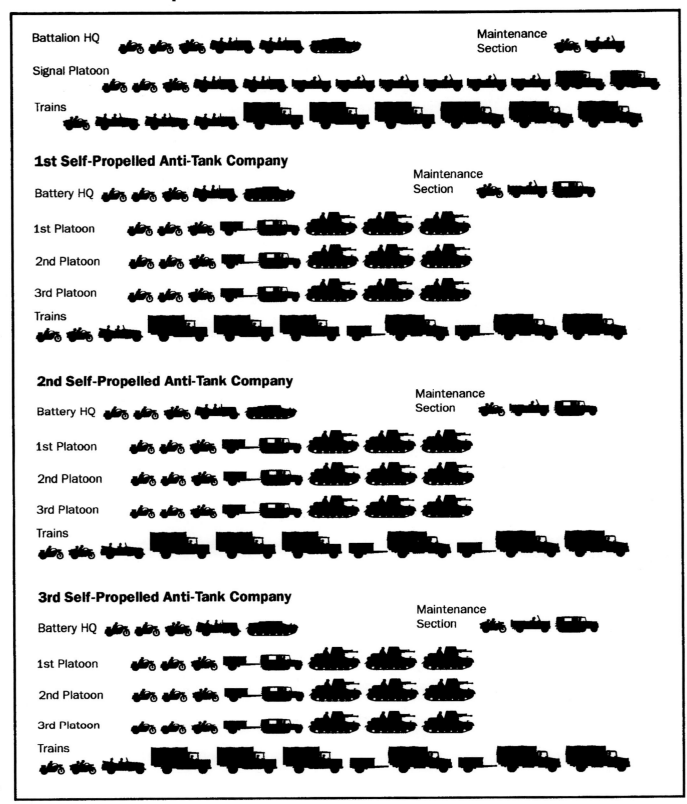

5th Light Mechanized Division (cont'd)
606th Light Anti-Aircraft Battalion

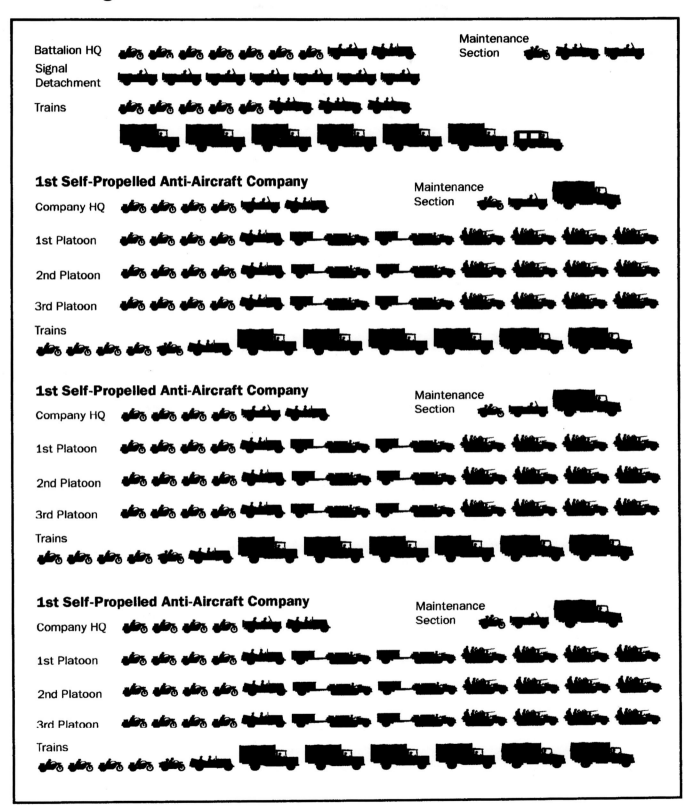

Battalion HQ

Maintenance Section

Signal Detachment

Trains

1st Self-Propelled Anti-Aircraft Company

Company HQ

Maintenance Section

1st Platoon

2nd Platoon

3rd Platoon

Trains

1st Self-Propelled Anti-Aircraft Company

Company HQ

Maintenance Section

1st Platoon

2nd Platoon

3rd Platoon

Trains

1st Self-Propelled Anti-Aircraft Company

Company HQ

Maintenance Section

1st Platoon

2nd Platoon

3rd Platoon

Trains

Attached to 5th Light Division from Luftwaffe
1st Motorized Battalion / 33rd Flak Regiment (Lw)

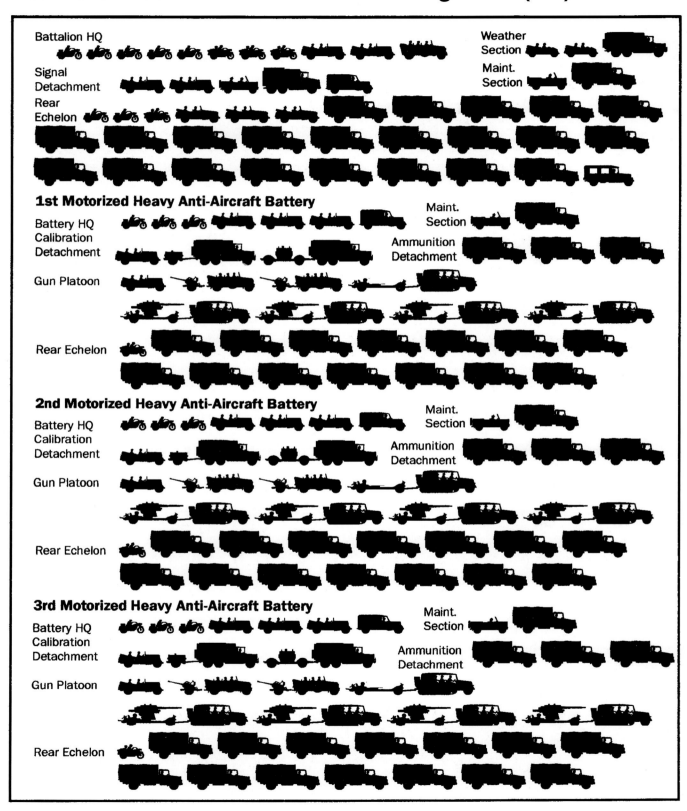

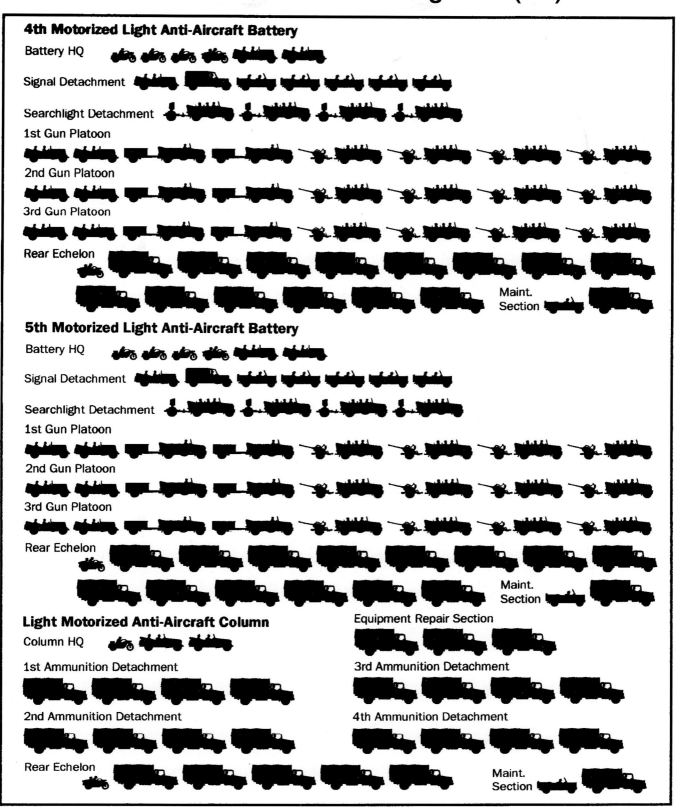

4th Motorized Light Anti-Aircraft Battery

Battery HQ

Signal Detachment

Searchlight Detachment

1st Gun Platoon

2nd Gun Platoon

3rd Gun Platoon

Rear Echelon

Maint. Section

5th Motorized Light Anti-Aircraft Battery

Battery HQ

Signal Detachment

Searchlight Detachment

1st Gun Platoon

2nd Gun Platoon

3rd Gun Platoon

Rear Echelon

Maint. Section

Light Motorized Anti-Aircraft Column

Column HQ

1st Ammunition Detachment

2nd Ammunition Detachment

Rear Echelon

Equipment Repair Section

3rd Ammunition Detachment

4th Ammunition Detachment

Maint. Section

15th PANZER DIVISION: May 27, 1942
15. PANZER DIVISION

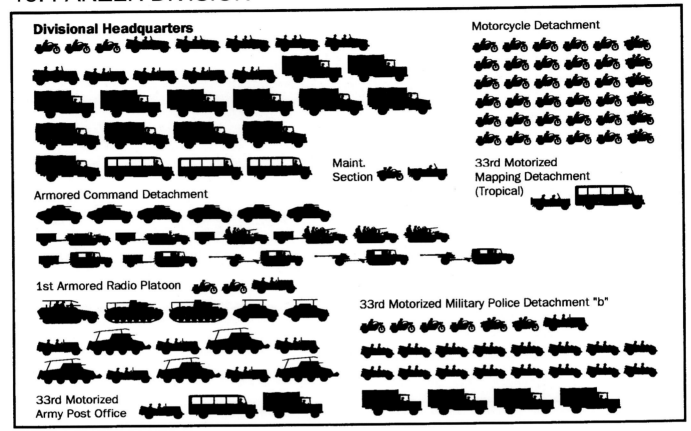

Divisional Headquarters

Motorcycle Detachment

Maint. Section

33rd Motorized Mapping Detachment (Tropical)

Armored Command Detachment

1st Armored Radio Platoon

33rd Motorized Military Police Detachment "b"

33rd Motorized Army Post Office

8th Panzer Regiment

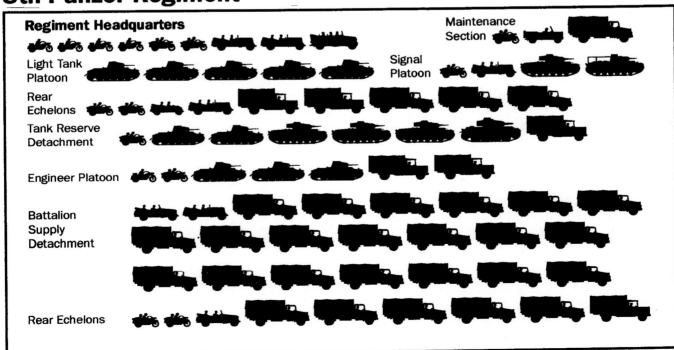

Regiment Headquarters

Maintenance Section

Light Tank Platoon

Signal Platoon

Rear Echelons

Tank Reserve Detachment

Engineer Platoon

Battalion Supply Detachment

Rear Echelons

8th Panzer Regiment (cont'd)

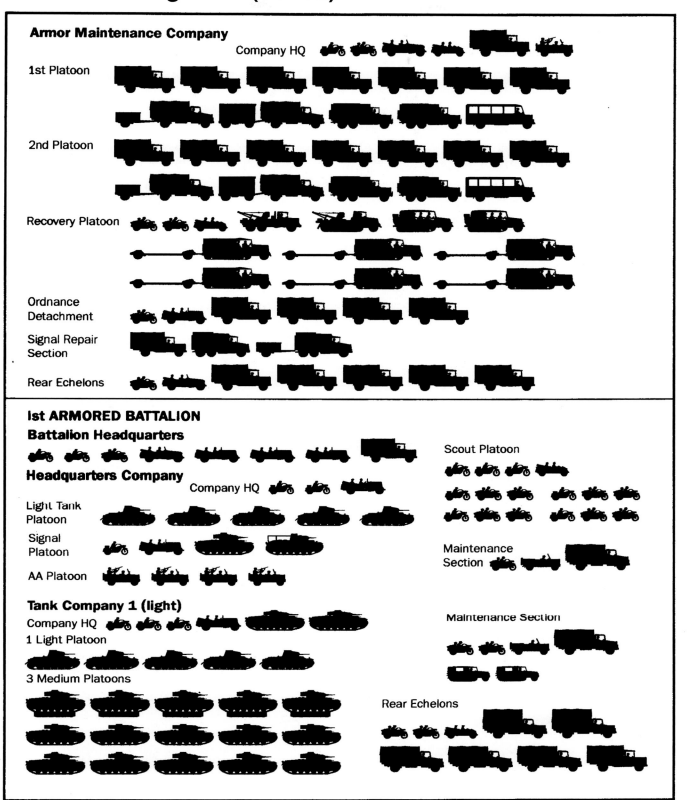

Armor Maintenance Company

Company HQ

1st Platoon

2nd Platoon

Recovery Platoon

Ordnance Detachment

Signal Repair Section

Rear Echelons

1st ARMORED BATTALION

Battalion Headquarters

Headquarters Company

Company HQ

Light Tank Platoon

Signal Platoon

AA Platoon

Scout Platoon

Maintenance Section

Tank Company 1 (light)

Company HQ

1 Light Platoon

3 Medium Platoons

Maintenance Section

Rear Echelons

15th Panzer Division (cont'd)
8th Panzer Regiment (cont'd)

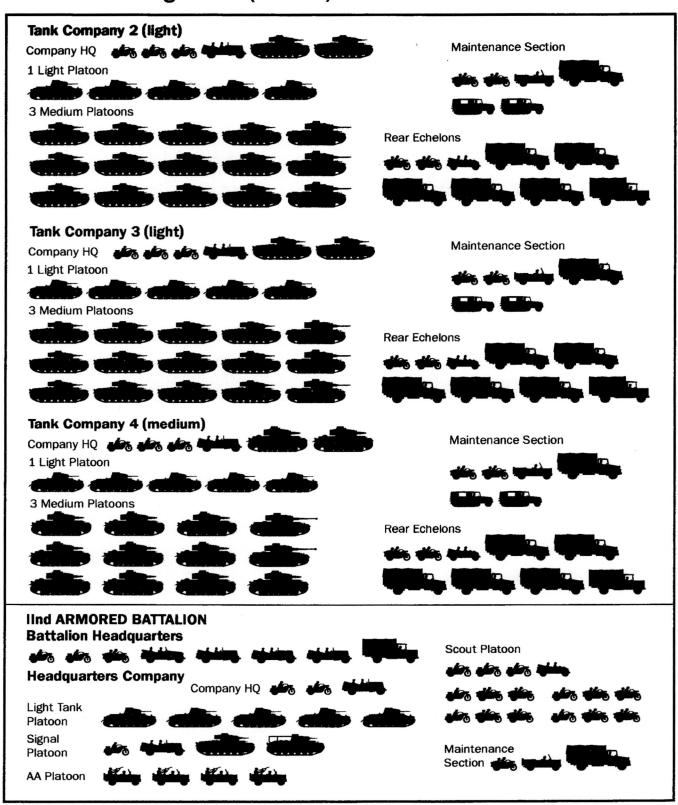

Tank Company 2 (light)
Company HQ

1 Light Platoon

3 Medium Platoons

Maintenance Section

Rear Echelons

Tank Company 3 (light)
Company HQ

1 Light Platoon

3 Medium Platoons

Maintenance Section

Rear Echelons

Tank Company 4 (medium)
Company HQ

1 Light Platoon

3 Medium Platoons

Maintenance Section

Rear Echelons

IInd ARMORED BATTALION
Battalion Headquarters

Headquarters Company
Company HQ

Light Tank Platoon

Signal Platoon

AA Platoon

Scout Platoon

Maintenance Section

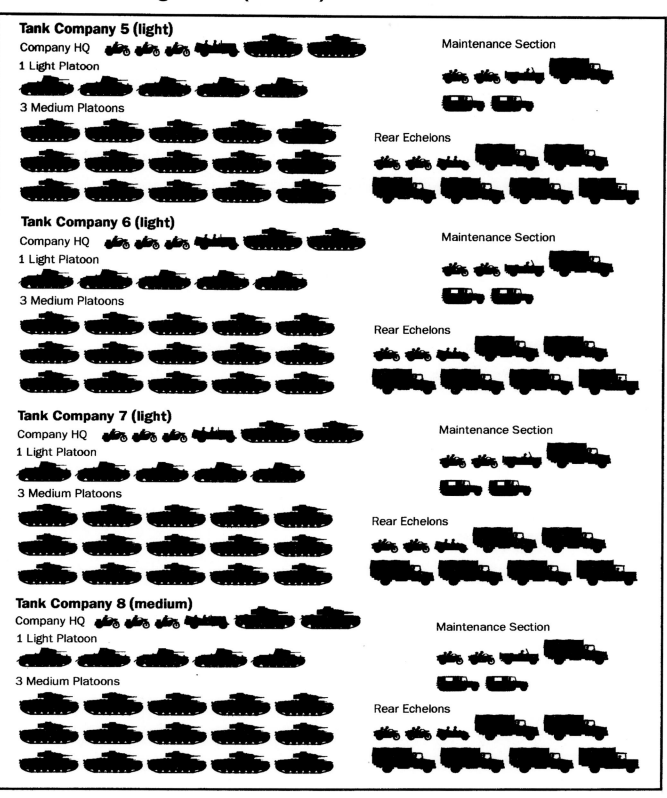

Tank Company 5 (light)
Company HQ

1 Light Platoon

3 Medium Platoons

Maintenance Section

Rear Echelons

Tank Company 6 (light)
Company HQ

1 Light Platoon

3 Medium Platoons

Maintenance Section

Rear Echelons

Tank Company 7 (light)
Company HQ

1 Light Platoon

3 Medium Platoons

Maintenance Section

Rear Echelons

Tank Company 8 (medium)
Company HQ

1 Light Platoon

3 Medium Platoons

Maintenance Section

Rear Echelons

15th Panzer Division (cont'd)
115th Motorized Infantry Regiment

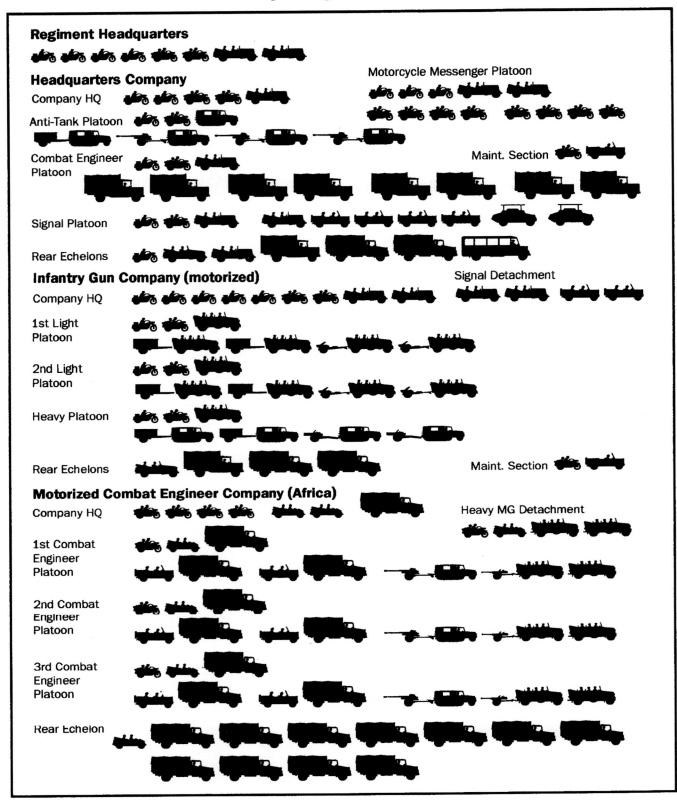

Regiment Headquarters

Headquarters Company

Company HQ

Anti-Tank Platoon

Combat Engineer Platoon

Signal Platoon

Rear Echelons

Motorcycle Messenger Platoon

Maint. Section

Infantry Gun Company (motorized)

Company HQ

1st Light Platoon

2nd Light Platoon

Heavy Platoon

Rear Echelons

Signal Detachment

Maint. Section

Motorized Combat Engineer Company (Africa)

Company HQ

1st Combat Engineer Platoon

2nd Combat Engineer Platoon

3rd Combat Engineer Platoon

Rear Echelon

Heavy MG Detachment

15th Panzer Division (cont'd)
115th Motorized Infantry Regiment (cont'd)

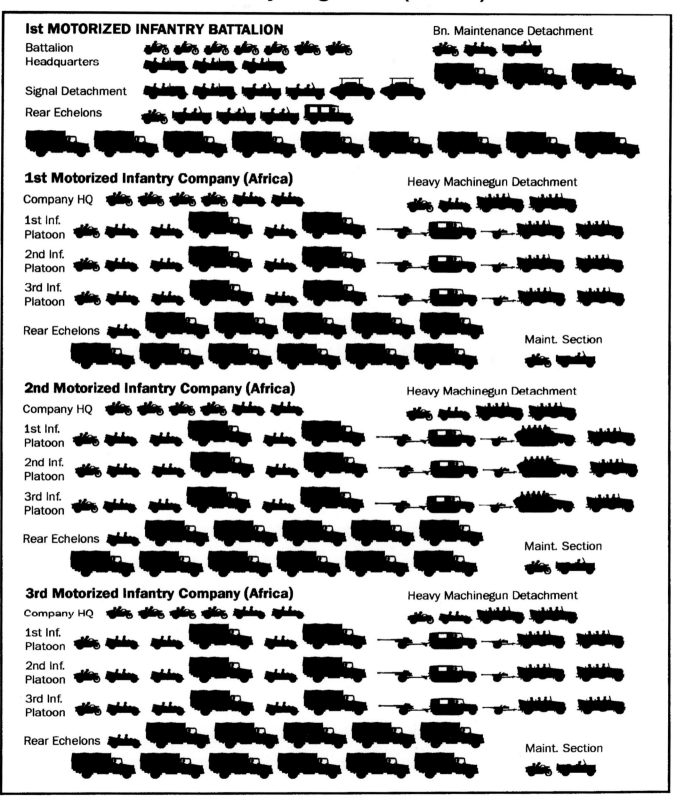

1st MOTORIZED INFANTRY BATTALION

Battalion Headquarters

Bn. Maintenance Detachment

Signal Detachment

Rear Echelons

1st Motorized Infantry Company (Africa)

Company HQ

Heavy Machinegun Detachment

1st Inf. Platoon

2nd Inf. Platoon

3rd Inf. Platoon

Rear Echelons

Maint. Section

2nd Motorized Infantry Company (Africa)

Company HQ

Heavy Machinegun Detachment

1st Inf. Platoon

2nd Inf. Platoon

3rd Inf. Platoon

Rear Echelons

Maint. Section

3rd Motorized Infantry Company (Africa)

Company HQ

Heavy Machinegun Detachment

1st Inf. Platoon

2nd Inf. Platoon

3rd Inf. Platoon

Rear Echelons

Maint. Section

115th Motorized Infantry Regiment (cont'd)

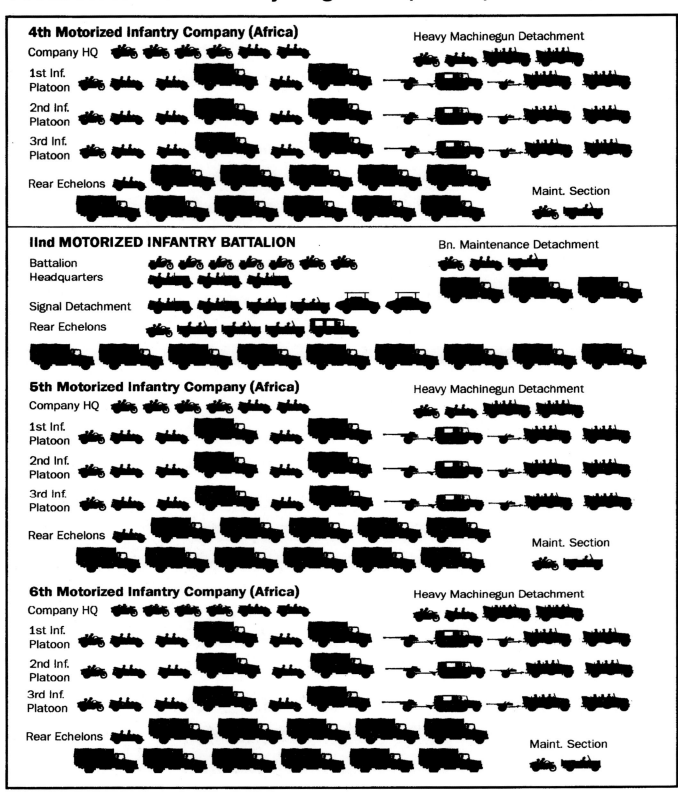

4th Motorized Infantry Company (Africa)
Company HQ

Heavy Machinegun Detachment

1st Inf. Platoon

2nd Inf. Platoon

3rd Inf. Platoon

Rear Echelons

Maint. Section

IInd MOTORIZED INFANTRY BATTALION
Battalion Headquarters

Bn. Maintenance Detachment

Signal Detachment

Rear Echelons

5th Motorized Infantry Company (Africa)
Company HQ

Heavy Machinegun Detachment

1st Inf. Platoon

2nd Inf. Platoon

3rd Inf. Platoon

Rear Echelons

Maint. Section

6th Motorized Infantry Company (Africa)
Company HQ

Heavy Machinegun Detachment

1st Inf. Platoon

2nd Inf. Platoon

3rd Inf. Platoon

Rear Echelons

Maint. Section

15th Panzer Division (cont'd)
115th Motorized Infantry Regiment (cont'd)

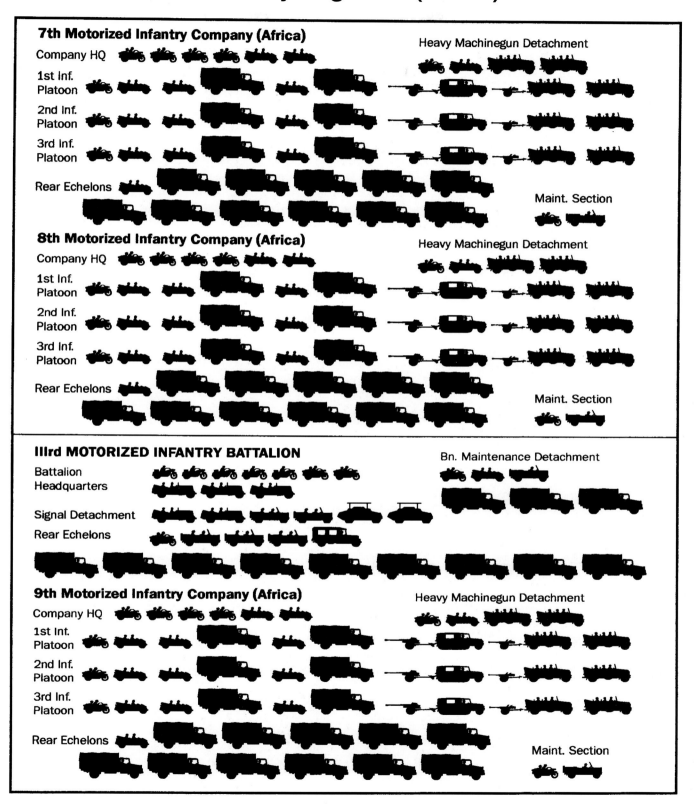

7th Motorized Infantry Company (Africa)
Company HQ
1st Inf. Platoon
2nd Inf. Platoon
3rd Inf. Platoon
Rear Echelons
Heavy Machinegun Detachment
Maint. Section

8th Motorized Infantry Company (Africa)
Company HQ
1st Inf. Platoon
2nd Inf. Platoon
3rd Inf. Platoon
Rear Echelons
Heavy Machinegun Detachment
Maint. Section

IIIrd MOTORIZED INFANTRY BATTALION
Battalion Headquarters
Signal Detachment
Rear Echelons
Bn. Maintenance Detachment

9th Motorized Infantry Company (Africa)
Company HQ
1st Inf. Platoon
2nd Inf. Platoon
3rd Inf. Platoon
Rear Echelons
Heavy Machinegun Detachment
Maint. Section

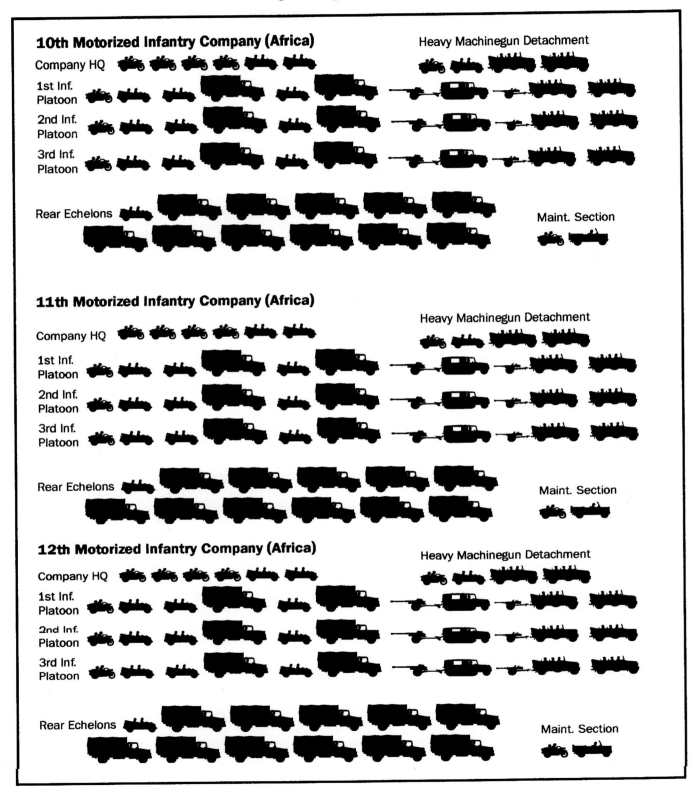

10th Motorized Infantry Company (Africa)

Company HQ

1st Inf. Platoon

2nd Inf. Platoon

3rd Inf. Platoon

Rear Echelons

Heavy Machinegun Detachment

Maint. Section

11th Motorized Infantry Company (Africa)

Company HQ

1st Inf. Platoon

2nd Inf. Platoon

3rd Inf. Platoon

Rear Echelons

Heavy Machinegun Detachment

Maint. Section

12th Motorized Infantry Company (Africa)

Company HQ

1st Inf. Platoon

2nd Inf. Platoon

3rd Inf. Platoon

Rear Echelons

Heavy Machinegun Detachment

Maint. Section

15th Panzer Division (cont'd)
33rd Motorized Artillery Regiment

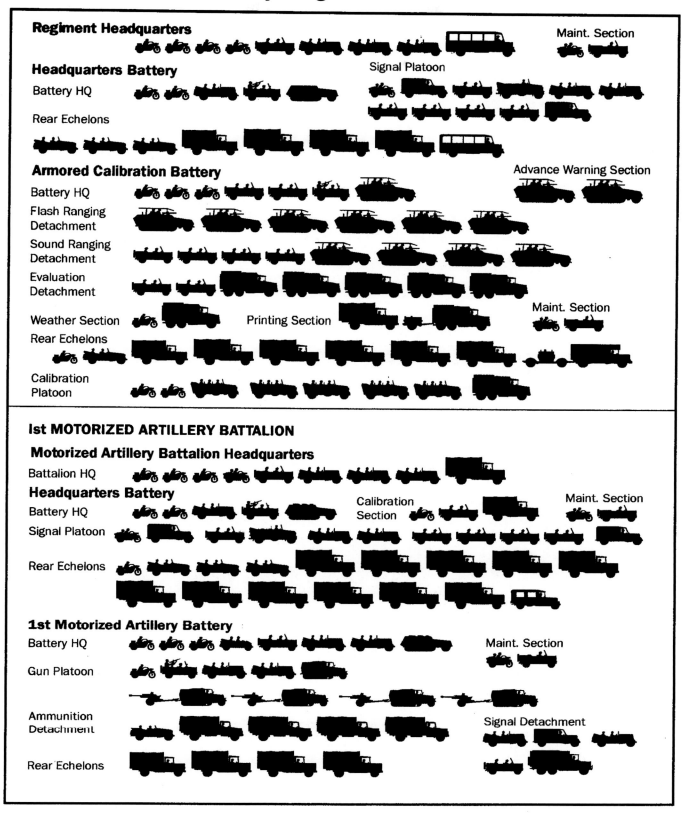

Regiment Headquarters

Maint. Section

Headquarters Battery

Signal Platoon

Battery HQ

Rear Echelons

Armored Calibration Battery

Advance Warning Section

Battery HQ

Flash Ranging Detachment

Sound Ranging Detachment

Evaluation Detachment

Weather Section   Printing Section   Maint. Section

Rear Echelons

Calibration Platoon

1st MOTORIZED ARTILLERY BATTALION

Motorized Artillery Battalion Headquarters

Battalion HQ

Headquarters Battery

Battery HQ   Calibration Section   Maint. Section

Signal Platoon

Rear Echelons

1st Motorized Artillery Battery

Battery HQ   Maint. Section

Gun Platoon

Ammunition Detachment   Signal Detachment

Rear Echelons

15th Panzer Division (cont'd)
33rd Motorized Artillery Regiment (cont'd)

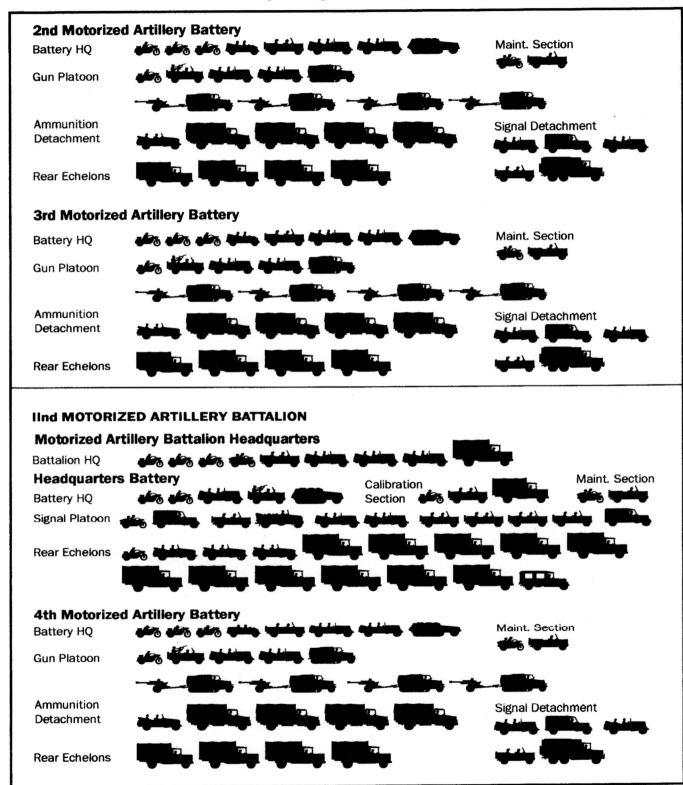

2nd Motorized Artillery Battery

Battery HQ

Gun Platoon

Ammunition Detachment

Rear Echelons

Maint. Section

Signal Detachment

3rd Motorized Artillery Battery

Battery HQ

Gun Platoon

Ammunition Detachment

Rear Echelons

Maint. Section

Signal Detachment

IInd MOTORIZED ARTILLERY BATTALION

Motorized Artillery Battalion Headquarters

Battalion HQ

Headquarters Battery

Battery HQ

Signal Platoon

Rear Echelons

Calibration Section

Maint. Section

4th Motorized Artillery Battery

Battery HQ

Gun Platoon

Ammunition Detachment

Rear Echelons

Maint. Section

Signal Detachment

15th Panzer Division (cont'd)
33rd Motorized Artillery Regiment (cont'd)

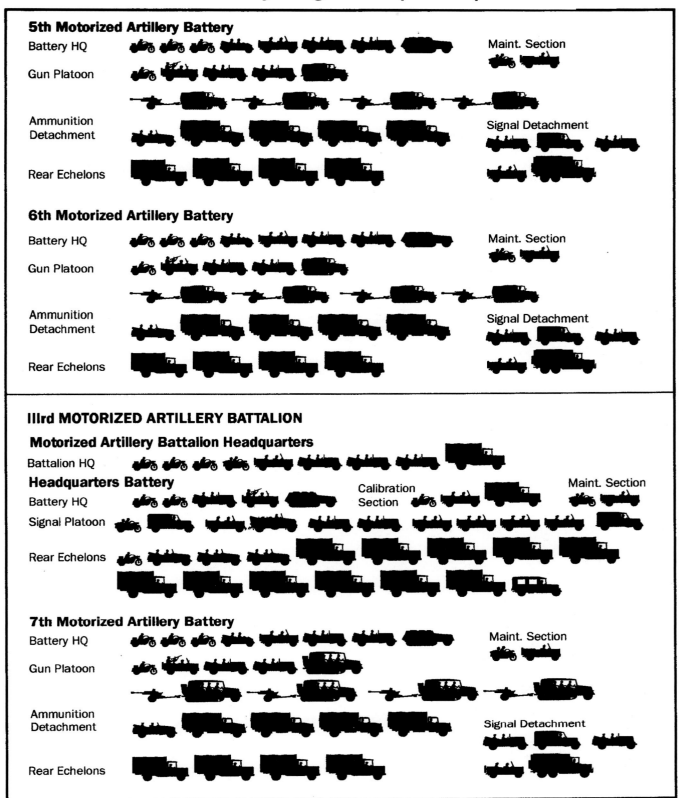

5th Motorized Artillery Battery
Battery HQ
Gun Platoon
Ammunition Detachment
Rear Echelons
Maint. Section
Signal Detachment

6th Motorized Artillery Battery
Battery HQ
Gun Platoon
Ammunition Detachment
Rear Echelons
Maint. Section
Signal Detachment

IIIrd MOTORIZED ARTILLERY BATTALION
Motorized Artillery Battalion Headquarters
Battalion HQ
Headquarters Battery
Battery HQ
Signal Platoon
Rear Echelons
Calibration Section
Maint. Section

7th Motorized Artillery Battery
Battery HQ
Gun Platoon
Ammunition Detachment
Rear Echelons
Maint. Section
Signal Detachment

33rd Motorized Artillery Regiment (cont'd)

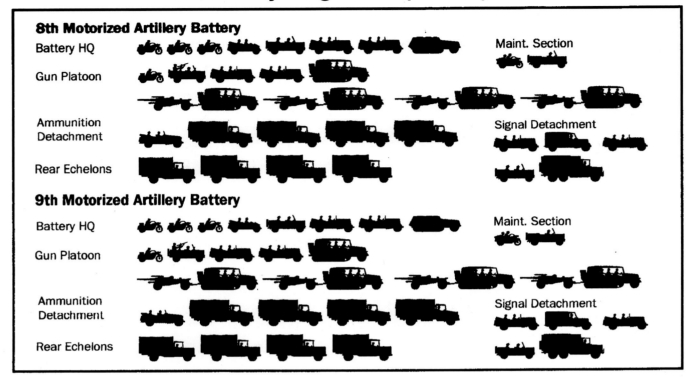

8th Motorized Artillery Battery

Battery HQ

Gun Platoon

Ammunition Detachment

Rear Echelons

Maint. Section

Signal Detachment

9th Motorized Artillery Battery

Battery HQ

Gun Platoon

Ammunition Detachment

Rear Echelons

Maint. Section

Signal Detachment

33rd Motorized Reconnaissance Battalion

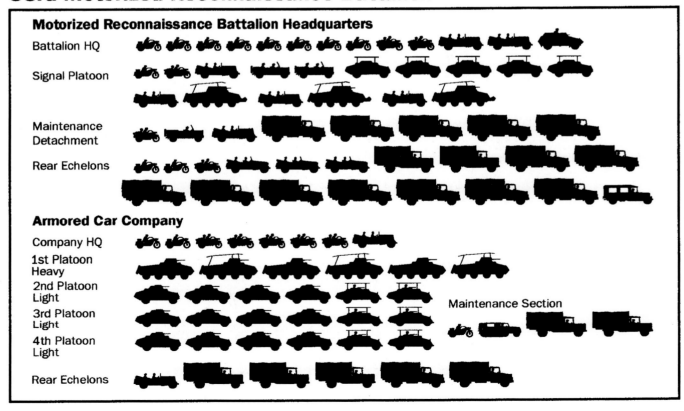

Motorized Reconnaissance Battalion Headquarters

Battalion HQ

Signal Platoon

Maintenance Detachment

Rear Echelons

Armored Car Company

Company HQ

1st Platoon Heavy

2nd Platoon Light

3rd Platoon Light

4th Platoon Light

Maintenance Section

Rear Echelons

15th Panzer Division (cont'd)
33rd Motorized Reconnaissance Battalion (cont'd)

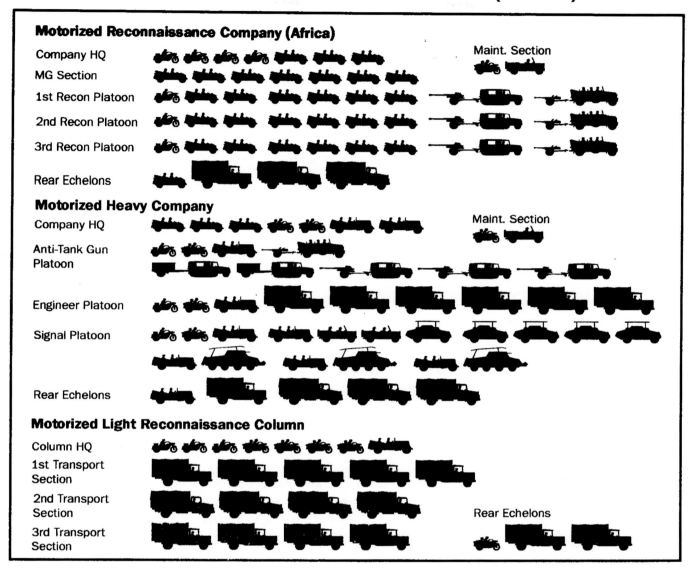

Motorized Reconnaissance Company (Africa)
Company HQ
MG Section
1st Recon Platoon
2nd Recon Platoon
3rd Recon Platoon
Rear Echelons

Maint. Section

Motorized Heavy Company
Company HQ
Anti-Tank Gun Platoon
Engineer Platoon
Signal Platoon
Rear Echelons

Maint. Section

Motorized Light Reconnaissance Column
Column HQ
1st Transport Section
2nd Transport Section
3rd Transport Section

Rear Echelons

33rd Motorized Combat Engineer Battalion

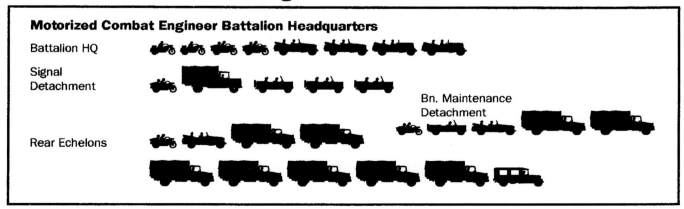

Motorized Combat Engineer Battalion Headquarters
Battalion HQ
Signal Detachment
Rear Echelons

Bn. Maintenance Detachment

15th Panzer Division (cont'd)
33rd Motorized Reconnaissance Battalion (cont'd)

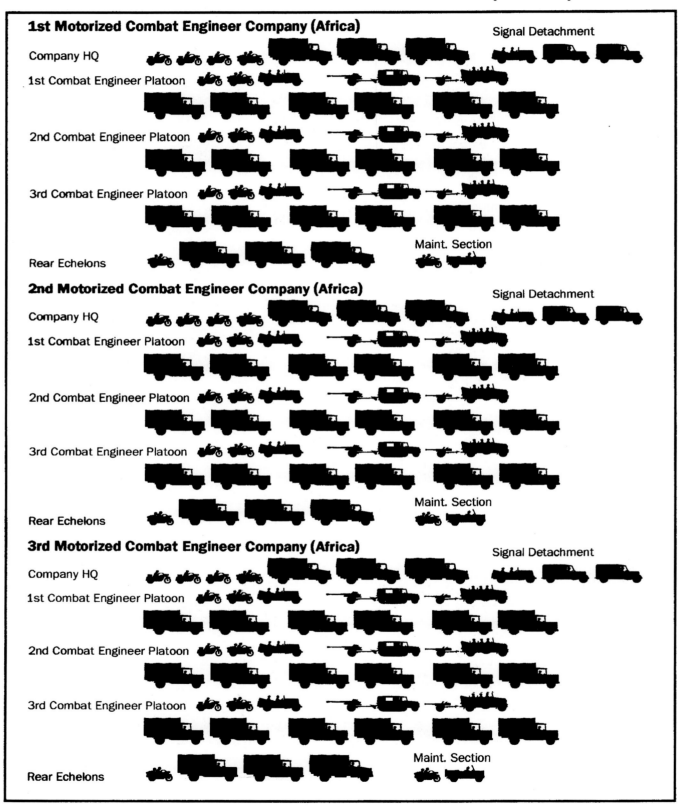

1st Motorized Combat Engineer Company (Africa)

Company HQ — Signal Detachment

1st Combat Engineer Platoon

2nd Combat Engineer Platoon

3rd Combat Engineer Platoon

Rear Echelons — Maint. Section

2nd Motorized Combat Engineer Company (Africa)

Company HQ — Signal Detachment

1st Combat Engineer Platoon

2nd Combat Engineer Platoon

3rd Combat Engineer Platoon

Rear Echelons — Maint. Section

3rd Motorized Combat Engineer Company (Africa)

Company HQ — Signal Detachment

1st Combat Engineer Platoon

2nd Combat Engineer Platoon

3rd Combat Engineer Platoon

Rear Echelons — Maint. Section

15th Panzer Division (cont'd)
33rd Motorized Combat Engineer Battalion (cont'd)

Motorized Light Engineer Column

78th Motorized Anti-Tank Battalion

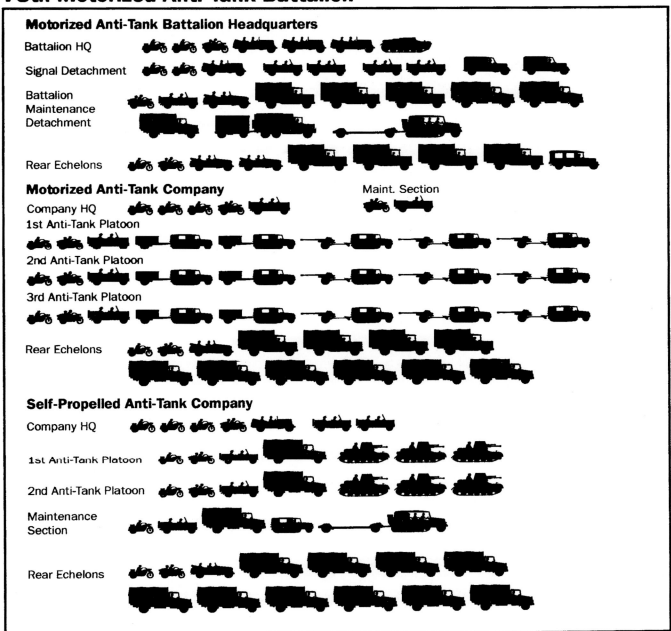

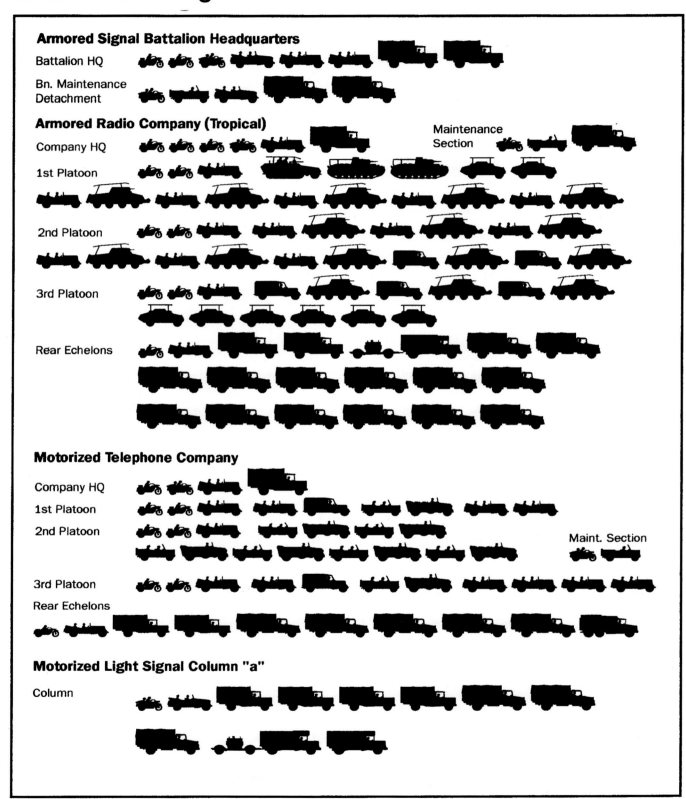

Armored Signal Battalion Headquarters

Battalion HQ

Bn. Maintenance Detachment

Armored Radio Company (Tropical)

Company HQ

Maintenance Section

1st Platoon

2nd Platoon

3rd Platoon

Rear Echelons

Motorized Telephone Company

Company HQ

1st Platoon

2nd Platoon

Maint. Section

3rd Platoon

Rear Echelons

Motorized Light Signal Column "a"

Column

21st Panzer Division: May 27, 1942
21. PANZER DIVISION

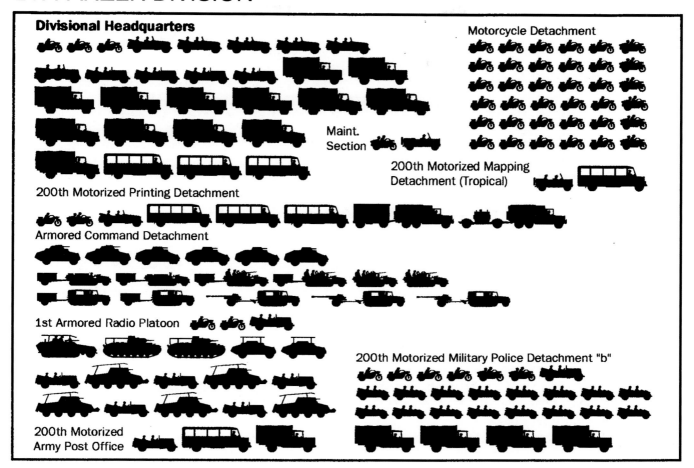

Divisional Headquarters

Motorcycle Detachment

Maint. Section

200th Motorized Mapping Detachment (Tropical)

200th Motorized Printing Detachment

Armored Command Detachment

1st Armored Radio Platoon

200th Motorized Military Police Detachment "b"

200th Motorized Army Post Office

5th Panzer Regiment

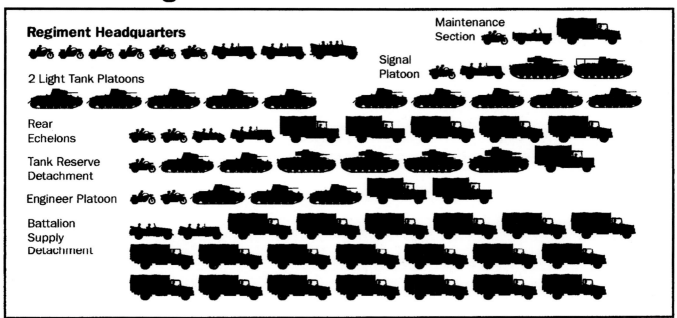

Regiment Headquarters

Maintenance Section

Signal Platoon

2 Light Tank Platoons

Rear Echelons

Tank Reserve Detachment

Engineer Platoon

Battalion Supply Detachment

21st Panzer Division (cont'd)
5th Panzer Regiment (cont'd)

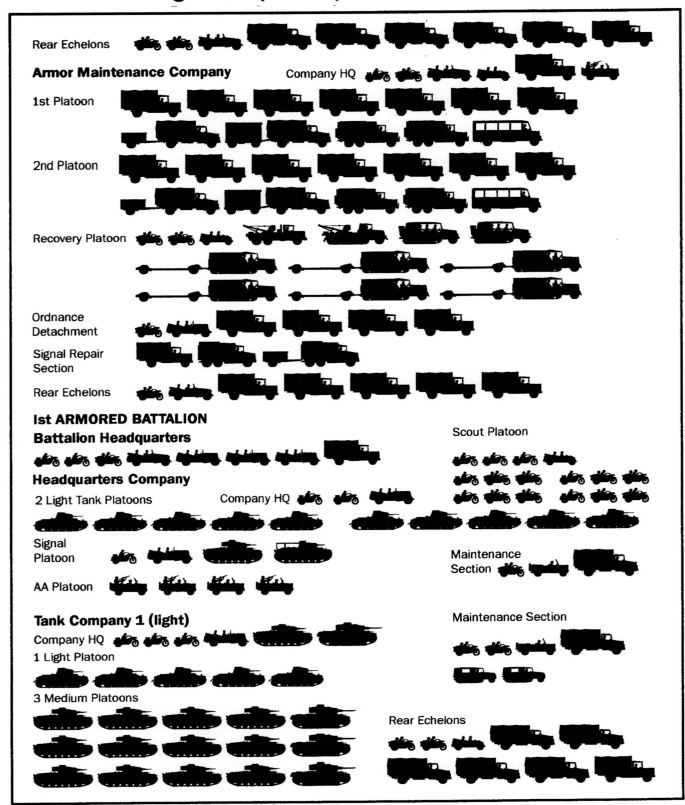

Rear Echelons

Armor Maintenance Company
Company HQ

1st Platoon

2nd Platoon

Recovery Platoon

Ordnance
Detachment

Signal Repair
Section

Rear Echelons

1st ARMORED BATTALION
Battalion Headquarters

Scout Platoon

Headquarters Company

2 Light Tank Platoons
Company HQ

Signal
Platoon

Maintenance
Section

AA Platoon

Tank Company 1 (light)
Company HQ
1 Light Platoon

Maintenance Section

3 Medium Platoons

Rear Echelons

21st Panzer Division (cont'd)
5th Panzer Regiment (cont'd)

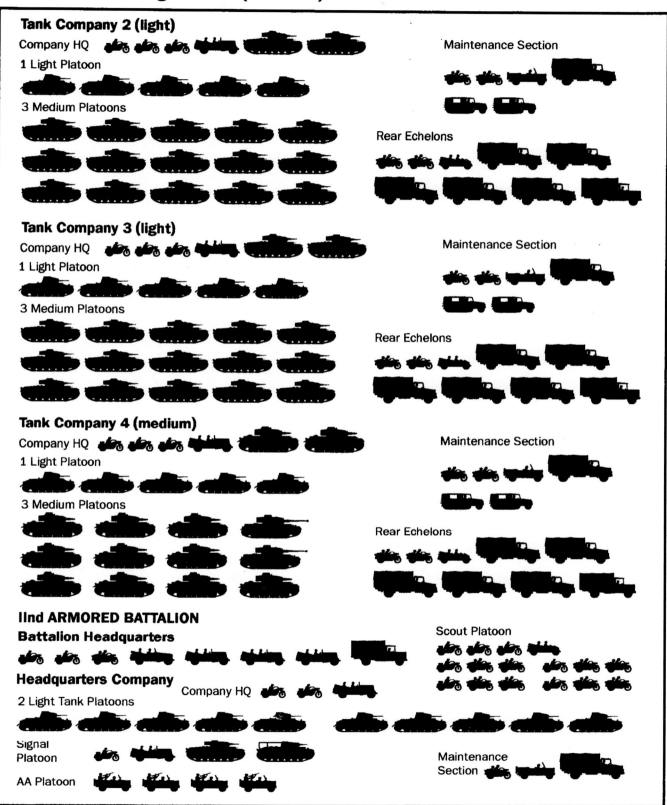

Tank Company 2 (light)
Company HQ
1 Light Platoon
3 Medium Platoons

Maintenance Section

Rear Echelons

Tank Company 3 (light)
Company HQ
1 Light Platoon
3 Medium Platoons

Maintenance Section

Rear Echelons

Tank Company 4 (medium)
Company HQ
1 Light Platoon
3 Medium Platoons

Maintenance Section

Rear Echelons

IInd ARMORED BATTALION
Battalion Headquarters

Scout Platoon

Headquarters Company
2 Light Tank Platoons
Company HQ

Signal Platoon

Maintenance Section

AA Platoon

21st Panzer Division (cont'd)
5th Panzer Regiment (cont'd)

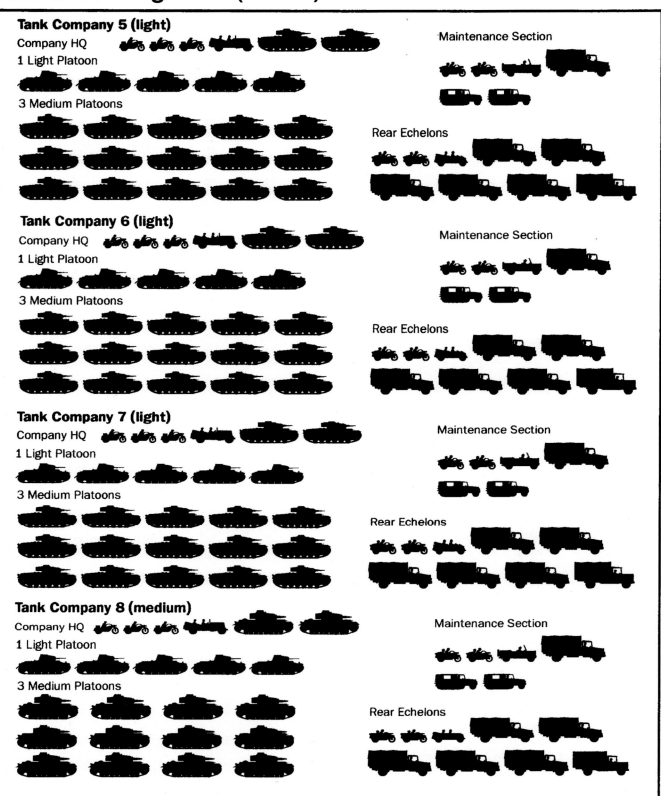

Tank Company 5 (light)
Company HQ
1 Light Platoon
3 Medium Platoons

Maintenance Section

Rear Echelons

Tank Company 6 (light)
Company HQ
1 Light Platoon
3 Medium Platoons

Maintenance Section

Rear Echelons

Tank Company 7 (light)
Company HQ
1 Light Platoon
3 Medium Platoons

Maintenance Section

Rear Echelons

Tank Company 8 (medium)
Company HQ
1 Light Platoon
3 Medium Platoons

Maintenance Section

Rear Echelons

21st Panzer Division (cont'd)
104th Motorized Infantry Regiment

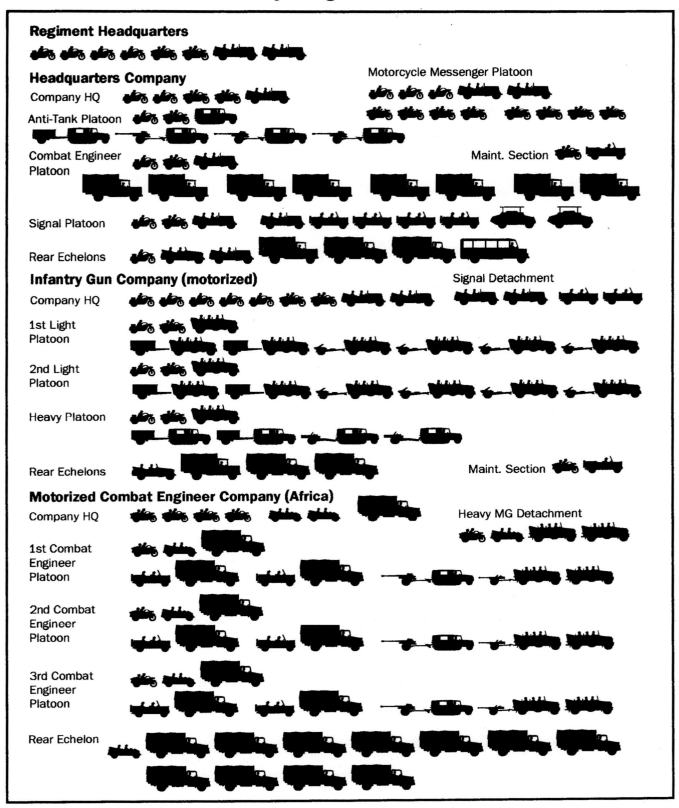

Regiment Headquarters

Headquarters Company

Company HQ

Motorcycle Messenger Platoon

Anti-Tank Platoon

Combat Engineer Platoon

Maint. Section

Signal Platoon

Rear Echelons

Infantry Gun Company (motorized)

Signal Detachment

Company HQ

1st Light Platoon

2nd Light Platoon

Heavy Platoon

Rear Echelons

Maint. Section

Motorized Combat Engineer Company (Africa)

Company HQ

Heavy MG Detachment

1st Combat Engineer Platoon

2nd Combat Engineer Platoon

3rd Combat Engineer Platoon

Rear Echelon

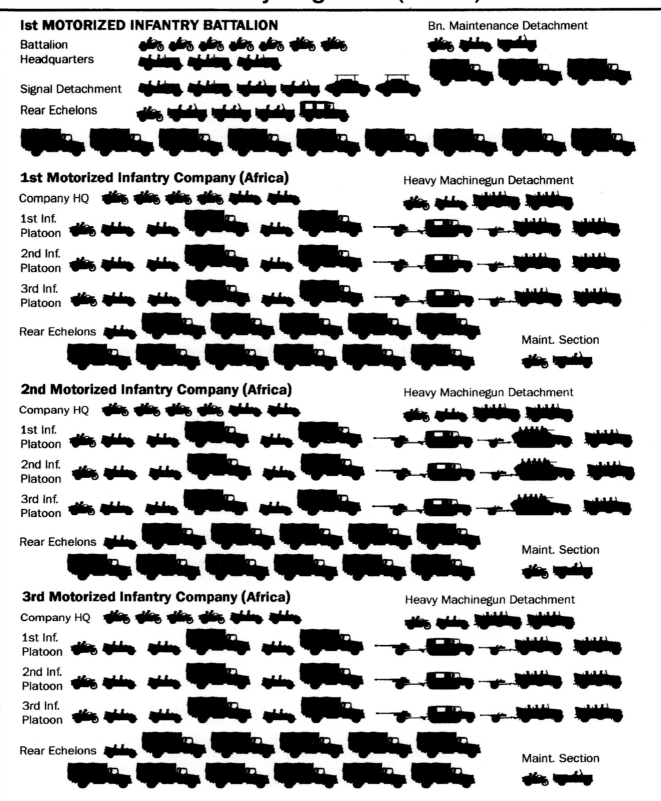

1st MOTORIZED INFANTRY BATTALION

Battalion Headquarters

Signal Detachment

Rear Echelons

Bn. Maintenance Detachment

1st Motorized Infantry Company (Africa)

Company HQ

1st Inf. Platoon

2nd Inf. Platoon

3rd Inf. Platoon

Rear Echelons

Heavy Machinegun Detachment

Maint. Section

2nd Motorized Infantry Company (Africa)

Company HQ

1st Inf. Platoon

2nd Inf. Platoon

3rd Inf. Platoon

Rear Echelons

Heavy Machinegun Detachment

Maint. Section

3rd Motorized Infantry Company (Africa)

Company HQ

1st Inf. Platoon

2nd Inf. Platoon

3rd Inf. Platoon

Rear Echelons

Heavy Machinegun Detachment

Maint. Section

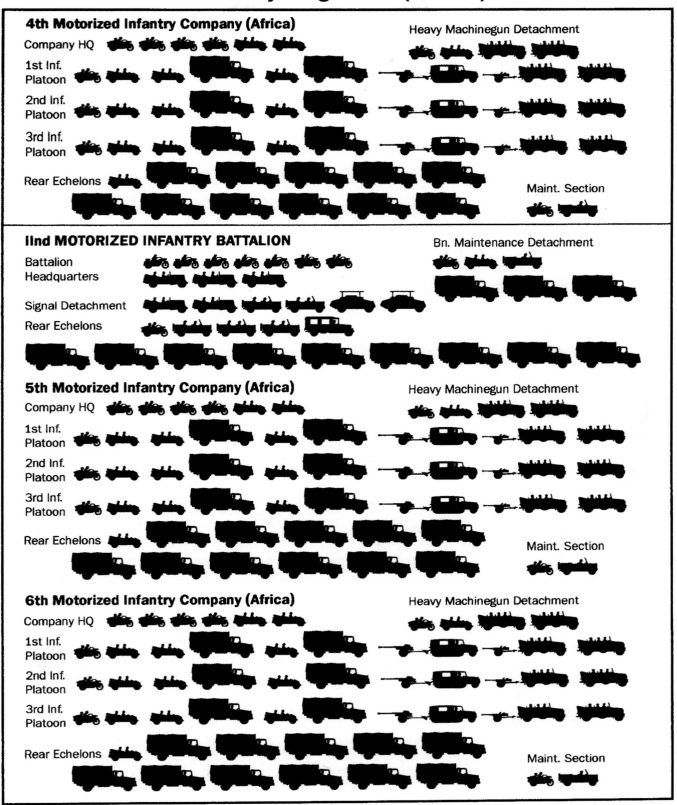

4th Motorized Infantry Company (Africa)

Company HQ

1st Inf. Platoon

2nd Inf. Platoon

3rd Inf. Platoon

Rear Echelons

Heavy Machinegun Detachment

Maint. Section

IInd MOTORIZED INFANTRY BATTALION

Battalion Headquarters

Signal Detachment

Rear Echelons

Bn. Maintenance Detachment

5th Motorized Infantry Company (Africa)

Company HQ

1st Inf. Platoon

2nd Inf. Platoon

3rd Inf. Platoon

Rear Echelons

Heavy Machinegun Detachment

Maint. Section

6th Motorized Infantry Company (Africa)

Company HQ

1st Inf. Platoon

2nd Inf. Platoon

3rd Inf. Platoon

Rear Echelons

Heavy Machinegun Detachment

Maint. Section

21st Panzer Division (cont'd)
104th Motorized Infantry Regiment (cont'd)

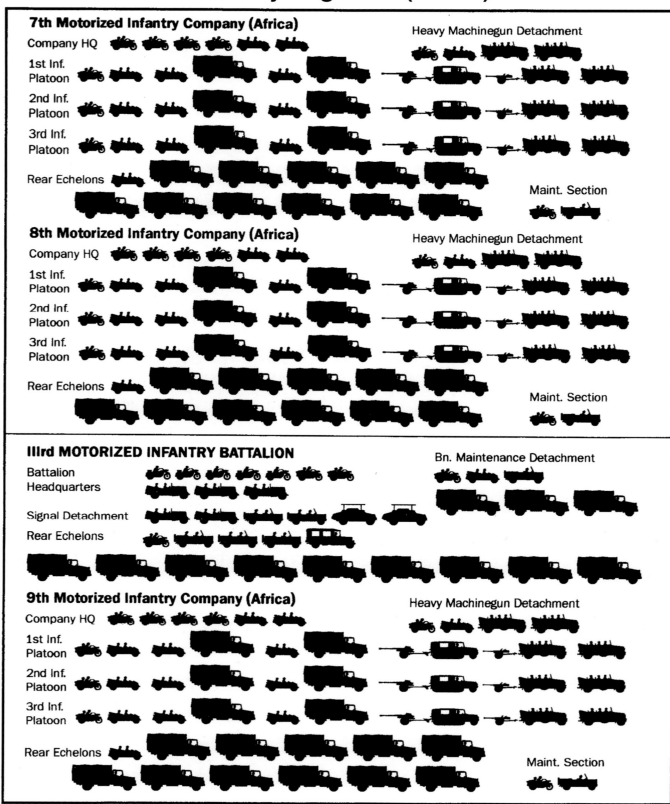

7th Motorized Infantry Company (Africa)

Company HQ

1st Inf. Platoon

2nd Inf. Platoon

3rd Inf. Platoon

Rear Echelons

Heavy Machinegun Detachment

Maint. Section

8th Motorized Infantry Company (Africa)

Company HQ

1st Inf. Platoon

2nd Inf. Platoon

3rd Inf. Platoon

Rear Echelons

Heavy Machinegun Detachment

Maint. Section

IIIrd MOTORIZED INFANTRY BATTALION

Battalion Headquarters

Signal Detachment

Rear Echelons

Bn. Maintenance Detachment

9th Motorized Infantry Company (Africa)

Company HQ

1st Inf. Platoon

2nd Inf. Platoon

3rd Inf. Platoon

Rear Echelons

Heavy Machinegun Detachment

Maint. Section

21st Panzer Division (cont'd)
104th Motorized Infantry Regiment (cont'd)

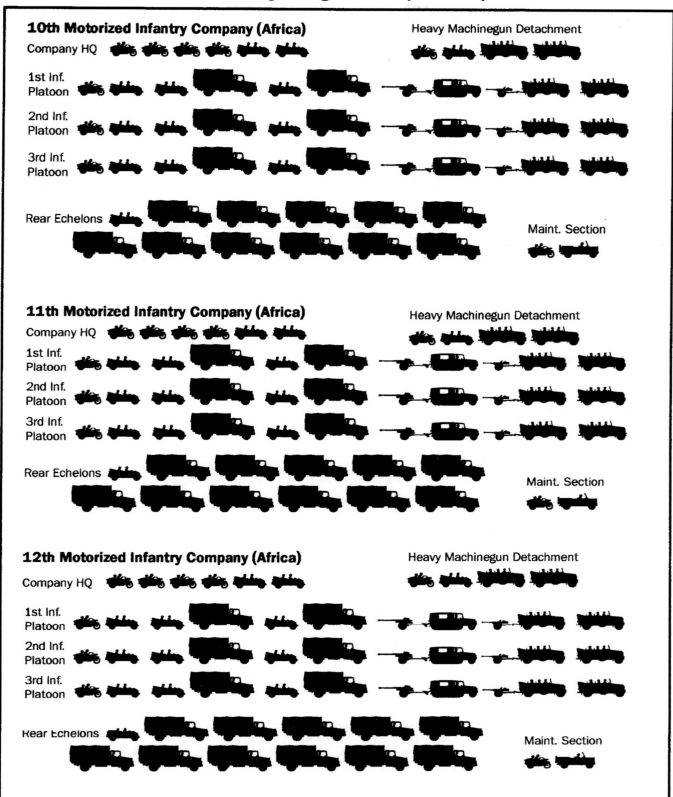

10th Motorized Infantry Company (Africa)

Company HQ

Heavy Machinegun Detachment

1st Inf. Platoon

2nd Inf. Platoon

3rd Inf. Platoon

Rear Echelons

Maint. Section

11th Motorized Infantry Company (Africa)

Company HQ

Heavy Machinegun Detachment

1st Inf. Platoon

2nd Inf. Platoon

3rd Inf. Platoon

Rear Echelons

Maint. Section

12th Motorized Infantry Company (Africa)

Company HQ

Heavy Machinegun Detachment

1st Inf. Platoon

2nd Inf. Platoon

3rd Inf. Platoon

Rear Echelons

Maint. Section

21st Panzer Division (cont'd)
155th Motorized Artillery Regiment

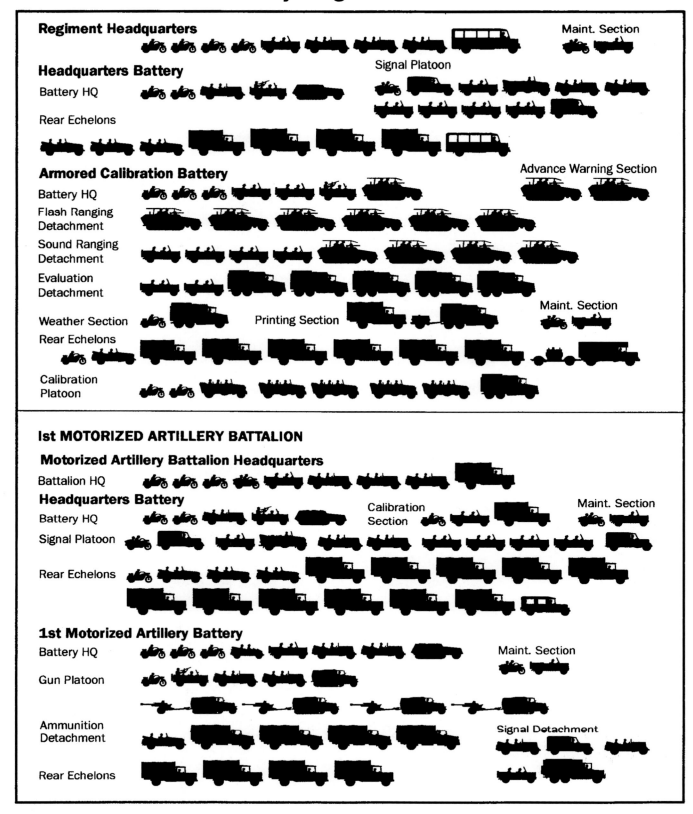

Regiment Headquarters   Maint. Section

Headquarters Battery   Signal Platoon

Battery HQ

Rear Echelons

Armored Calibration Battery   Advance Warning Section

Battery HQ

Flash Ranging Detachment

Sound Ranging Detachment

Evaluation Detachment

Weather Section   Printing Section   Maint. Section

Rear Echelons

Calibration Platoon

1st MOTORIZED ARTILLERY BATTALION

Motorized Artillery Battalion Headquarters

Battalion HQ

Headquarters Battery   Calibration   Maint. Section
Battery HQ   Section

Signal Platoon

Rear Echelons

1st Motorized Artillery Battery

Battery HQ   Maint. Section

Gun Platoon

Ammunition Detachment   Signal Detachment

Rear Echelons

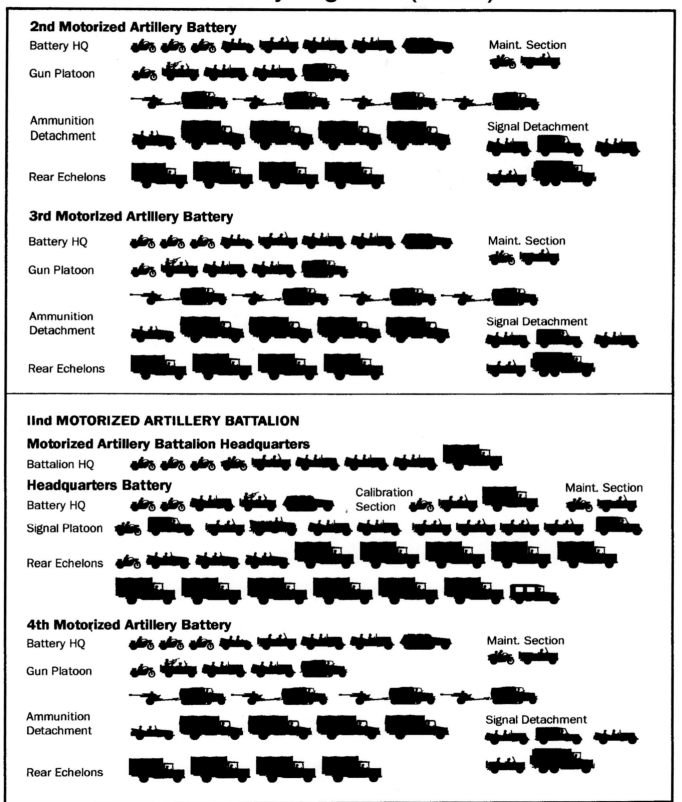

2nd Motorized Artillery Battery
Battery HQ

Gun Platoon

Ammunition Detachment

Rear Echelons

Maint. Section

Signal Detachment

3rd Motorized Artillery Battery
Battery HQ

Gun Platoon

Ammunition Detachment

Rear Echelons

Maint. Section

Signal Detachment

IInd MOTORIZED ARTILLERY BATTALION

Motorized Artillery Battalion Headquarters
Battalion HQ

Headquarters Battery
Battery HQ

Signal Platoon

Rear Echelons

Calibration Section

Maint. Section

4th Motorized Artillery Battery
Battery HQ

Gun Platoon

Ammunition Detachment

Rear Echelons

Maint. Section

Signal Detachment

155th Motorized Artillery Regiment (cont'd)

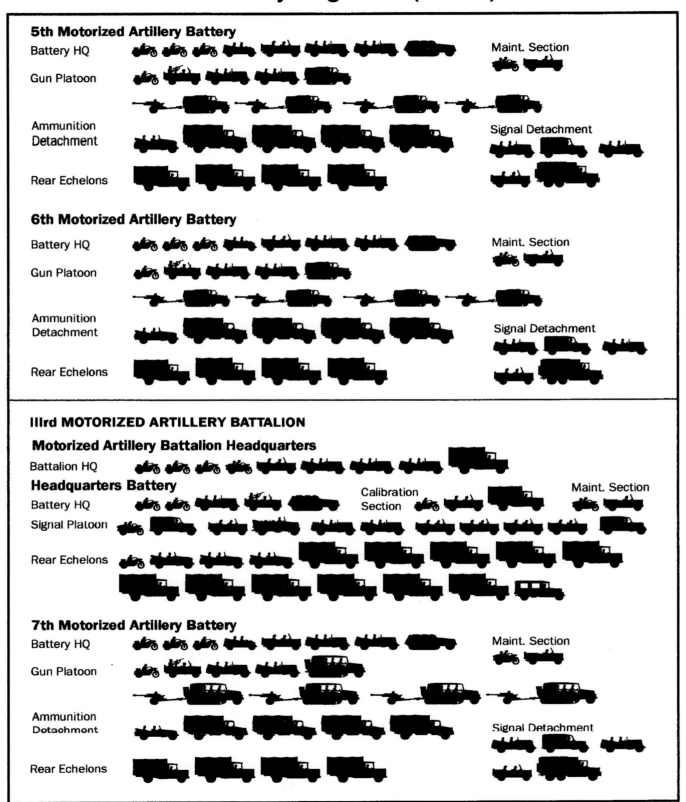

5th Motorized Artillery Battery
Battery HQ

Maint. Section

Gun Platoon

Ammunition Detachment

Signal Detachment

Rear Echelons

6th Motorized Artillery Battery
Battery HQ

Maint. Section

Gun Platoon

Ammunition Detachment

Signal Detachment

Rear Echelons

IIIrd MOTORIZED ARTILLERY BATTALION
Motorized Artillery Battalion Headquarters
Battalion HQ

Headquarters Battery
Battery HQ

Calibration Section

Maint. Section

Signal Platoon

Rear Echelons

7th Motorized Artillery Battery
Battery HQ

Maint. Section

Gun Platoon

Ammunition Detachment

Signal Detachment

Rear Echelons

155th Motorized Artillery Regiment (cont'd)

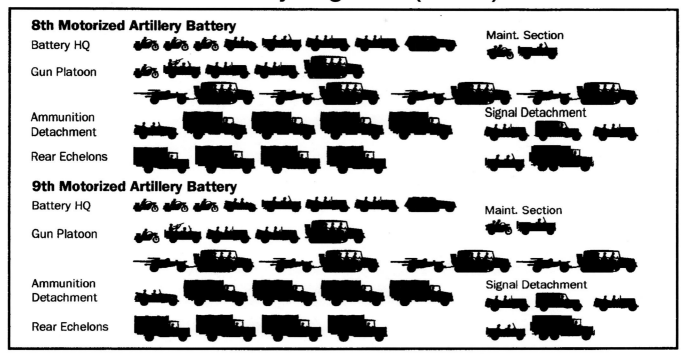

8th Motorized Artillery Battery

Battery HQ

Gun Platoon

Maint. Section

Ammunition Detachment

Signal Detachment

Rear Echelons

9th Motorized Artillery Battery

Battery HQ

Gun Platoon

Maint. Section

Ammunition Detachment

Signal Detachment

Rear Echelons

3rd Motorized Reconnaissance Battalion

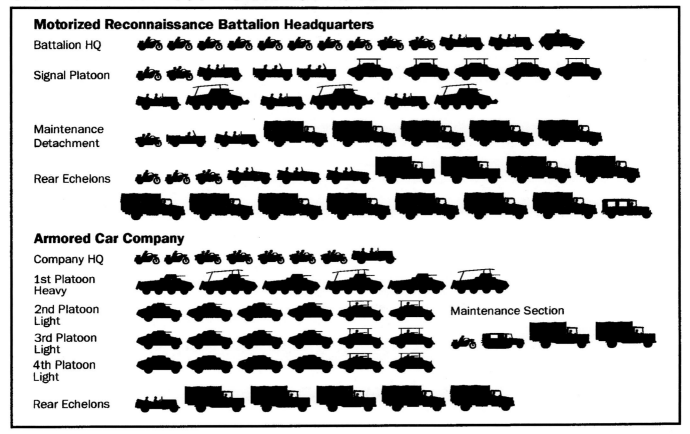

Motorized Reconnaissance Battalion Headquarters

Battalion HQ

Signal Platoon

Maintenance Detachment

Rear Echelons

Armored Car Company

Company HQ

1st Platoon Heavy

2nd Platoon Light

Maintenance Section

3rd Platoon Light

4th Platoon Light

Rear Echelons

21st Panzer Division (cont'd)
3rd Motorized Reconnaissance Regiment (cont'd)

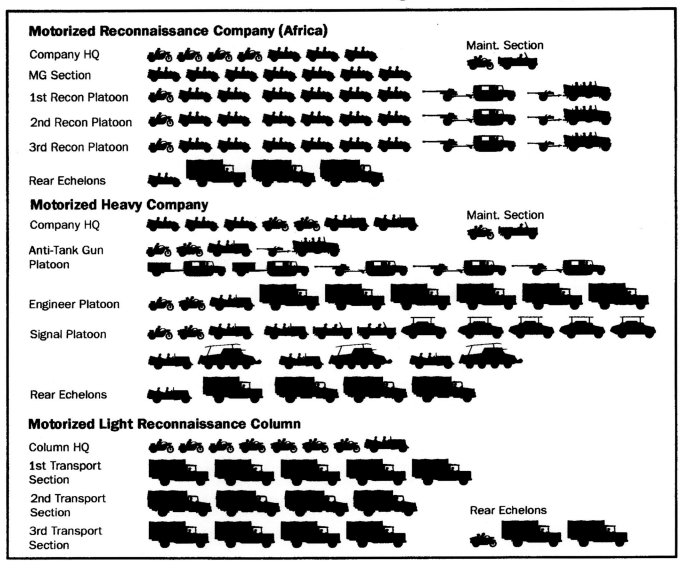

Motorized Reconnaissance Company (Africa)

Company HQ

MG Section

1st Recon Platoon

2nd Recon Platoon

3rd Recon Platoon

Rear Echelons

Maint. Section

Motorized Heavy Company

Company HQ

Anti-Tank Gun Platoon

Engineer Platoon

Signal Platoon

Rear Echelons

Maint. Section

Motorized Light Reconnaissance Column

Column HQ

1st Transport Section

2nd Transport Section

3rd Transport Section

Rear Echelons

200th Motorized Combat Engineer Battalion

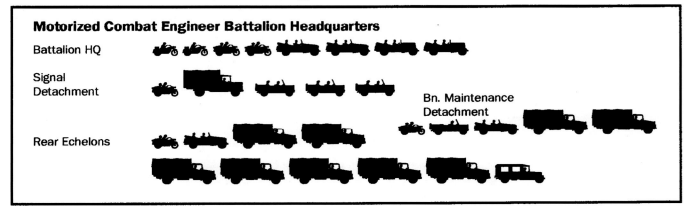

Motorized Combat Engineer Battalion Headquarters

Battalion HQ

Signal Detachment

Rear Echelons

Bn. Maintenance Detachment

200th Motorized Combat Engineer Battalion (cont'd)

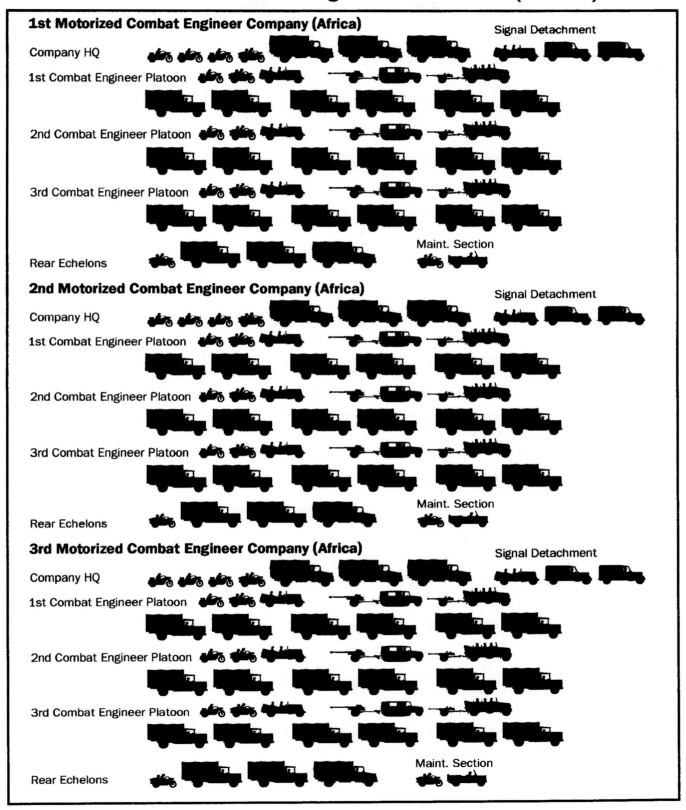

21st Panzer Division (cont'd)
200th Motorized Combat Engineer Battalion (cont'd)

Motorized Light Engineer Column

39th Motorized Anti-Tank Battalion

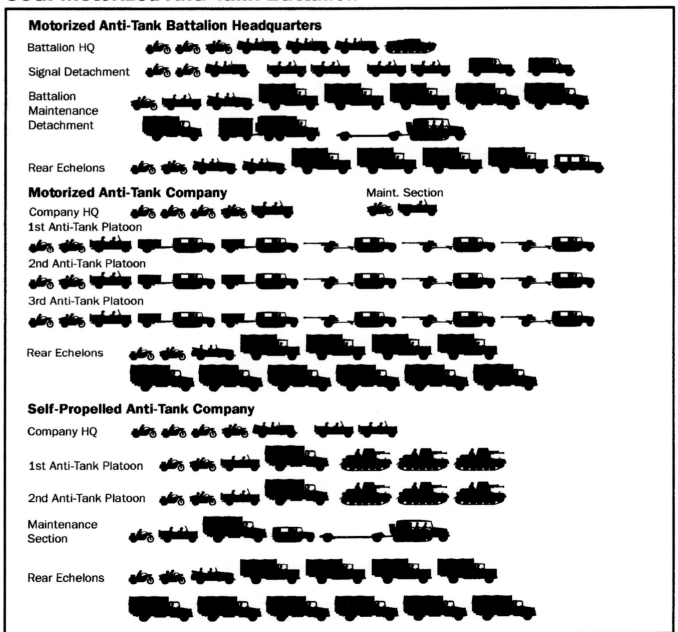

Motorized Anti-Tank Battalion Headquarters

Battalion HQ

Signal Detachment

Battalion Maintenance Detachment

Rear Echelons

Motorized Anti-Tank Company

Company HQ

1st Anti-Tank Platoon

2nd Anti-Tank Platoon

3rd Anti-Tank Platoon

Rear Echelons

Maint. Section

Self-Propelled Anti-Tank Company

Company HQ

1st Anti-Tank Platoon

2nd Anti-Tank Platoon

Maintenance Section

Rear Echelons

21st Panzer Division (cont'd)
200th Armored Signal Battalion

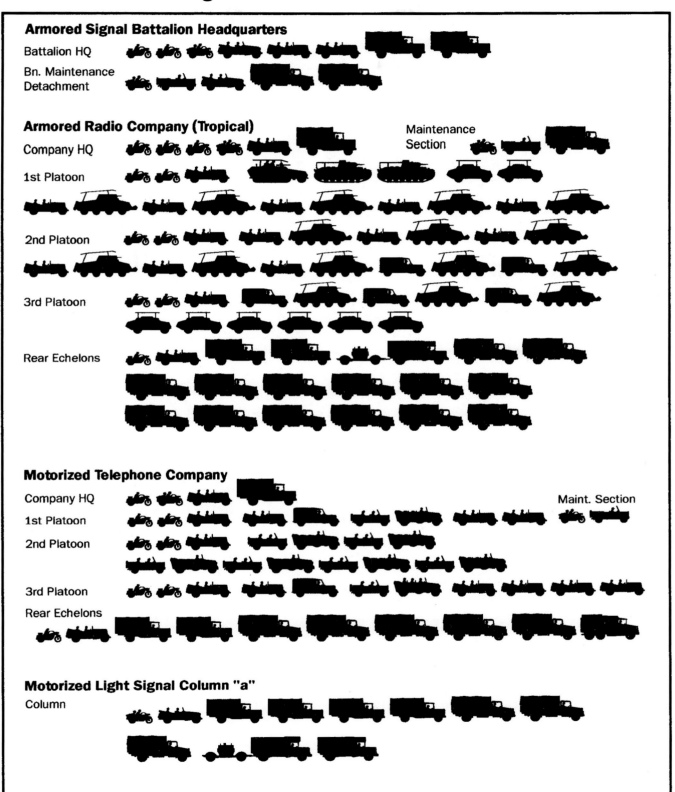

Armored Signal Battalion Headquarters

Battalion HQ

Bn. Maintenance Detachment

Armored Radio Company (Tropical)

Company HQ

Maintenance Section

1st Platoon

2nd Platoon

3rd Platoon

Rear Echelons

Motorized Telephone Company

Company HQ

Maint. Section

1st Platoon

2nd Platoon

3rd Platoon

Rear Echelons

Motorized Light Signal Column "a"

Column

187

90th Light "Africa" Division: May 27, 1942
90. LEICHTE-AFRIKA-DIVISION

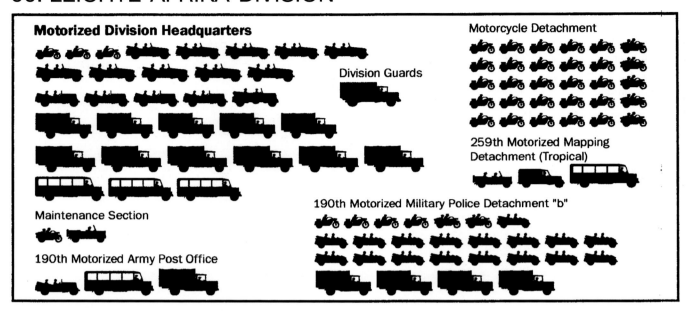

Motorized Division Headquarters

Division Guards

Maintenance Section

190th Motorized Army Post Office

Motorcycle Detachment

259th Motorized Mapping Detachment (Tropical)

190th Motorized Military Police Detachment "b"

155th Motorized Infantry Regiment

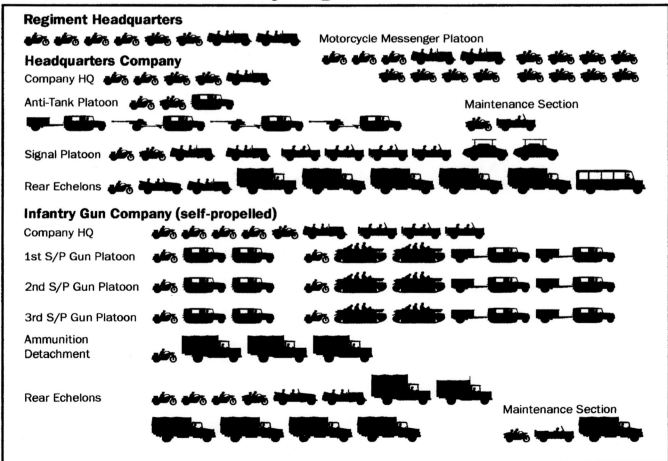

Regiment Headquarters

Motorcycle Messenger Platoon

Headquarters Company

Company HQ

Anti-Tank Platoon

Maintenance Section

Signal Platoon

Rear Echelons

Infantry Gun Company (self-propelled)

Company HQ

1st S/P Gun Platoon

2nd S/P Gun Platoon

3rd S/P Gun Platoon

Ammunition Detachment

Rear Echelons

Maintenance Section

90th Light "Africa" Division (cont'd)
155th Motorized Infantry Regiment (cont'd)

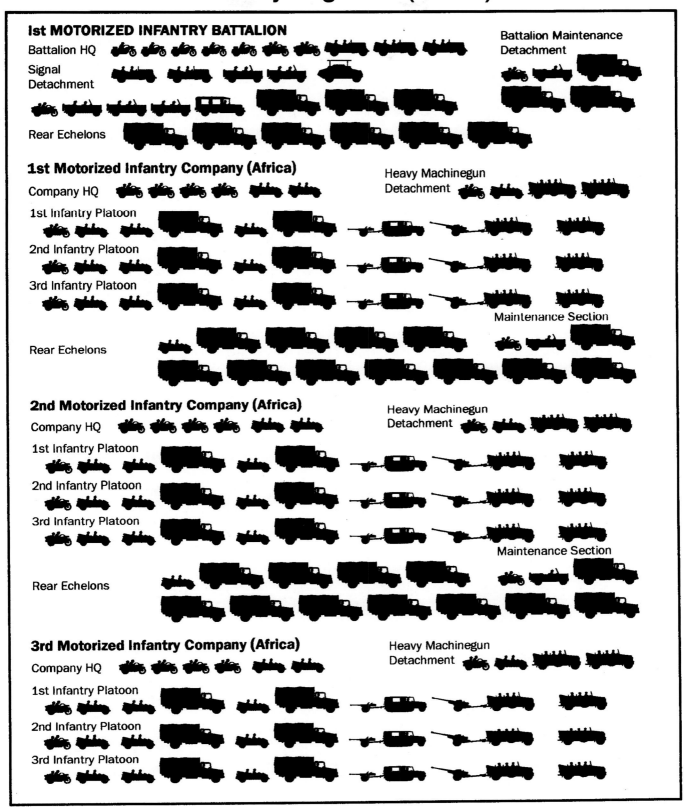

189

90th Light "Africa" Division (cont'd)
155th Motorized Infantry Regiment (cont'd)

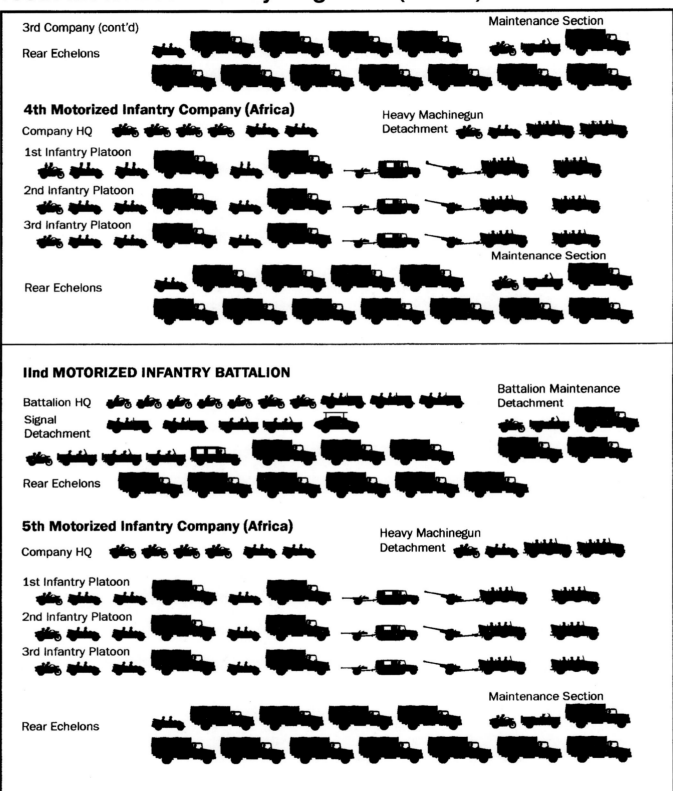

3rd Company (cont'd)

Rear Echelons

Maintenance Section

4th Motorized Infantry Company (Africa)

Company HQ

Heavy Machinegun Detachment

1st Infantry Platoon

2nd Infantry Platoon

3rd Infantry Platoon

Maintenance Section

Rear Echelons

IInd MOTORIZED INFANTRY BATTALION

Battalion HQ

Signal Detachment

Battalion Maintenance Detachment

Rear Echelons

5th Motorized Infantry Company (Africa)

Company HQ

Heavy Machinegun Detachment

1st Infantry Platoon

2nd Infantry Platoon

3rd Infantry Platoon

Maintenance Section

Rear Echelons

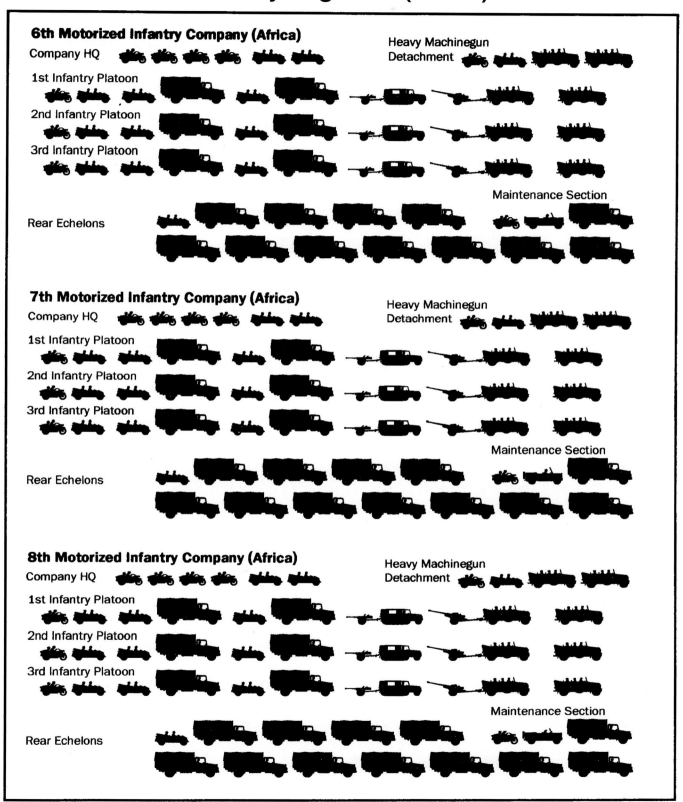

6th Motorized Infantry Company (Africa)

Company HQ

Heavy Machinegun Detachment

1st Infantry Platoon

2nd Infantry Platoon

3rd Infantry Platoon

Maintenance Section

Rear Echelons

7th Motorized Infantry Company (Africa)

Company HQ

Heavy Machinegun Detachment

1st Infantry Platoon

2nd Infantry Platoon

3rd Infantry Platoon

Maintenance Section

Rear Echelons

8th Motorized Infantry Company (Africa)

Company HQ

Heavy Machinegun Detachment

1st Infantry Platoon

2nd Infantry Platoon

3rd Infantry Platoon

Maintenance Section

Rear Echelons

90th Light "Africa" Division (cont'd)
1st Battalion/190th Motorized Artillery Regiment

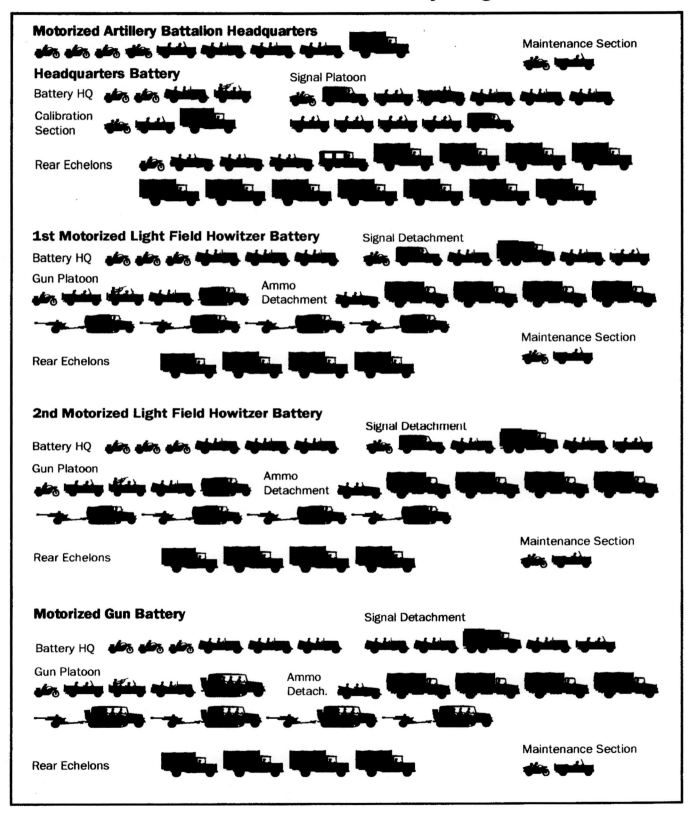

Motorized Artillery Battalion Headquarters

Maintenance Section

Headquarters Battery

Battery HQ

Calibration Section

Signal Platoon

Rear Echelons

1st Motorized Light Field Howitzer Battery

Battery HQ

Signal Detachment

Gun Platoon

Ammo Detachment

Maintenance Section

Rear Echelons

2nd Motorized Light Field Howitzer Battery

Battery HQ

Signal Detachment

Gun Platoon

Ammo Detachment

Maintenance Section

Rear Echelons

Motorized Gun Battery

Battery HQ

Signal Detachment

Gun Platoon

Ammo Detach.

Maintenance Section

Rear Echelons

90th Light "Africa" Division (cont'd)
900th Motorized Combat Engineer Battalion

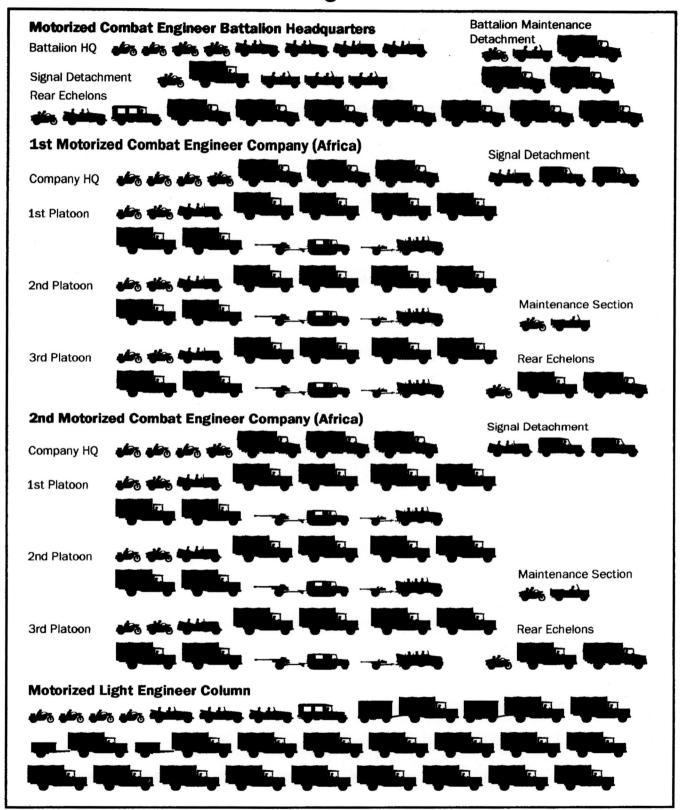

Motorized Combat Engineer Battalion Headquarters

Battalion HQ

Signal Detachment
Rear Echelons

Battalion Maintenance Detachment

1st Motorized Combat Engineer Company (Africa)

Company HQ

1st Platoon

2nd Platoon

3rd Platoon

Signal Detachment

Maintenance Section

Rear Echelons

2nd Motorized Combat Engineer Company (Africa)

Company HQ

1st Platoon

2nd Platoon

3rd Platoon

Signal Detachment

Maintenance Section

Rear Echelons

Motorized Light Engineer Column

90th Light "Africa" Division (cont'd)
580th Motorized Mixed Reconnaissance Company

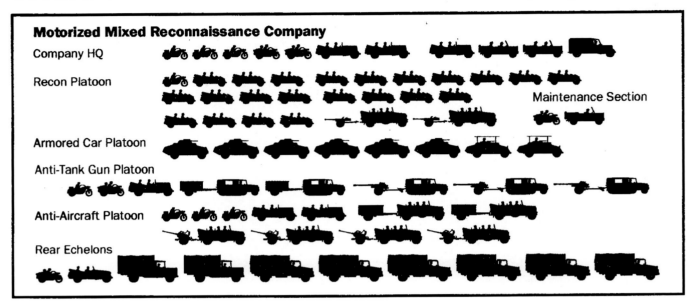

190th Motorized Anti-Tank Battalion

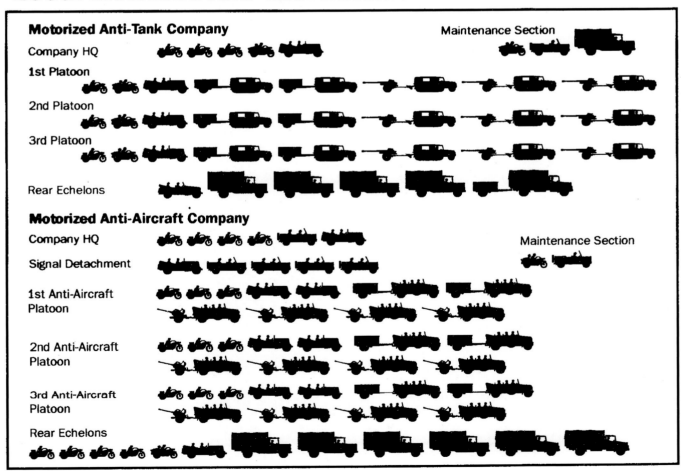

90th Light "Africa" Division (cont'd)
2nd Company/190th Armored Signal Battalion

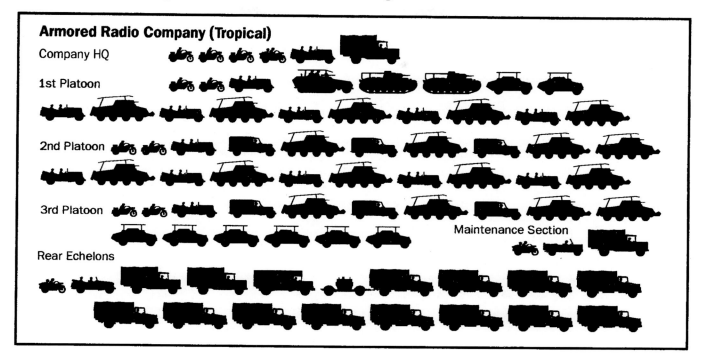

Armored Radio Company (Tropical)

Company HQ

1st Platoon

2nd Platoon

3rd Platoon

Maintenance Section

Rear Echelons

132nd Ariete Armored Division: May 27, 1942
132 DIVISIONE CORAZZATA

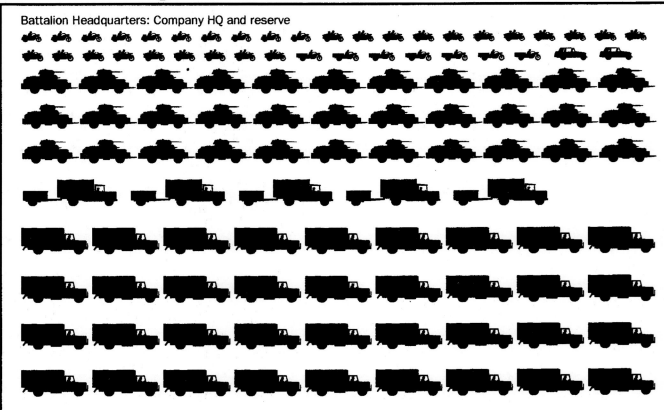

Divisional Headquarters

Tactical Command Unit

Brigade Headquarters Company

132nd Tank Regiment

Battalion Headquarters: Company HQ and reserve

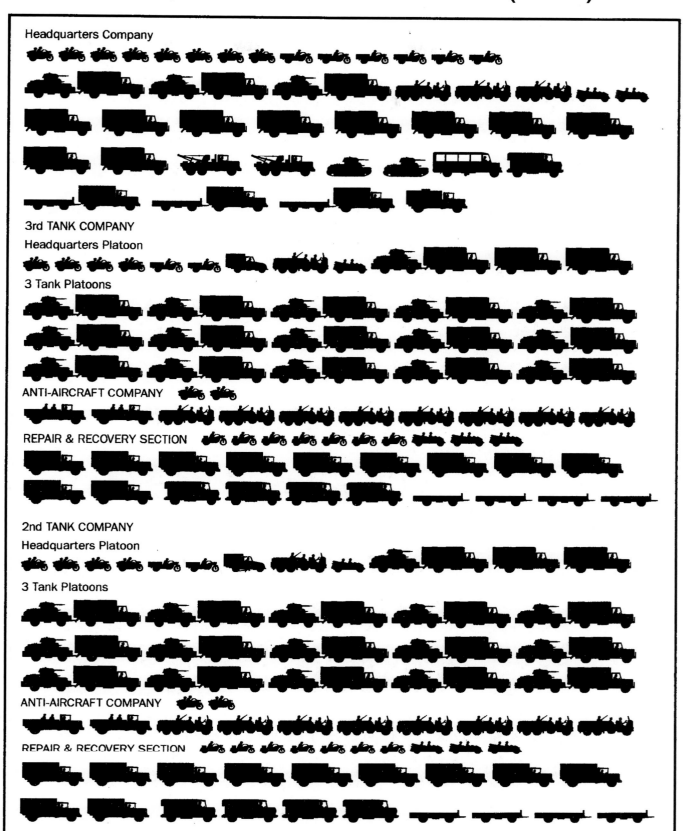

Headquarters Company

3rd TANK COMPANY

Headquarters Platoon

3 Tank Platoons

ANTI-AIRCRAFT COMPANY

REPAIR & RECOVERY SECTION

2nd TANK COMPANY

Headquarters Platoon

3 Tank Platoons

ANTI-AIRCRAFT COMPANY

REPAIR & RECOVERY SECTION

VIII Tank Battalion: Ariete Armored Division (cont'd)

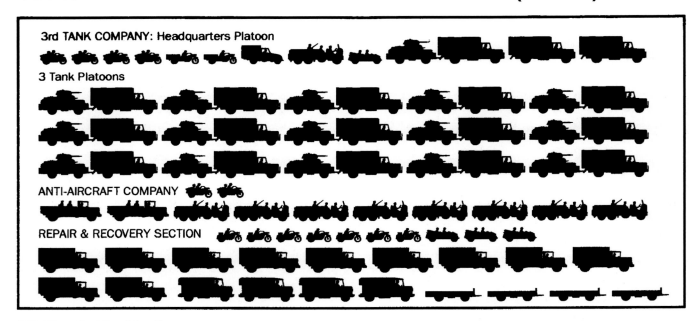

3rd TANK COMPANY: Headquarters Platoon

3 Tank Platoons

ANTI-AIRCRAFT COMPANY

REPAIR & RECOVERY SECTION

IX Tank Battalion

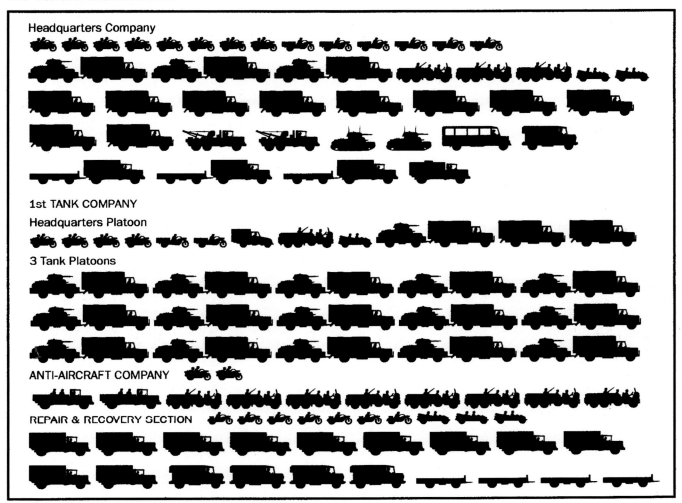

Headquarters Company

1st TANK COMPANY

Headquarters Platoon

3 Tank Platoons

ANTI-AIRCRAFT COMPANY

REPAIR & RECOVERY SECTION

IX Tank Battalion: Ariete Armored Division (cont'd)

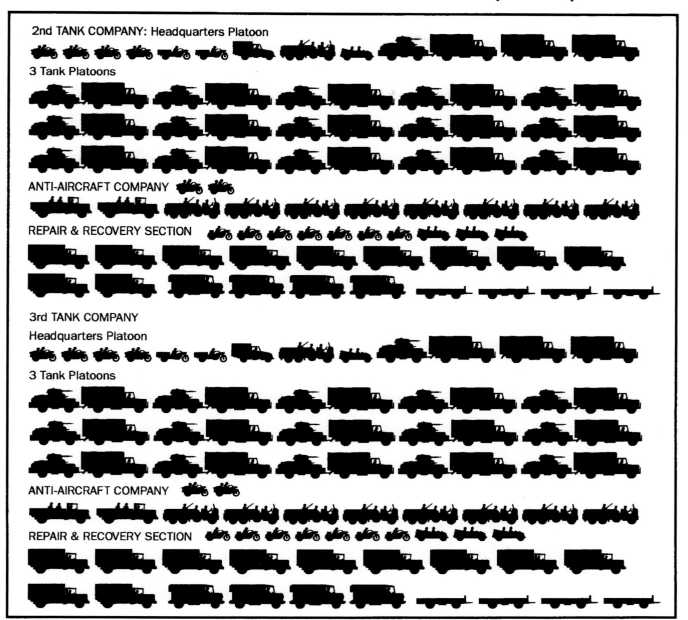

2nd TANK COMPANY: Headquarters Platoon

3 Tank Platoons

ANTI-AIRCRAFT COMPANY

REPAIR & RECOVERY SECTION

3rd TANK COMPANY

Headquarters Platoon

3 Tank Platoons

ANTI-AIRCRAFT COMPANY

REPAIR & RECOVERY SECTION

X Tank Battalion

Headquarters Company

X Tank Battalion: Ariete Armored Division (cont'd)

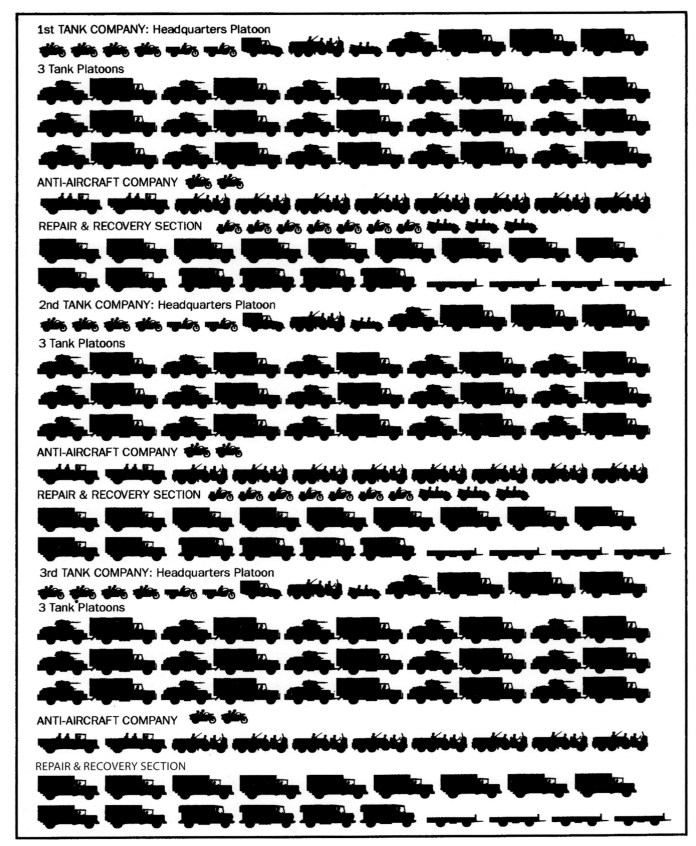

1st TANK COMPANY: Headquarters Platoon

3 Tank Platoons

ANTI-AIRCRAFT COMPANY

REPAIR & RECOVERY SECTION

2nd TANK COMPANY: Headquarters Platoon

3 Tank Platoons

ANTI-AIRCRAFT COMPANY

REPAIR & RECOVERY SECTION

3rd TANK COMPANY: Headquarters Platoon

3 Tank Platoons

ANTI-AIRCRAFT COMPANY

REPAIR & RECOVERY SECTION

8th Bersaglier Regt. (Mech. Inf.): Ariete Armored Division

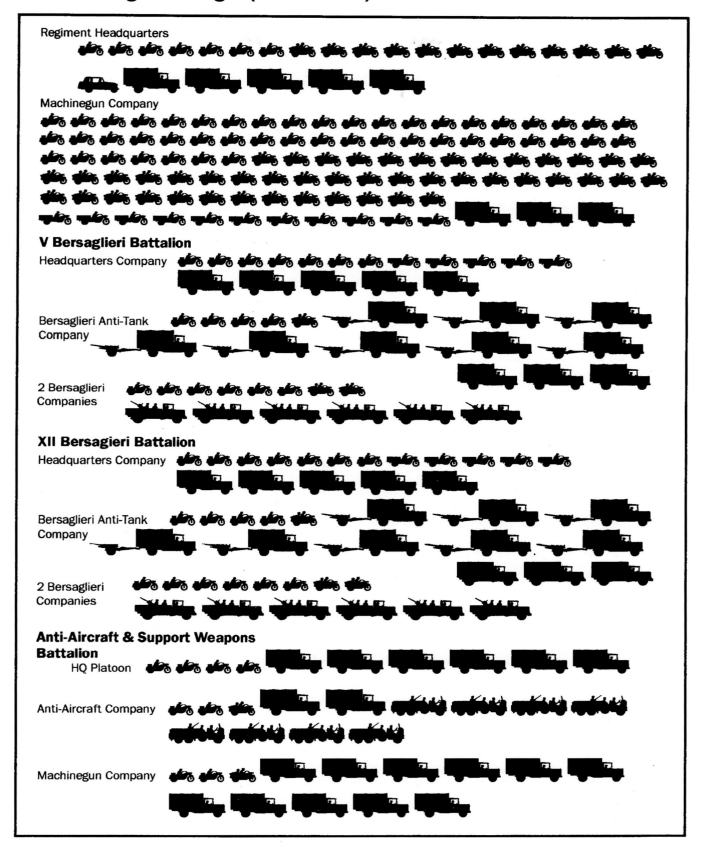

Regiment Headquarters

Machinegun Company

V Bersaglieri Battalion

Headquarters Company

Bersaglieri Anti-Tank Company

2 Bersaglieri Companies

XII Bersagieri Battalion

Headquarters Company

Bersaglieri Anti-Tank Company

2 Bersaglieri Companies

Anti-Aircraft & Support Weapons Battalion

HQ Platoon

Anti-Aircraft Company

Machinegun Company

8th Bersaglier Regtiment: Ariete Armored Div. (cont'd)

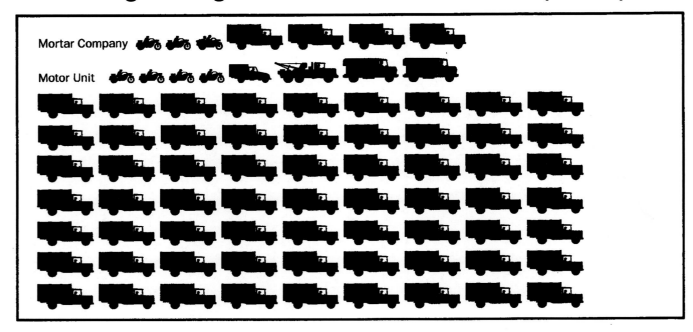

132nd Artillery Regiment

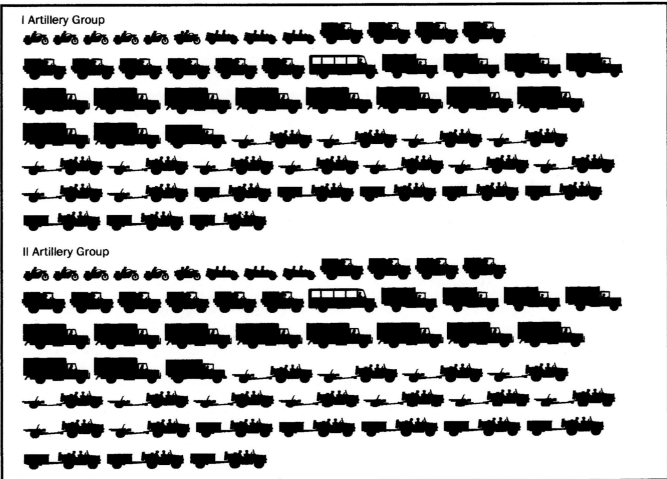

132nd Artillery Regt. (cont'd): Ariete Armored Division

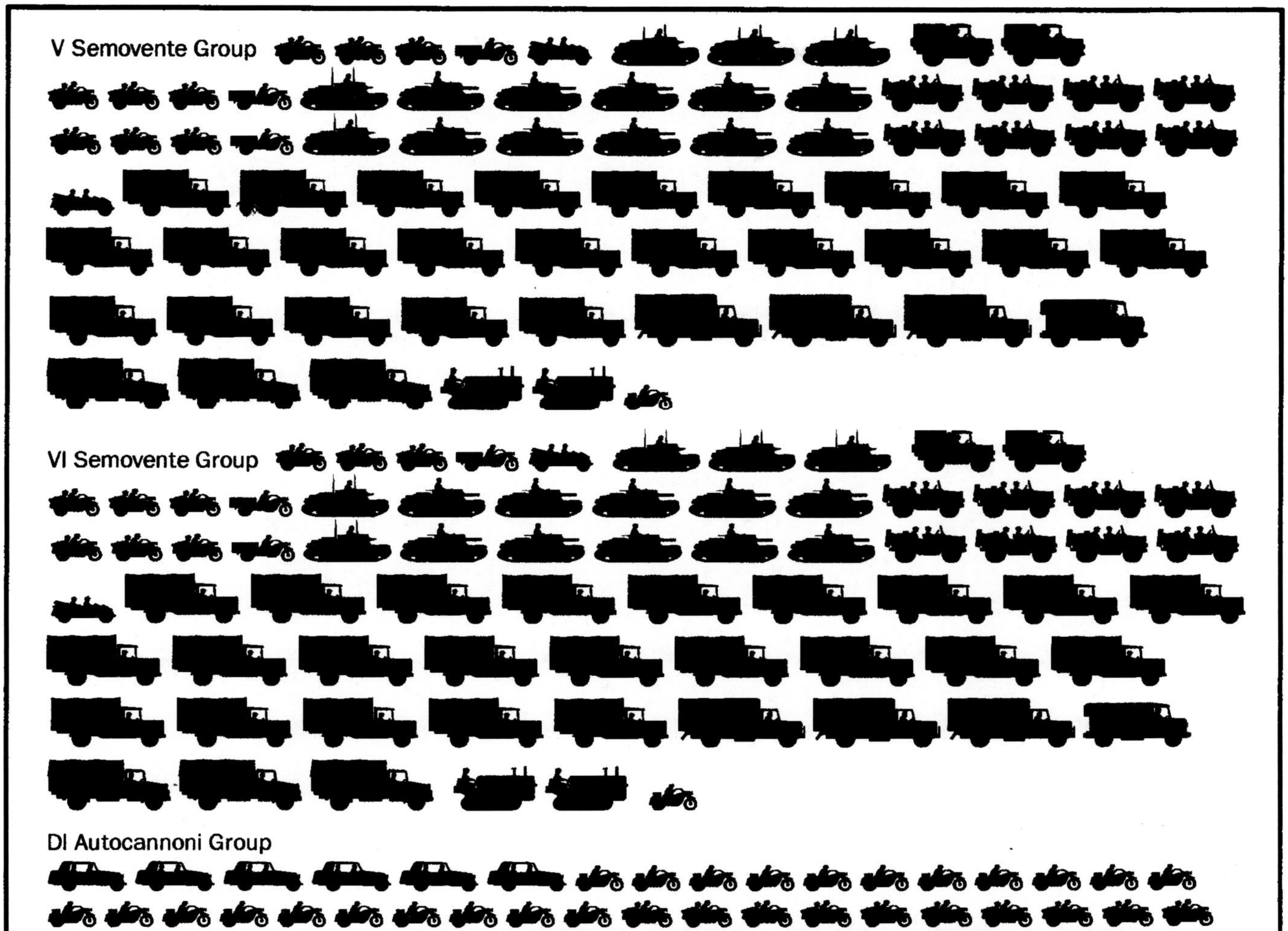

V Semovente Group

VI Semovente Group

DI Autocannoni Group

British 1st Armoured Division: May 27, 1942

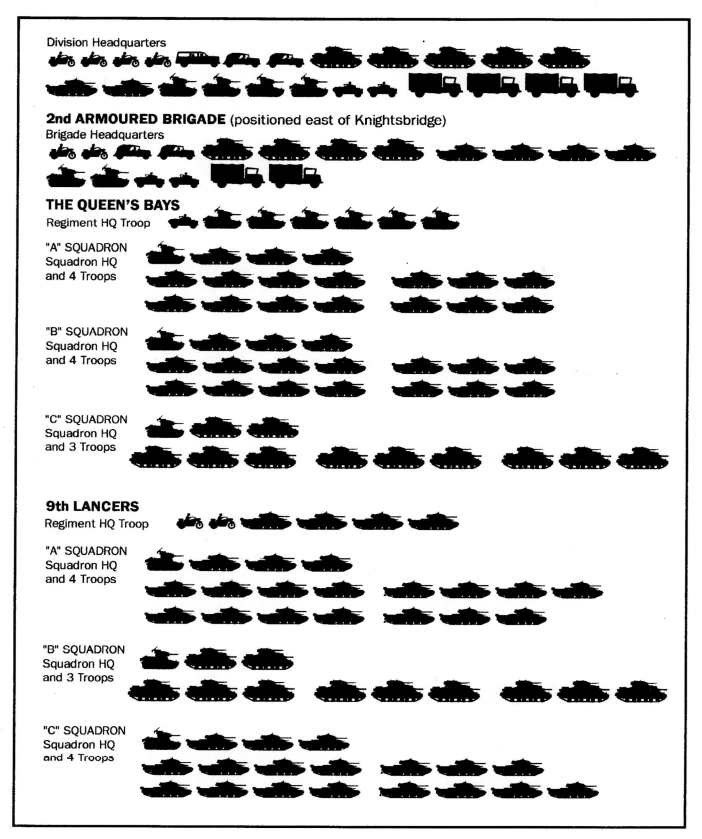

Division Headquarters

2nd ARMOURED BRIGADE (positioned east of Knightsbridge)
Brigade Headquarters

THE QUEEN'S BAYS
Regiment HQ Troop

"A" SQUADRON
Squadron HQ
and 4 Troops

"B" SQUADRON
Squadron HQ
and 4 Troops

"C" SQUADRON
Squadron HQ
and 3 Troops

9th LANCERS
Regiment HQ Troop

"A" SQUADRON
Squadron HQ
and 4 Troops

"B" SQUADRON
Squadron HQ
and 3 Troops

"C" SQUADRON
Squadron HQ
and 4 Troops

British 1st Armoured Division (cont'd)

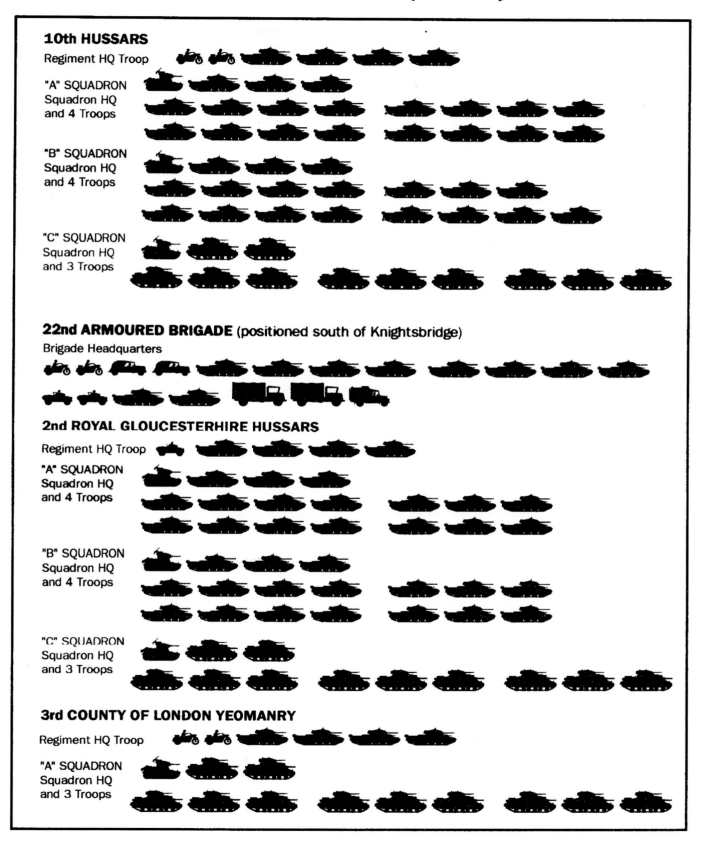

10th HUSSARS

Regiment HQ Troop

"A" SQUADRON
Squadron HQ
and 4 Troops

"B" SQUADRON
Squadron HQ
and 4 Troops

"C" SQUADRON
Squadron HQ
and 3 Troops

22nd ARMOURED BRIGADE (positioned south of Knightsbridge)

Brigade Headquarters

2nd ROYAL GLOUCESTERHIRE HUSSARS

Regiment HQ Troop

"A" SQUADRON
Squadron HQ
and 4 Troops

"B" SQUADRON
Squadron HQ
and 4 Troops

"C" SQUADRON
Squadron HQ
and 3 Troops

3rd COUNTY OF LONDON YEOMANRY

Regiment HQ Troop

"A" SQUADRON
Squadron HQ
and 3 Troops

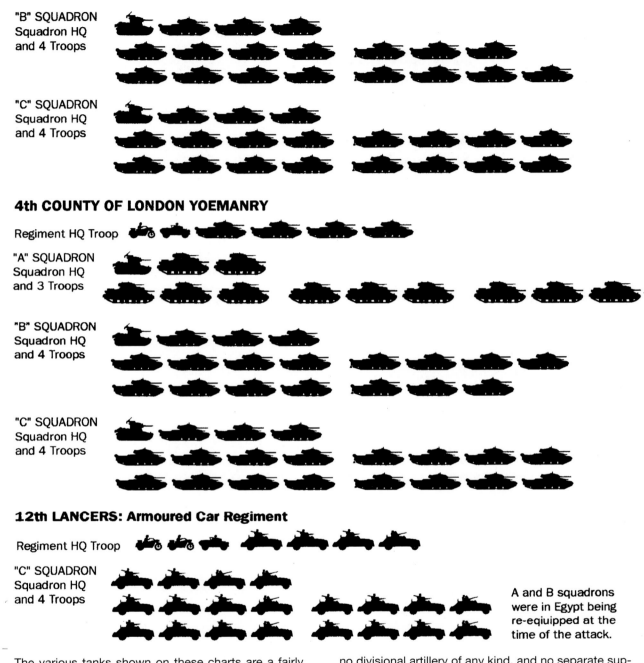

"B" SQUADRON
Squadron HQ
and 4 Troops

"C" SQUADRON
Squadron HQ
and 4 Troops

4th COUNTY OF LONDON YOEMANRY

Regiment HQ Troop

"A" SQUADRON
Squadron HQ
and 3 Troops

"B" SQUADRON
Squadron HQ
and 4 Troops

"C" SQUADRON
Squadron HQ
and 4 Troops

12th LANCERS: Armoured Car Regiment

Regiment HQ Troop

"C" SQUADRON
Squadron HQ
and 4 Troops

A and B squadrons
were in Egypt being
re-eqiupped at the
time of the attack.

The various tanks shown on these charts are a fairly accurate representation of the tank strength of the British 1st A.D., May 27, 1941. However, the support elements are merely abbreviated representations of their full complement because of space limitations. The Royal Dragoons acted as its reconnaissance unit, and divisional troops included 201st Guards Motor Infantry Brigade with 3rd Bn. Coldstream Guards, 2nd Bn. Scot's Guards, and 9th Bn. Rifle Brigade. They had no divisional artillery of any kind, and no separate support group.

During the desert war the individual units of the RTR were called battalions (e.g. 3rd RTR was 3rd Bn. RTR). Other armored formations such as the various Yeomanry and cavaly units (e.g. 9th Lancers or 10th Hussars) were referred to as regiments. However, the basic organization of each RTR Bn and Yeomanry or cavalry unit was quite similar.

British 7th Armoured Division: May 27, 1942

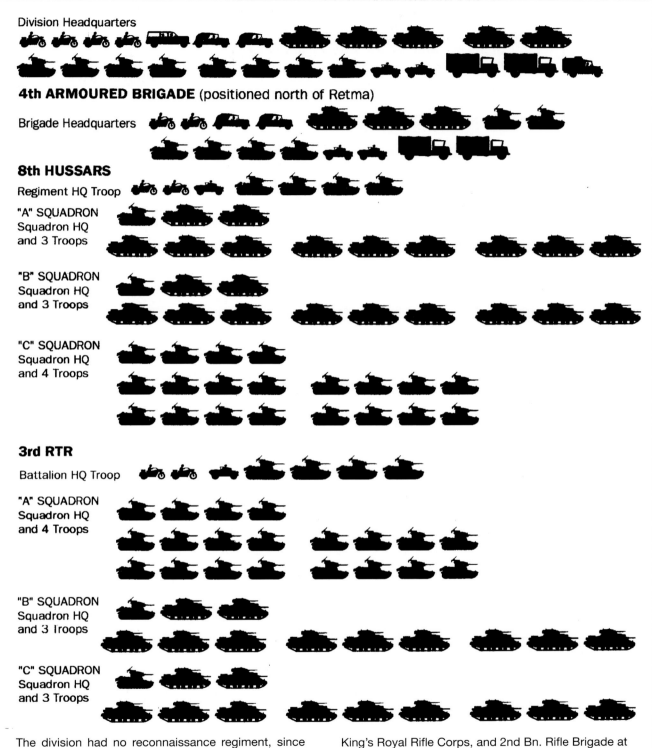

Division Headquarters

4th ARMOURED BRIGADE (positioned north of Retma)

Brigade Headquarters

8th HUSSARS

Regiment HQ Troop

"A" SQUADRON
Squadron HQ
and 3 Troops

"B" SQUADRON
Squadron HQ
and 3 Troops

"C" SQUADRON
Squadron HQ
and 4 Troops

3rd RTR

Battalion HQ Troop

"A" SQUADRON
Squadron HQ
and 4 Troops

"B" SQUADRON
Squadron HQ
and 3 Troops

"C" SQUADRON
Squadron HQ
and 3 Troops

The division had no reconnaissance regiment, since the 11th Hussars were in Persia at this time. The divisional troops included the 7th Motor Brigade with 3 battalions of fully motorized infantry, 1st and 9th Bn. King's Royal Rifle Corps, and 2nd Bn. Rifle Brigade at this time. There was no support group, and apparently no divisional field artillery or anti-tank units of any kind either.

British 7th Armoured Division (cont'd)

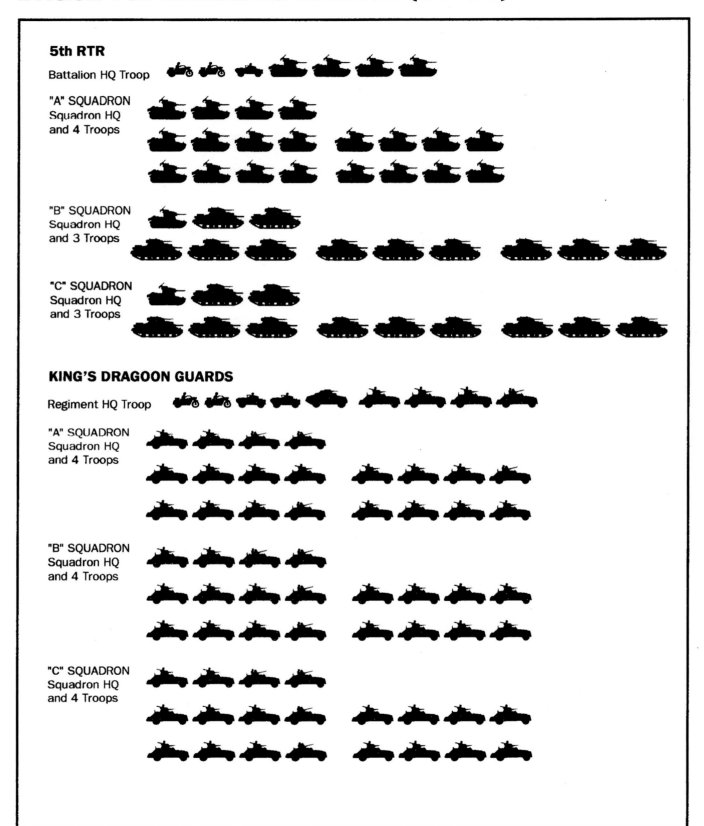

5th RTR

Battalion HQ Troop

"A" SQUADRON
Squadron HQ
and 4 Troops

"B" SQUADRON
Squadron HQ
and 3 Troops

"C" SQUADRON
Squadron HQ
and 3 Troops

KING'S DRAGOON GUARDS

Regiment HQ Troop

"A" SQUADRON
Squadron HQ
and 4 Troops

"B" SQUADRON
Squadron HQ
and 4 Troops

"C" SQUADRON
Squadron HQ
and 4 Troops

British 7th Armoured Division (cont'd)

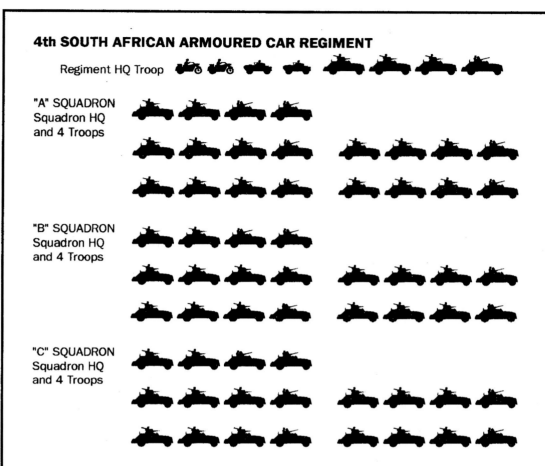

4th SOUTH AFRICAN ARMOURED CAR REGIMENT

Regiment HQ Troop

"A" SQUADRON
Squadron HQ
and 4 Troops

"B" SQUADRON
Squadron HQ
and 4 Troops

"C" SQUADRON
Squadron HQ
and 4 Troops

The arrival of the American-built M3 Grant on the Gazala Line battlefield had come as a nasty shock to the advancing DAK. These tanks had arrived in the Middle East several months before the crew training programs that were carried out in the Cairo area had uncovered a number of significant failings. The Grant's 75mm gun fired both high-explosive and armor-piercing rounds, and the gunnery techniques for the HE were more akin to field artillery fire. Since the 75mm gun had no range scale or clinometer, notches had to be filed into the elevation handwheel to mark the different range settings, and the azimuth was marked in a similar manner on the traversing wheel. Vane and bore sights also had to be improvised, and to shield the periscope from the desert sun, custom hoods had to be added.

Continuous use during this training period also revealed that the engines on the first Grants were burning out in their initial 25 hours of operation.

The tank itself was slightly underpowered to begin with, and the fine desert dust, along with the wrong grade of oil was playing havoc with engine life. To correct this, a special airlift of replacement engines had to be flown in from the USA. Suitable filters were added to the engine air intakes, and they eventually overcame the problem. Serious problems with the HE ammunition were also encountered during this training program. The available stockpiles in Egypt turned out to be of World War I vintage, and some of it had deteriorated so badly that the gunners experienced premature explosions, with a number of fatalities occurring.

By mid-May 1942 at least 167 Grants had been sent forward to equip the 1st and 7th Armoured Divisions. In an attempt to help boost morale, the limited number of Grants available were spread around the various fighting units as equally as possible.

Glossary of German-to-English Terminology

German	Abbr.	English
A		
Abteilung	Abt	Battalion
Armeekorps	AK	Army Corps
Armeeoberkommando	AOK	Army High Command
Artillerie-Regiment	AR	Artillery Regiment
Aufklärung		Reconnaissance
Aufklärungs-Abteilung	A.A.	Recon battalion
Ausfärung	Ausf.	Model or Mark
B		
Batterie	Battr	Battery
Batallion	Batl	Battalion
Beobachtung	Beob	Observation
Brigade	Brig	Brigade
D		
Deutsches-Afrika-Korps	DAK	German Africa Corps
Division	Div	Division
E		
Einheits	E	Standard
F		
Fallschirmjäger-Regiment	FJR	Parachute Regiment
Feldhaubitze	FH	Field Howitzer
Fla-Batallion		Anti-Aircraft bn. (Army)
Fla-Kompanie		Anti-Aircraft co. (Army)
Flak-Abteilung		Anti-Aircraft bn. (Luftwaffe)
Flak-Batterie		Anti-Aircraft bty. (Luftwaffe)
Flugabwehr	Fla	Anti-Aircraft
Flugabwehrkanone	Flak	Anti-Aircraft Gun
Funk	Fu	Radio
G		
Gebirgsjäger-Regiment	GebRgt	Mountain Regiment
gemischter Aufklärüngs-Kompanie		Motorized mixed recon co.
Generalkommando	GenKdo	Corps Headquarters
Geschütz	Gesch	Gun / Cannon
grosser	gr	Large
H		
Haubitze	H	(gun)-Howitzer
Heeres-Flak-Abteilung		Anti-Aircraft Battalion (Army)
Heeresgruppe	Hgr	Army Group
I		
Infanterie	Inf	Infantry
Infanterie-Geschütze	IG	Infantry Gun
K		
Kampfgruppe	KGr	Combat Team
Kampfwagenkanone	KwK	Tank Cannon
klein	kl	Small
Kolonne	Kol	Column
Kompanie	Ko	Company
Kradschützen-Batallion		Motorcycle Battalion
Kraftfahrzeug	Kfz	Softskin Motor Vehicle
Kraftrad	krad	Motorcycle
Kriegsstärkenachwisung	KStN	Table of Organization
L		
Land-Wasser-Schlepper	LWS	Land & Water Tractor
leicht	le	Light
leichte Division (mot)		Light Mechanized Div.
M		
Machinengewehr	MG	Machinegun
Mammut		Mammoth
mittler	m	Medium
motorisiert	mot	Motorized
O		
Oberkommando	OK	High Command
P		
Panzer	Pz	Tank / Armor
Panzerabwehrkanone	Pak	Anti-Tank Gun
Panzer-Artillerie-Regiment		Armored Artillery Regt.
Panzerarmee		Tank Army
Panzerbefehlswagen	Pz-Bef	Command Tank
Panzerbüsche	PzB	Anti-Tank Rifle
Panzer-Division	PD	Armored Division
Panzerkampfwagen	PzKpfw	Tank
Panzergrenadier-Division		Armored Motorized Division
Panzergruppe	PzGr	Armored Group
Panzerjäger-Abteilung	PzJgAbt	Anti-Tank Battalion
Panzer-Korps	PzK	Armored Corps
Panzer-Nachrichten-Abteilung		Armored Signal Battalion
Panzer-Pionier-Batallion		Arm'd Combat Engineer Bn.
Panzer-Regiment		Armored Regiment
Panzerspähwagen	PzSpWg	Armored Scout Car
Pionier	Pi	Engineer
Personenkraftwagen	PKW	Personnel Carrier (car)
R		
Regiment	Rgt	Regiment
S		
Schlepper		Tractor
Schützen	(S)	Rifle / Infantry
Schützenpanzerwagen	SPW	Armored Personnel Carrier
Schützen-Regiment		Motorized Infantry Regt.
schwers		Heavy
Sonder	Sd	Special
Sonder-Kraftfahrzeug	SdKfz	Special Motor Vehicle
Sonderverband	Sd.Verb	Special Service Unit
Stab	Stb	Headquarters Staff
Sturmgeschütz	StuG	Assault Gun (S/P)
T		
Trinkwasser		Drinking Water
Tropenhelm		Pith Helmet
W		
Wehrkreis	WK	Military District
Wolfsangel		Wolf's Hook / Trap
Z		
Zug	Zug	Platoon
Zugkraftwagen	Zgkw	Halftrack Towing Vehicle

Bibliography

Balin, George, *Afrika Korps, Tanks Illustrated No. 17*, Arms & Armour Press, 1985.

Bellis, Malcolm A., *British Tanks and Formations 1939–45*, published by Malcolm Bellis.

Bender, James and R. Law, *Uniforms, Organization and History of the Afrikakorps*. R.James Bender Pub. 1973.

Bierman, John and Colin Smith. *War Without Hate*. Penguin Books Ltd. 2002.

Bradford, George R., *Armour Camouflage & Markings, North Africa 1941-43*. Arms & Armour Press, 1974.

Chamberlain, Peter and Hilary Doyle. *Encyclopedia of German Tanks of World War Two*. Arms & Armour Press, 1979.

Cockle, Tom, *Armor of the Deutsches Afrikakorps*, Concord Publications Co., 2000.

Collier, Richard. *The War in the Desert*. Time-Life Books Inc., 1977.

Cowles, Virginia, *The Phantom Major: The Story of David Stirling and the SAS*. William Collins Co., 1959.

Crisp, Robert, *Brazen Chariots*. WW Norton & Company Inc., 1961.

Ellis, Chris and Hilary Doyle, *Panzerkampfwagen: German Combat Tanks 1933–1945*. Bellona Publications, 1976.

Fletcher, David, *Tanks in Camera, 1940–43*. Sutton Publishing Limited, 1998.

Forty, George, *Afrika Korps at War: Volumes 1 & 2*, Ian Allan Publishing, 1978

Greene, Jack, *Mare Nostrum*. Typesetting etc. 1990.

Heckmann, Wolf. *Rommel's War in Africa*. Konecky & Konecky, Doubleday & Company, 1981.

Icks, Robert J., *Famous Tank Battles*, Doubleday & Company, Inc., 1972.

Irving, David, *The Trail of the Desert Fox*. E.P. Dutton, 1977.

Jentz, Thomas, *Tank Combat in North Africa*, Schiffer Publishing Ltd., Atglen, USA. 1998.

Jorgensen, Christer, *Rommel's Panzers*, MBI Publishing, 2003

Kühn, Volkmar, *Rommel in the Desert*. Schiffer Publishing Ltd., 1991.

Law, Richard and C. Luther, *Rommel: A Narative & Pictorial History*. R.James Bender Publishing, 1980.

Macksey, Kenneth, *Rommel: Battles and Campaigns*, Thomas Nelson & Sons (Canada) 1979.

McGuirk, Dal, *Rommel's Army in Africa*, Motorbooks International, 1993.

Mitcham, Samuel W. Jr., *Triumphant Fox*. Cooper Square Press, NY, 2000.

Montgomery, Bernard Law, *The Memoirs of Field Marshal Montgomery*. William Collins Sons & Co., 1958.

Münich, Raif, *Panzer in Nord-Afrika 1941–1943*. Podzun-Pallas-Verlag, 1977.

Nagliere, Valerio, *Carri Armati nel Deserto*, Ermano Albertelli Editore, 1972.

Niehorster, Leo W.G., *German World War II Organizational Series, Vol. 2/1*. Pub by Dr. Leo W. Niehorster, 1990.

Niehorster, Leo W.G., *German World War II Organizational Series, Vol. 3/1*. Pub by Dr. Leo W. Niehorster, 1990.

Oliver, Dennis, *Codename Swallow: British Sherman Tanks at Alamein*. Stratus s.c., Poland, Green Series, 2006.

Orpen, Neil, *War in the Desert*, Vol. III, Pumel, Capetown, 1971.

Pafi, B., C. Falessi and G. Fiore, *Corazzati Italiani 1939–45*. D'Anna Editore, 1968.

Perrett, Bryan, *The Valentine in North Africa 1942–1943*. Ian Allan Ltd., 1972.

Pignato, Nicola, *Dalla Libia al Libano*, Editrice Scorpione, 1992.

Platz, William, *Desert Tracks*, Baron Publishing, 1978.

Plowman, Jeffrey, M. Thomas, *2nd New Zealand Divisional Cavalry Regiment in the Mediterranean*. Kiwi Armour 3, Christchurch, NZ, 2002.

Quarrie, Bruce, *Panzers in the Desert*, Patrick Stephens Limited, 1988.

Riccio, Ralph, *Italian Tanks and Fighting Vehicles of World War 2*. Pique Pubs. Kristall Productions Ltd., 1975.

Rutherford, Ward, *The Biography of Field Marshal Erwin Rommel*. Bison Books Limited, 1981.

Strawson, John. *The Battle for North Africa*. Charles Scribner's Sons, New York, 1969.

Von Luck, Hans, *Panzer Commander*. Praeger Publishers, 1989

Walker, Ian W., *Iron Hulls, Iron Hearts*. The Cromwell Press, Trowbridge, UK, 2006.

War Diary of the German Afrika Korps: from Air Historical Branch Translations, 1950.

War Diary of Panzerarmee Afrika: from Air Historical Branch translations, 1951.

Watson, Bruce Allen, *Exit Rommel*, Stackpole Books, 2007

Williamson, Gordon, *Afrikakorps 1941–43*, Osprey Elite Series No. 34, Osprey Pub. 1991.

Young, Desmond, *Rommel the Desert Fox*. Harper & Row Publishers, 1978.

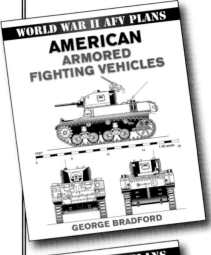

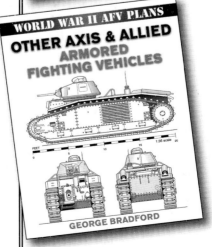
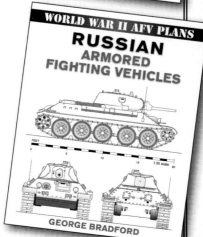